THE FAULT LINES OF
EMPIRE

New World in the Atlantic World
Jack P. Greene and Amy Turner Bushnell, Series Editors

THE FAULT LINES OF
EMPIRE

POLITICAL DIFFERENTIATION IN MASSACHUSETTS AND NOVA SCOTIA, CA. 1760–1830

ELIZABETH MANCKE

Routledge
NEW YORK • LONDON

Published in 2005 by
Routledge
Taylor & Francis Group
270 Madison Avenue
New York, NY 10016
www.routledge-ny.com

Published in Great Britain by
Routledge
Taylor & Francis Group
2 Park Square
Milton Park, Abingdon
Oxon OX14 4RN
www.routledge.co.uk

10 9 8 7 6 5 4 3 2 1

Library of Congress Cataloging-in-Publication Data
    Mancke, Elizabeth, 1954-
        The fault lines of empire : political differentiation in Massachusetts and Nova Scotia, ca.
    1760–1830 / by Elizabeth Mancke.
            p. cm. — (New world in the Atlantic world)
    Includes bibliographical references.
        ISBN 0-415-95000-7 (hb : alk. paper) — ISBN 0-415-95001-5 (pbk. : alk. paper)
    1. Massachusetts—Politics and government—1775–1865. 2. Nova Scotia—Politics and
    government—1763–1867. 3. Political socialization—Massachusetts—History. 4. Political
    socialization—Nova Scotia—History. 5. Land grants—Massachusetts—History. 6. Land
    grants—Nova Scotia—History. 7. Local government—Massachusetts—History. 8. Local
    government—Nova Scotia—History. I. Title. II. Series.
    F69.M36 2004
    320.744'09'033—dc22   2004019521

Contents

List of Illustrations

List of Tables

Acknowledgments

The research and writing of this study, which I did in two countries, involved its own kind of comparative research as I sought ways to bridge two national historiographies and an imperial one. Many people assisted my labors, answered my questions, questioned my answers, and provided good-humored laughter at inexplicable cultural differences. Their influence is on every page of this book, even if their names never appear in it. An acknowledgment is an admittedly partial recognition of some of them; over the years many unnamed people asked a provocative question, corrected a detail, recommended a source, offered encouragement, or simply displayed the generosity of spirit that makes scholarly work pleasurable.

This project bears the imprint of two graduate programs in history, one at the University of British Columbia, where I received a Master's degree, and the other at The Johns Hopkins University, where I received a PhD. At UBC, Skip Ray, Bob McDonald, Peter Ward, and Keith Ralston made sure I could recognize a Canadian perspective on the history of North America. Through UBC connections, I also made my first Atlantic Canadian connections, particularly with Graeme Wynn and George Rawlyk (now deceased), both of whom provided invaluable encouragement over the years. Alan Tully unexpectedly provided a link between UBC and JHU. At JHU, Jack P. Greene introduced me to Atlantic history, which offered a vantage point on North America that was neither Canadian nor American and which subsequently shaped my outlook on the history of the early modern era. As well, Jack's extensive research on the political and constitutional history of early modern British America has been invaluable to my own work, and no number of citations or words of thanks would exhaust my respect of, and debt to, his scholarship. In the two years I was in residence at JHU, I found that the seminar system raised more historical problems than could be solved in a lifetime of scholarship. This study only provides partial answers to Toby Ditz's question about public and private spheres and Ron Walter's query about values. As well, Ashraf Ghani told me unequivocally to risk new conceptualizations of old problems; I hope his injunction finds some resonance in these pages.

A fellowship from the Department of History at JHU funded my first two years of doctoral study. A Jacob Javits doctoral fellowship from the U.S. Department of Education allowed for lengthy sojourns in Boston, Halifax, and Machias where I did most of the research and writing. In Boston, I worked in the Massachusetts Historical Society and the Commonwealth of Massachusetts Archives. Conversations with Dick Ryerson always proved stimulating. Cynthia Col provided me a house key so I always had a place to stay in Boston even after we no longer shared an abode.

In Halifax, I did most of my research at the Public Archives of Nova Scotia (now the Nova Scotia Archives and Record Management), with excursions to the Dalhousie University Library. The staff at the NSARM offered exemplary service and encouragement. Jack Crowley proved a soft touch for discussing any early modern topic. Debra McNabb sensitized me to differences among Maritimers, quietly insisted that I could learn to see landscapes as would a historical geographer, and taught me basic cartographic skills. In Liverpool, Gary Hartlan, at the Queens County Museum, clarified puzzling details about the town. The Atlantic Canada workshops, Atlantic Canadian Studies conferences, and the Planters Studies conferences offered scholarly venues to discuss my work and invaluable contacts with other scholars of the region, in particular David Bell, Rusty Bittermann, Ernie Clarke, Margaret Conrad, Julian Gwyn, David Jaffee, Barry Moody, Del Muise, Rosemary Ommer, Allen Robertson, and Deb Trask.

In Machias, Ilze Balodis made working in the Washington County Court House a pleasure, and she and Charlie Duncan provided lodging for the times I was just passing through town. The Machias and East Machias town clerks gave me generous access to the town records. The genealogist for the Machias chapter of the Daughters of the American Revolution, Scotty Chalmers (now deceased), was a fund of information and good company well into the ninth decade of her life. Randall Kindelberger, a historian of early modern France, was an equally skilled discussant of early modern North America. James Leamon and Ed Churchill, both of whose work informs my interpretation of the Revolution in Machias, provided scholarly counsel and encouragement. For my occasional trips back to Baltimore, Chris Daniels and Steve Whitman provided me a room and intellectual companionship.

After I completed the core of this project, I set it aside and worked on developing a conceptualization of the early modern British Empire that could encompass Machias and Liverpool, as well as Boston and Bombay, the Carolinas and the Caribbean, New York and West Africa. That endeavor took far longer than the research on Liverpool and Machias, and indeed is ongoing. I am grateful to my colleagues at the University of Akron who accepted the merits of that detour, even though it was an unusual career choice. A number of people were particularly helpful during that phase: among them are David Armitage, Bob Babcock, Mike Braddick, Lige Gould, Jack Greene, Stephen

Hornsby, Richard Johnson, Ken Lockridge, Peter, J. Marshall, Malyn Newitt, John G. Reid, and Steve Whitman.

In the summer of 1995, I had a summer research grant from UA, part of which I used for research on this project. I finished revisions of the manuscript during part of a UA faculty improvement leave. Moira Kloster read the work in transition. John Reid kindly reviewed the penultimate version of the manuscript and helped to catch many of the small errors and infelicities that an author can no longer see. The ones that remain are my responsibility. Stephen Hornsby arranged for Michael J. Hermann, a cartographer at the University of Maine, to provide a map of northeast North America. Deanna Bonner-Ganter at the Maine State Museum and Scott Robson at the Nova Scotia Museum helped in the acquisition of illustrations. Amy Bushnell reassuringly kept tabs on the project in its last stages of preparation. At Routledge and CRC Press the editorial staffs have been unfailingly patient and helpful.

With all long-term projects, a few people see one through all the stages. Alan Tully, Tina Loo, Bob McDonald, Moira Kloster, Richard and Jane Nelson, and Jack Greene have engaged the small and large problems that come with all scholarship. Their steady counsel, patient advice, and faithful friendships have proved invaluable over the years and I am deeply grateful to all of them.

Introduction

The Fault Lines of Empire: Political Differentiation in Massachusetts and Nova Scotia, ca. 1760–1830, is a comparative study of the impact of state formation and state centralization in the early modern British Empire. The study focuses on two towns settled by New Englanders in the 1760s: Machias, Massachusetts (Maine after 1820), and Liverpool, Nova Scotia. Strong similarities in their social, cultural, and economic circumstances make it possible to analyze how imperial- and provincial-level changes in the structures of power in the British Empire were refracted down to localities. The divergences in the political cultures of Machias and Liverpool, the study shows, originated in the seventeenth- and eighteenth-century attempts by the British metropolitan government to redefine center–periphery relations in the British Atlantic world. Thus the political divergence between the United States and Canada dates not from the American Revolution but from developments that began decades earlier. By analyzing governmental systems of power from the perspective of localities, it becomes possible to see that state formation and centralization in the Anglo-Atlantic world were far from uniform and that the constitutional and political fault lines in the British Empire long predated the American Revolution.

The towns of Liverpool and Machias were settled in 1760 and 1763, respectively, by New Englanders, most of whom made their livelihoods in the fishing and timber trades. Sited on large harbors, these towns soon became the largest settlements in their regions, county seats, and ports of entry for foreign trade. In sailing time they were roughly the same distance from Boston. The first churches were Congregationalist and initially all residents were assessed to support them. The most distinguishing difference between the two towns was not social, cultural, or economic, but jurisdictional. Liverpool was in the relatively new colony of Nova Scotia, conquered from the French in the War of the Spanish Succession (1702–1713), and Machias was in one of the oldest British American colonies, Massachusetts, settled by Puritans in the 1630s.

Throughout this work the grammar, spelling, and punctuation of all quoted material strictly adhere to the originals.

Nova Scotia remained within the British Empire after 1783, whereas Massachusetts was in the new United States.

With such strong social, cultural, and economic similarities, this study asked if the jurisdictional differences at the provincial/state and imperial/national levels were simply externally imposed administrative artifices, or if they reflected substantive political differences at the local level. If there were differences down to the local level, at what point in time did they emerge given the shared New England legacy of Liverpool and Machias and the ongoing economic and cultural similarities? In the 1760s when the towns were settled? In 1775 when fighting broke out between British regulars and colonial militias? When thirteen colonies, but not Nova Scotia, declared their independence? When peace arrived in 1783? At some even later point in time? Or at some earlier time that was unrelated to the particular settlement of either town?

These questions relate to more general questions scholars have raised about political and social change in early modern British America. Given the disparate origins of the British American colonies, scholars have tried to assess the degree of developmental convergence among them. The uniting of thirteen colonies in a war for independence suggests a reasonably high degree of convergence, but scholars vary on its nature. Was it social, economic, cultural, or political?[1] If convergence was true for thirteen colonies, to what extent can we conclude that their patterns of development can be applied to other British colonies? Was developmental convergence normative throughout British America, or was there also developmental divergence? Were developments in Massachusetts and Nova Scotia converging or diverging in the 1760s, and if they were converging, why did Nova Scotia not rebel? If they were diverging, how do we explain it?[2]

The Fault Lines of Empire is an exploration of the patterns of political convergence and divergence in Anglo-America. It began as an attempt to gain fresh purchase on understanding the differences in Canadian and American political cultures. A handful of scholars have written on the topic, most of them following the framework set by Louis Hartz in *The Liberal Tradition in America* and then in *The Founding of New Societies*. He argues that a new society—such as the United States, Canada, Brazil, Mexico, or South Africa—was but a fragment of its home society and transplanted only a portion of its ideological spectrum. In the United States and Canada, liberalism is the dominant ideological fragment that defines the political culture of both countries.[3] Depending on the scholar, the French Canadian and Loyalist political influences qualify liberalism in Canada so that it differs qualitatively from American liberalism. Significantly, the qualifiers of Canadian liberalism that scholars have identified happened relatively late in the eighteenth century and were largely influences originating in North America as much as in Europe.[4] Most studies of the historical roots of Canadian and American political differences work within a Hartzian framework that emphasizes ideological transplantation followed by internal growth and elaboration.[5]

Generally scholars have accepted unquestioningly that the American Revolution was the critical moment of divergence in the political cultures of Canada and the United States.[6] Initially I, too, accepted that assumption, but sought to identify and analyze the particular factors from the revolutionary era that contributed to divergence. Researching those factors, however, was not straightforward. Abundant sources exist for studying the rebelling colonies, while sources for the northern loyal colonies are scarcer. To minimize the distortions that source disparities might cause, I decided to do a comparative study of two towns, essentially applying a variant of social history methodology to political history. That decision had two collateral benefits. One, political differentiation is generally studied as a state-level phenomenon, for example, comparisons of state formation in Russia, France, and China or in Britain and France, rather than from the perspective of localities.[7] Local studies, however, provide a way to analyze how large-scale processes, many of them determined at the state level, manifested themselves at the local level where people experienced them day to day.[8] Two, a focus on localities weighted my analysis toward identifying patterns of institutional divergence, in contrast to most other studies on political differences between the United States and Canada that are weighted toward explanations of ideological divergence.[9]

To make the study systematically comparative and analytically rigorous, I posed a series of questions that applied to both Liverpool and Machias. How were group resettlements organized and land grants given by the governments of Nova Scotia and Massachusetts? How was land distributed within the townships? How did people respond to the intensifying imperial dispute between the British government and the American colonies? How did each town use armed force when fighting began in 1775? What were the local factors influencing the sundering of the bonds between church and community? What were the structures and responsibilities of local governments?

The answers to each question produced six discrete comparative studies, and the results of each could be checked against others. Significantly, all six comparisons show that divergences in political culture did not originate in the localities, but existed before the initial granting and settlement of Machias and Liverpool. The salient causal factors shaping divergences were the institutional modifications to New England practices that the British implemented in Nova Scotia. Both settlements were granted to groups, but the grantees of Machias had corporate rights as tenants-in-common, whereas in Liverpool they did not. In Machias, the undivided land was held in common by the proprietors as a corporation, and in Liverpool each grantee had a right to one 500-acre share held in severalty (or individual) ownership. The British government's proscription of municipal corporations in newer colonies, beginning with Nova Scotia, sharply curtailed communications among settlements, which were critical to sustaining the revolutionary resistance to Britain. The absence of town governments in Nova Scotia accelerated the collapse of New England Congregationalism, whereas in Massachusetts town governments provided critical buttressing of the established church. In New England, and indeed throughout the colonies that became the United States, the importance of local government, both town and county, vested the provisioning of most social services, whether schools, care of the poor, the building of roads, or the construction and maintenance of jails, with localities, whether towns or counties. In Nova Scotia, and then throughout post-1783 British North America, the fiscal powers of local governments were sharply curtailed, and provincial governments became more important in providing various services. In all six comparative cases, changes in the institutions within which people operated—and which generally were not determined at the local level, although they were locally modified—were critical factors in explaining long-term patterns of political differentiation between Nova Scotia and New England, including ideological shifts.

The institutional legacy of Machias had its origins in seventeenth-century Massachusetts, whereas Liverpool's had been influenced by a century of piecemeal attempts by British officials to bind colonies more closely to the metropolitan government. Those endeavors had the greatest chance of effecting change in the newest colonies, such as Nova Scotia, rather than in older colonies, such as Massachusetts, where customary practices proved powerful deterrents. The sources of institutional differentiation that I documented for Liverpool and Machias did not begin with their founding in the 1760s or at the time of the American Revolution, but rather originated in long-term reconfigurations of power in the British Atlantic world.

This study of micro-level political behavior reinforces macro-level analyses that show that the extension of British state power overseas was not a precipitous development after the Seven Years' War, but had been episodically continuous and incrementally cumulative from at least the time of the revocation of the Virginia Company charter in 1624.[10] The growing involvement of the metropolitan government in overseas enterprises, however, was not guided by a well-articulated policy, such as characterized French overseas policy under Cardinal Richelieu or Jean-Baptiste Colbert, but tended to be piecemeal and reactive. Nonetheless, an accumulation of discrete actions created discernible patterns, even without clearly articulated policy.[11] Over the seventeenth century, the Privy Council and King's Bench gradually pared back the privileges that had been delegated to colonial promoters in royal charters. The assertion of royal prerogative over the civil governance of subjects was reflected in decisions such as the royalization of many colonies and the proscription of municipal governments in newer colonies, such as Nova Scotia. In the early seventeenth century, chartered overseas enterprises had great latitude to pursue diplomacy with foreigners and wage war in the extra-European world. By the end of the century, the Crown had asserted its prerogative over foreign policy with Europeans. Diplomacy with and war-making against non-European peoples continued to be powers delegated to colonies and companies, although by the mid eighteenth century, relations with native peoples in North America were being increasingly centralized at the level of the metropolitan government and the autonomy of colonial governments to craft their own policy was formally curtailed, most notably with the appointment of Indian Superintendents in 1754 and the Proclamation of 1763.[12]

The implementation of these changes varied enormously, and was least effective in the North American colonies established in the seventeenth century, because customary practices carried constitutional legitimacy, at least in the minds of colonists. New England colonies, for example, maintained a vibrant tradition of town government, even though metropolitan officials long recognized the centrifugal tendencies of towns. Throughout British America the power of assemblies grew and repeatedly challenged the power of governors.[13] The large mainland colonies continued to exercise considerable discretion over foreign policy, whether planning an attack on Louisbourg or sending the Virginia militia into the Ohio River Valley. Precedent gave legitimacy and a growing colonial demographic and economic base made these military forays feasible. Older colonies could also resist developments such as Crown claims to naval stores on ungranted land, whereas in a newer colony such as Nova Scotia, and later Lower Canada, Upper Canada, New Brunswick, and Newfoundland, people acknowledged the legitimacy of the policy because it predated their arrival.[14]

The other cluster of important variables that contributed to political and constitutional divergence within the early modern Empire was the way Britain acquired territory and when it received a government. Of the colonies that rebelled, only New York and New Jersey began as conquered colonies, whereas on the eve of the Revolution the North American colonies of Nova Scotia, the Island of St. John (renamed Prince Edward Island in 1799), Quebec, and East and West Florida were all conquered colonies. Newfoundland was a commercial territory (without a year-round colonial governor until 1824), as was Rupert's Land (the Hudson Bay drainage basin). Over the eighteenth century, France and Spain contested British claims to these territories, militarily, at the treaty table, or both. British claims were confirmed—if not established—by international agreement, and thus by state action. All of the colonies and territories that became Canada, therefore, had been under greater metropolitan control since the time of their acquisition by Britain than had been the colonies chartered and settled in the seventeenth century. The first British colonial government in the future state of Canada was in Nova Scotia after the conquest of Acadia in 1710. Consequently, the governments of all these colonies were established after the Glorious Revolution (1688–1689) and development of the Crown-in-Parliament, and thus colonists could not claim a constitutional autonomy from Parliament and an allegiance to the Crown alone in the way the people in the older colonies did.[15]

Constitutional and political developments within Britain also contributed to the metropolitan government's ability to increase its power over overseas enterprises. Between the granting of Pennsylvania in 1681, the last proprietary colony, and the next colonial acquisition, Acadia/Nova Scotia which the French ceded in 1713, sovereignty came to reside in the Crown-in-Parliament, most immediately a consequence of Parliament's role in the abdication of James II and the accession of Mary Stuart and William of Orange to the throne. In 1707, the English state became the British state with the Union of the Kingdoms. The Treasury, facing a debilitating debt accrued during the Nine Years' War (1689–1697) and the War of the Spanish Succession (1702–1713), devised a stable financial system to fund the public debt.[16] Although these reorganizations and consolidations of power within Britain did not result in a willingness to fund colonial developments, they did reinforce the emerging fault lines in the British Empire between the seventeenth-century practice of privately chartered colonies and the eighteenth-century practice of keeping colonies under tighter metropolitan control.

Machias lay on the seventeenth-century side of the fault line and Liverpool lay on the eighteenth-century side. These two communities did not create the constitutional fault line that lay between them, although their settlement—and the settlement of other towns in northern New England and Nova Scotia—made the divide more apparent to eighteenth-century observers. Liverpool and Machias, therefore, were not on North American frontiers devoid of European political definition, and hence places where societies could be made anew, but rather were in quite distinctive political spaces shaped by a long and ongoing struggle among Europeans to define and control the Americas. Before the first New England settler surveyed a lot or set a foundation stone for a house, the influences on the development of Machias and Liverpool would be external as much as internal, and reflected divergent patterns of British Atlantic governance.

1

Corporate Structure and Private Interest: The Mid-Eighteenth-Century Expansion of New England

As the French made their last defenses of New France in the late 1750s and early 1760s, New Englanders, who had long fought them, believed that the end of French influence in North America would open for settlement a band of land stretching from eastern New York across Vermont and New Hampshire and out to the Atlantic in Maine and Nova Scotia. For over a hundred years the area had served as a buffer, and at times a battleground, between British settlements in New England and New York and French settlements in New France.[1] The Mi'kmaq, Wulstukwiuk, and Wabanaki nations remained the dominant day-to-day military power in Nova Scotia and Maine, but three years of successive French defeats at Louisbourg, Quebec, and Montreal, in 1758, 1759, and 1760, respectively, made it easier for the British to exact modest and contested permission from the Mi'kmaq in 1760 and 1761 to allow some settlement on their lands in Nova Scotia, particularly those previously settled by the Acadians.[2]

Native claims notwithstanding, land-hungry New Englanders responded almost immediately to the French capitulations at Louisbourg (1758) and Quebec (1759). Rather than going home after being discharged, a group of Massachusetts soldiers settled on "some of the Lands they had Conquered" in Maine. In their petition for a grant of land, they reasoned that as no English

An earlier version of this essay appeared as "Corporate Structure and Private Interest: The Expansion of New England in the 1760s," in *They Planted Well: New England Planters in Maritime Canada,* Margaret Conrad, ed. (Fredericton, NB: Acadiensis Press, 1988).

inhabitants had ever settled there the land "would be as likely to fall to their share as to others." A group organized in 1759 in the towns of Duxborough, Pembrook, Kingston, and Plympton, Massachusetts, reasoned in their petition that "having small and very poor farms or Tenements … and some of us not one foot of Land in the world," they very much desired a grant on the Penobscot River in Maine. Thomas Pownall, governor of Massachusetts, advised the General Court in his January 1760 address "that now every other obstacle is removed," namely, the century-old conflict with the French, the council and assembly should resolve all title disputes in Maine to facilitate the orderly and legal settlement of the region. New Hampshire's Governor Benning Wentworth busily granted dozens of townships in what are now Vermont and New Hampshire. In October 1758 Nova Scotia's governor, Charles Lawrence, circulated a proclamation throughout New England inviting settlers to immigrate to that colony, from where, only three years before, he had ordered the deportation of the Acadian population—French-speaking colonists whose ancestors had settled in the region more than a century earlier.[3]

Between 1755 and 1775 over 200 townships were granted in Vermont, New Hampshire, the District of Maine, western Massachusetts, and Nova Scotia. Bernard Bailyn counted the granting of 283 townships in New England between 1760 and 1776. An extremely conservative estimate of the number of grantees involved is 10,000 for New England and Nova Scotia, assuming 200 grants and fifty men per grant, or nearly one out of every ten men in New England between the ages of sixteen and sixty.[4] The number was certainly higher. Many townships had more than 50 grantees; Machias, Maine, and Liverpool, Nova Scotia, had 80 and 164 grantees respectively.[5] When settlers, including women, children, and nongrantees, are counted the number of uprooted grows. The 1767 Nova Scotia census identified 6,913 people as "Americans," most of whom were from New England. During the 1760s New Hampshire's population increased by 22,000 or 58 percent, mostly in the western counties. In the early 1760s Vermont had only a few dozen families; by 1776 it had 20,000 inhabitants. In Lincoln County, Maine, stretching from the Androscoggin River to the St. Croix River, there were over 15,000 souls, most of them recent settlers. Thus the migration into northern New England and Nova Scotia in the 1760s and 1770s involved upwards of 60,000 of New England's 500,000 residents.[6]

Demographic conditions in lower New England encouraged this demand for land. By the mid eighteenth century, many New England towns settled in the seventeenth century had reached land-to-people ratios of one adult man to approximately forty acres. Some towns diversified their economies to absorb displaced agricultural labor, but many New Englanders preferred to move in search of new land. To compound the demographic pressure, massive fires burned across lower New Hampshire and southern Maine during the

Fig. 1.1 "A Sketch of Mechios Mills," from *Atlantic Neptune III* by Joseph F. W. Des Barres, 1776. (Courtesy of the Maine State Museum.)

summers of 1761 and 1762, destroying the forests and livelihood of many timbermen and thus intensifying the demand for land, especially downeast in Maine where the access to the sea and water transportation made the timber trade viable.[7]

Demographic pressure and ecological catastrophe explain the high demand for land. The deportation of the Acadians from Nova Scotia and the collapse of French power in North America explain the interest in the lands north and east of lower New England. But the causes of the rapid expansion of New England in the mid eighteenth century do not explain the pronounced group character of expansion. The petitions and grants listing hundreds and thousands of New Englanders are conspicuous in the public record, largely because governments granted townships to groups and people relocated in groups.

At a logistical level, the magnitude of the petitioning process alone is impressive. Groups had to be organized, decisions made as to where to ask for land and which colonial government to petition for a grant, a petition drafted, signatures collected, and money raised to send an agent to the appropriate colonial assembly or governor and council. Evidence of how that process took place is nearly nonexistent, but its result is clearly evident and the conclusion inescapable that New Englanders had enormous organizational aptitude and a willingness to act as groups. The corporate structure of New England expansion, through both the granting and settlement processes, drew in so many settlers so fast. New Englanders' preference for group grants shaped the interactions of individuals, groups, and governments, reflecting prevailing cultural patterns and influencing the establishment of new settlements.

Group grants also became a point of political tension and dispute in northeastern North America. In New England, group grants had carried legislatively created corporate rights since the late seventeenth century, including the right to tax corporate members for the expenses of resettlement. The grant of a township (the physical space) also implied the eventual extension of political recognition by the colonial government, including the right to have a township's residents incorporated as a town with rights to pass bylaws, raise taxes, build roads, hire a minister, establish schools, and send representatives to the legislative assembly. These New England customs for establishing communities had concerned officials in Britain for most of a century, because group grants engendered cohesive political units that had proved themselves adept at evading the wishes of metropolitan planners.

The right to grant land was a form of power signifying who controlled major sections of North America, a power the Board of Trade wanted under its final purview, rather than under a colonial assembly or governor. The granting of land by townships to large groups of people carried enormous implications for whether the public sphere in northeastern British America would be reproduced on existing New England models or whether it would be reconstructed on a new metropolitan-defined model. In both Nova Scotia and eastern Maine, the Board of Trade found itself trying to control the granting of land, including the elimination of the corporate privileges of group grants.

* * *

The deportation of the Acadians between 1755 and 1762 opened for settlement large tracts of land in Nova Scotia before land became widely available through the governments of New Hampshire or Massachusetts.[8] New Englanders, long wary of moving there, did not head north just because land was available. J. Hector St. John de Crevecoeur contended that "the power of the crown in conjunction with the musketos has prevented men from settling here."[9] Commercially and militarily, Nova Scotia had come within the orbit of Bay Colony interests: Massachusetts merchants had traded with the Acadians along the Bay of Fundy and the French in Louisbourg; New England fishers frequented Nova Scotia's harbors and shores; and New England soldiers fought to bring the region under the British flag.[10] But since the French cession of Nova Scotia in 1713, London, not Boston, controlled the government of the colony. With a predominantly French-speaking Catholic population until the founding of Halifax in 1749 and the subsequent deportation of the Acadians, the colony lacked the necessary Protestant population base to establish the full apparatus of a British colonial government, including an assembly. Instead, a governor and executive council governed the colony, hardly a selling point for New Englanders with a strong commitment to self-government.[11] When, in 1749, the British moved the seat of government from Annapolis Royal on the Bay of Fundy to Halifax on Chebucto Bay, they peopled the new capital by subsidizing the immigration of British, German, French, and Swiss Protestants, many of whom later moved west down the coast to found Lunenburg.[12]

In 1758, under pressure from the Board of Trade and New England merchants residing in Halifax, Governor Charles Lawrence called a representative assembly, which met for the first time on October 2.[13] Ten days later, on October 12, he issued a proclamation published in New England newspapers inviting colonists to submit proposals for settling in Nova Scotia. He received sufficient inquiries about the nature of the colony's government to issue a second proclamation on January 11, 1759 stating,

> That the Government of Nova Scotia is constituted like those of the neighbouring colonies, the Legislature consisting of Governor Council and Assembly, and every township as soon as it shall consist of Fifty Families will be entitled to send two representatives to the General Assembly. The Courts of Justice are also constituted in like manner with those of the Massachusetts, Connecticut and other Northern colonies.[14]

For many observers the proclamation appeared to be an about-face to a long-standing British policy not to develop Nova Scotia as a "New New England." Whenever the British had considered initiating a more broadly based government, official opinion held that a more centralized government, similar to Virginia's with royally appointed county magistrates and officials, would be superior to the decentralized New England practice of town government and locally elected officers. The proclamation, however, convinced many prospective settlers and some merchants residing in Halifax that the British intended to allow New England–style town government in Nova Scotia.[15]

The language of the proclamation allowed for generous interpretation, without promising more than had been achieved with the establishment of the colonial assembly.[16] Indeed, the Board of Trade had insisted to Governor Lawrence and the executive officers in Nova Scotia that an assembly had to be called. In 1755 His Majesty's attorney general and solicitor general, at the request of the Board of Trade, reviewed the legality of governing Nova Scotia without an assembly and concluded that the governor and council "have not Power to enact Laws for the publick Peace, Welfare and Good Government of the said Province and the People and Inhabitants thereof." When Lawrence observed that the colony of Virginia had been governed "in the same manner" when first established, the Board of Trade responded that it had been of "very short Duration," and that "since the Constitution of the Country has been restored to its true principles, [it] has never been thought advisable to be executed." For two years the two sides argued the case, with the Board of Trade insisting that an assembly be called and contending that representative government would encourage the settlement of the colony. In 1758, Lawrence finally capitulated, but not before an agent for the freeholders had pleaded their case in London.[17] Thus, Lawrence's issuance of the proclamation inviting settlers to Nova Scotia, just ten days after convening the first assembly, and the later proclamation noting that the colony had a government "like those of the neighbouring colonies," referred not to town government, but to a legislative assembly with townships serving as electoral ridings.

Those who drafted the proclamation almost certainly chose the term "township" rather than "town" carefully. In New England usage, a township is a unit of land that can be defined by survey whether peopled or not. A town is the incorporated political entity comprised of residents within a township. Although the distinction between the two terms may have been lost on some prospective settlers, or considered a slip in usage, it was not lost on British officialdom. In 1749 the Board of Trade instructed the governor of Nova Scotia, as it also instructed the governors of East and West Florida and Quebec after 1763, to lay out townships for new settlers, instructions which, in various forms, remained in effect until at least 1773. The Board of Trade reasoned that "it has been found by experience that the settling of planters in townships hath very much redounded to their advantage, not only with respect to the assistance they have been able to afford each other in their civil concerns, but likewise with regard to the security they have thereby acquired against the insults and incursions of neighboring Indians or other enemies."[18] Instructions to lay out townships implied nothing about the form of local government in these new colonies, although in "their civil," or private, concerns, such as building homes and clearing land, settlers would derive benefit from grouping together. New Englanders, however, with their close association between township and town government, labored under the misimpression that town government would be allowed and took up land in Nova Scotia with that expectation. Among them was Captain John Dogget, who secured a grant for the township of Liverpool for himself and 163 other men from Massachusetts.

The language of the Liverpool grant and the subsequent organization of the township's proprietors indicate how shrewdly officials in Halifax used the form but not the substance of New England practice. In style and organization the grant read as would one from Massachusetts. It noted the four primary organizers who had applied for the grant of a township on behalf of themselves and the within-named grantees. The grant's text stated the location of the township, and stipulated the number of families to be settled and the amount of land they were to clear within a given time. Important, although subtle, differences existed. The township was "given, Granted and confirmed … unto the Several Persons hereafter Named," thus in severalty, or individually, to each of the 164 men named. The government did not grant the land to them as "tenants-in-common," the language used in the Massachusetts grants. The grantees were to divide the land among themselves in 500-acre shares; if a majority could not agree upon adequate procedures, the governor would appoint a committee to divide the land. To minimize speculation, settlers could not sell or alienate their land within ten years except by license from the governor, lieutenant governor, or commander-in-chief.

As a further block to speculation, the grant remained conditional upon the settlement of "Forty One of the said Grantees with their Wives, Children, Servants and Effects" by September 30, 1760 and another sixty grantees and their families within the following twelve months. In contrast, the grant for Machias required the grantees to settle the township "with Eighty good Protestant Families" within six years of the King's approval of the grant, but it did not require that the grantees themselves had to be among the eighty families.[19] The Massachusetts phrasing allowed land speculators to be among the grantees, a time-honored tradition that many saw as a virtue; a few well-heeled and well-connected speculators could help to acquire a grant and could advance monies to cover the initial expenses of resettlement and land surveying. The British government, however, wanted to make sure that speculators did not thwart the establishment of stable settlements in Nova Scotia by engrossing land, a concern that continued after the American Revolution in Upper and Lower Canada.[20]

The Liverpool grant played upon the very strong corporate traditions in New England resettlement; the grant would become null or void if the grantees did not work together to ensure the necessary number of settlers. At the same time, the grant extended no legal corporate rights to the grantees as tenants-in-common, or a proprietorship, the legally incorporated entity created with the granting of townships in New England. The grant's language retained the grantees' corporate responsibilities for organizing the resettlement of New Englanders in Nova Scotia, while removing the corporate rights. If the change initially escaped the notice of most grantees, the government intended the modification. Had it desired to replicate faithfully a New England–type grant, then one could have been copied from the *Acts and Resolves* of Massachusetts, which printed all grants as acts of the legislature, and which were available in Halifax. The first Nova Scotia assembly modeled some of its initial legislation on Massachusetts laws only to have them disallowed by the Crown.[21] Government officials routinely copied, with slight modifications, documents from one colony to another colony. Anyone drafting a grant would have known that Britain and the New England governments had long-standing controversies over titles to land and the right to grant land.[22] Thus it is reasonable to conclude that subtle differences between New England grants and the Nova Scotia grants were constructed quite wittingly. Whether it was witting deception is less clear, but the proclamations and grants did deceive some New Englanders who went to Nova Scotia.

Colonial officials in Halifax and the Board of Trade in Britain continued to modify, restrain, and eliminate New England local practices after Yankee settlers arrived in Nova Scotia. In 1761 the King disallowed an act passed by the assembly the previous year to "enable the proprietors to divide their lands held in common and undivided." The executive council responded by appointing township committees to divide the forfeited lands of grantees who had not come. For over a year, however, settlers in many townships had organized themselves as self-governing proprietorships and took umbrage at the appointment of committees. In a memorial to the Council, eight Liverpool settlers protested the appointment of the committee, arguing that "we conceive we have right and authority invested in ourselves (or at least we pray we may) to nominate and appoint men among us to be our Committee," a right they perceived as theirs by virtue of being "born in a Country of Liberty." The appointed committee, they observed, created unease among the settlers, causing some to leave and others not to come. At the end of the memorial, they reiterated their right to choose their own committee and other officers, a privilege they "must insist on as it belongs to us alone to rule ourselves." The memorial reflected not just the colonial New England view that grantees constituted associations that had corporate rights of self-government, but also the men's understanding that those rights might not extend to Nova Scotia, captured in the parenthetical phrase "or at least we pray we may."[23] These Yankees were beginning to realize that the rights of British subjects in New England might not be the same as those in Nova Scotia, and indeed, what New Englanders thought of as rights might well be revocable privileges in the eyes of the British government. The colony was indeed a new public world, albeit one still being made operational as officials established its parameters and settlers maneuvered to work within them.

The Liverpool petition failed to move the Council. The difficulty in Halifax lay in deciding how many rights New England settlers might have without reproducing the New England practices that the Board of Trade opposed. The Council's appointment of proprietors' committees in 1761 acknowledged its growing awareness that the Crown's ministers would allow little latitude in the devolution of autonomous decision making to the level of the township. But in a 1763 evaluation of the status of the townships, Charles Morris, provincial surveyor, and Richard Bulkeley, provincial secretary, recommended to the Council that the New England settlers be allowed the political rights to which they had been accustomed. The allowance of these rights, they believed, was one of the conditions Governor Lawrence used to induce New Englanders to come to Nova Scotia. Morris and Bulkeley's reasoning did not persuade the

Council. Lawrence died in 1761, before the controversy arose, and thus his personal intentions are unknowable.[24] Perhaps Morris and Bulkeley were right when they argued that Lawrence had intended for the townships to have local self-government. But as the royal disallowance of the proprietors' act showed, and as was subsequently proved in Machias and eastern Maine, the Board of Trade would not permit any governor much discretion in granting settlers extra rights, whatever his personal predilections might have been. In 1767 the Nova Scotia assembly passed an act that required a writ for land to be distributed in the townships. That year a justice of the peace in Londonderry, Nova Scotia, issued a warrant allowing the settlers there to choose their own committee to divide the lands, a decision the Council in Halifax declared unlawful.[25] Authorities in neither Halifax nor London would willfully allow the extension of undesirable New England practices and privileges to Nova Scotia.

The settlement of Liverpool, the most successful of the South Shore fishing townships, proceeded rapidly. Seventy families with thirteen schooners and three sawmills arrived in 1760. Two years later, 90 families (504 individuals) had settled, 12 families short of the 102 required by the grant but enough to satisfy officials in Halifax and to ensure the settlement's survival. By the following year Liverpool had grown by another 10 families, making a total of 634 inhabitants. In 1764 the inhabitants of Liverpool gave up the 1759 grant, and the government issued one to conform to the families and individuals who had actually settled. The 1759 grant had named 164 individuals, whereas the 1764 grant named 142. Only 31 names carried over from one grant to the other. Although a small percentage of the original grantees (18.9 percent), the 31 provided a solid core of settlers.[26] Many of the original grantees may have thought that they could sell their share or have someone settle in their stead, as one could in New England. The sizeable number of nongrantees among the first settlers in Liverpool suggests that some variant of that practice had been operable among the first grantees. By issuing a new grant the government reinforced its opposition to land speculation by prohibiting absentee proprietors and sales of land during the first decade of settlement. The language of the second grant reproduced much of the first. It added one share for the first settled Anglican minister, the established church of Nova Scotia, and one share for the use of a school. The settlement stipulations changed slightly to require that each grantee settle himself or a family before November 30, 1765, reflecting a change in metropolitan policy on land grants in Nova Scotia.[27]

Throughout the 1760s and 1770s the governor and executive council retained the right to increase the number of grantees if they thought land was available, and they monitored the number of settled grantees through the reports submitted by the appointed proprietors' committee. On January 11, 1771, the government issued an amending grant to fifteen Liverpool men, as agreed upon by the proprietors' committee at a December 2, 1770 meeting.

A 1784 proprietors' report included the names of another ten men who had been locally admitted as proprietors at the December 2, 1770 meeting, but were not official grantees because they had been absent at the time or could not raise the money to pay their share of the cost for petitioning the government. The major caveat to the settlement requirement was that friends of the government could be absentee grantees and speculate in lands. Through Orders in Council the government granted another fourteen shares to men not on the grant, nine of which were for political favors to men from Halifax.[28] This involvement of Halifax in township affairs was part of the ongoing attempts to suppress unwanted New England political behavior and to shape it anew for Nova Scotia. The right to control some land grants in a township and for the governor and council to insert men of their choosing were significant enhancements of executive powers.

In one welcomed deviation from New England practice, the Nova Scotia government subsidized the expense of new settlements, particularly transportation and food. When New Englanders sent agents to view the available lands in Nova Scotia, the government paid to take them around the colony. Richard Bulkeley, the provincial secretary, instructed the appointed hosts to treat the agents well and provide good accommodations. One ship's captain received thirteen sets of bedding and boards to build a platform because he did "not have room enough to accommodate the whole [thirteen Gentlemen] in [his] cabbin." The government did not initiate all largesse. Agents from Connecticut and Rhode Island, representing over 300 people interested in settling the former Acadian lands in the Minas Basin, negotiated for provisions, arms, and ammunition for local defense, and free transport of livestock, furniture, and settlers. Governor Lawrence agreed to most of their requests, even though he did not have the power to authorize government expenditures for transportation and provisions.[29]

The Board of Trade reprimanded Lawrence for his settlement policy, first for giving away rather than selling the lands along the Bay of Fundy and then for agreeing to provide government assistance for transportation and provisions. It conceded, however, that once made the commitments should be honored. In the spring of 1760, the Nova Scotia government hired ships' captains, among them Silvanus Cobb, to go to New England to pick up settlers. Cobb, a native of Plymouth, Massachusetts, and a Liverpool grantee, had long been involved in the affairs of Nova Scotia including the attacks on Louisbourg and the deportation of the Acadians. He received sailing orders to pick up settlers in Plymouth waiting to go to Liverpool. In later instructions for transporting New England settlers, he was told to stop in Boston to receive a shipment of bricks to bring back to Nova Scotia, an indication that Lawrence was serious about providing the necessary goods to help settlements survive, despite the Board of Trade's resistance to his plans. In 1761, the government asked John

Dogget, the primary organizer for the township of Liverpool, to hire a ship to transport twenty families and their livestock from Nantucket to Liverpool.[30]

The fall of 1760, after the spring arrival of settlers, the government shipped 360 food rations to Liverpool to be distributed among the township's indigent population. The following March thirteen barrels of pork and thirty barrels of flour arrived, supplemented in April with another ten barrels of pork and forty barrels of flour. Regular government assistance halted after the first two years, although Halifax continued to assist destitute Liverpool settlers. In December 1762 Dogget requested assistance for a poor family of three and seven indigent children. In the summer of 1763 a committee from Halifax surveyed conditions in all the new settlements and reported that 1,000 bushels of Indian corn might be needed for the South Shore communities of Liverpool, Barrington, and Yarmouth.[31]

Government subsidies for transportation and food had the immediate effect of speeding settlement, as well as serving the long-term aim of encouraging a sense of local deference to government. As patronage, transportation and food funded by Halifax, but distributed by local elites, shifted some of the allegiance of local leaders from the township residents to the government. Officials in Halifax, not the townspeople, chose the committees that oversaw the distribution of food, thus reinforcing the right of the colonial government in Nova Scotia to determine local affairs, however beneficent the purposes. Most elites knew that the monies for these expenses came from parliamentary appropriations rather than from provincial sources, thus tying themselves not just to Halifax, but to Whitehall and Westminster, as well. In New England, well-to-do grantees, some of them speculators, helped with the initial costs of settlement. In Nova Scotia, parliamentary assistance helped achieve settlement survival, a subtle but important enhancement of the imperial public sphere, a notion of a commitment to imperial growth beyond the boundaries of a single colony. Subsidies also created the precedent that the colonial government, backed by the metropolitan government, provided some social goods, a position that was reinforced when the towns had virtually no power to raise taxes locally, except ironically for the poor.

* * *

In Nova Scotia, the newness of the colonial government, few customary rights that colonists would agitate to protect, and patronage networks tied to Britain provided the context for colonial officials and the Board of Trade to develop new land-granting practices without serious social or political dissent. Modifying policy in a relatively new colony was far easier than modifying it in older colonies where established elites and long-standing precedents could thwart the initiatives of metropolitan planners.[32] In the unsettled "backcountry" from eastern Maine to South Carolina, settlers found themselves in political vacuums as colonial governments and the Board of Trade contested jurisdictional control of Crown lands, quarreled over how the institutions of local government would be extended into new areas, and jeopardized land titles of settlers. In eastern Maine, Machias became the focus of the battle between Boston and London over control of the Territory of Sagadahoc, the land between the Penobscot and St. Croix Rivers that had been part of the Duke of York's holdings in the seventeenth century, and which reverted to the Crown in 1689 after the abdication of James II and the accession of Mary Stuart and William of Orange. They subsequently gave the territory to Massachusetts with the rechartering of the colony in 1691, with the proviso that all grants in the territory needed royal approval.[33] Although Machias was only one of dozens of new settlements established in Massachusetts in the 1760s, its story captures how metropolitan–periphery dynamics changed when the Board of Trade found itself on the defensive in its attempts to assert the royal prerogative against the customary land-granting practices of the long-established Massachusetts government.

During the summers of 1761 and 1762 drought plagued New England. The forest fires in New Hampshire and southern Maine, ignited by lightning and fueled to enormous size by the wood refuse remaining from profligate cutting, ravaged the forests and drove men eastward down the coast of Maine. In 1763, thirteen men from Scarborough, Maine, loaded a sawmill onto a boat, sailed downeast, and planted their mill on the falls on the West Machias River.[34] The following year, their families and others from Scarborough reinforced the nascent settlement. Thinking themselves on the Nova Scotia side of the border, the settlers reputedly applied to Halifax for a grant of a township encompassing the upper end of the Machias Bay, and the West, Middle, and East Machias Rivers. Upon learning they had settled within the jurisdiction of Massachusetts, in 1767 they petitioned the Massachusetts General Court for a grant, but the government rejected their request. The next year, they applied again; the House of Representatives and Council approved a grant, but the governor refused to sign it. Undaunted, they applied again in 1770. This time the grant received the approval of the House of Representatives, the Council, and Governor Thomas Hutchinson.[35] The proprietors subsequently sent the grant to London for the Crown's approval, where it was tabled. Only in 1784, after Massachusetts had gained uncontested jurisdiction over the eastern part of Maine, did the state's assembly confirm the grant and incorporate the township's inhabitants as the Town of Machias.

Machias became "the most noted plantation in Maine" in the dispute between Massachusetts and Britain over which governmental body had the right to initiate grants in the area of Maine between the Penobscot and St. Croix Rivers.[36] Massachusetts claimed that in the 1691 charter of William and Mary establishing the Province of Massachusetts Bay (after the 1684 revocation of the Massachusetts Bay Company charter), the Crown gave Maine to the Bay Colony in gratitude for its exertions in driving out the French. Even though hostilities between the French and the British discouraged settlement in Maine for the next seven decades, Massachusetts continued as the area's main source of British defense. Twice, the British government challenged Massachusetts's title to the Territory of Sagadahoc, and twice the attorney general and solicitor general found in favor of the colony. Then in the 1760s the Board of Trade challenged the title again, arguing that William and Mary had not possessed the territory in 1691 and, therefore, could not have granted it legitimately.[37] The argument reflected the metropolitan government's broad strategy to restructure and reform its North American colonies, including control of unsettled lands, whether in eastern Maine, the backcountry from New York to Georgia, or the trans-Appalachian West. The Board of Trade's challenge to Massachusetts's claim to the territory between the Penobscot and the St. Croix Rivers fitted within a larger pattern of ministerial attempts to curb the power of colonies.[38]

When the Massachusetts General Court began to receive petitions for land in Maine in 1759, Governor Thomas Pownall urged it to resolve all outstanding claims of private parties so that the area could be settled. In the seventeenth century, the Council of New England granted sections of Maine to prominent men; their descendants, or the descendants of men who had bought the claims, continued to assert their rights to the land. The multiple and conflicting land claims—of private individuals based on early-seventeenth-century grants, of the Massachusetts Bay Colony based on a 1691 charter, and of the British state—illustrate how dramatically metropolitan–periphery relations had changed over two centuries, and how the institutionalization of seventeenth-century practices blocked the ability of the metropolitan government to effect change. The stakes were high and all parties were prepared to defend their interests. The private claims between the Kennebec and Penobscot Rivers remained contested until well into the nineteenth century, but east of the Penobscot the Massachusetts government quickly resolved outstanding claims. In return for releasing and quitting all claim to the area between the Penobscot and St. Croix Rivers, the Massachusetts General Court granted the heirs of Brigadier Samuel Waldo a township on the Penobscot River. Having extinguished that last private claim, the General Court promptly granted twelve townships in the Territory of Sagadahoc.[39]

Francis Bernard succeeded Thomas Pownall as governor of Massachusetts in 1762, and it fell to him to decide whether to approve the twelve township grants in territory of disputed jurisdiction. He approved them and then had to explain his action to the Board of Trade. In a lengthy letter, written on April 8, 1763, Bernard acknowledged the jurisdictional conflict between Massachusetts and the Crown, including the dispute over the right to initiate grants. He felt, however, that the exigencies of settling the area speedily, and the good intentions of the Massachusetts government in achieving that end, overrode any serious complaints that the Board might raise. To demonstrate the General Court's good intentions, Bernard made three points. One, the grants were to further settlement, and so the General Court had given away, not sold, the land. The Massachusetts government, in turn, was not profiting from land sales. Two, the grants conformed to the restrictions in the 1691 charter, including the requirement that the grantees gain royal approval for all grants in the area. Thus, Bernard saw the grants as "recommendations" to the Crown, which, if not signed, would cease after the eighteen months the General Court had allowed for the grantees to gain royal approval.

As it happened, the Crown had the power to withhold approval and the General Court had the power to extend the time allowance for receiving royal approval. From 1762 to 1784 the grants of twelve townships in Maine, and thirteen after 1770 to include Machias, existed in a legal limbo. But in 1763 when Bernard wrote his justification of the grants he did not foresee the great stubbornness of both the Crown and the Massachusetts government. Bernard made the third point that the Massachusetts government required each grantee to give a £50 bond against fulfillment of the settlement requirements, therefore reinforcing his first point that the grants were for immediate settlement and not for long-term speculation. Bernard believed that it would take years to resolve the jurisdictional dispute between Boston and London, but he also thought it was worthwhile to open eastern Maine to settlers. The General Court had proceeded in good faith to achieve this end, and he saw no reason to withhold his approval of the grants.[40]

The House of Representatives had approved the first six grants on February 20, 1762, but Bernard did not write his letter to the Board of Trade until April 8, 1763, over a year later, perhaps after learning of the Crown's refusal to approve them. A week after sending his explanatory letter, he received a strong reprimand from the Board, written on December 24, 1762, for giving his approval to the grants.[41] Thus, by the spring of 1763, when the men from Scarborough, Maine, settled in Machias, the conflict over land grants in eastern Maine had reached an impasse beyond which neither the Massachusetts General Court nor the Crown and Board of Trade would move until after the American Revolution.

The dispute, however, did not keep settlers from moving downeast or from submitting petitions for land grants. In 1768 the Massachusetts House of Representatives and Council approved a grant to the settlers at Machias, but the governor vetoed it. Two years later the General Court passed the same grant and this time Governor Thomas Hutchinson approved it. Like his predecessor Francis Bernard, he had to explain his actions to the Board of Trade. By 1770 the area between the Penobscot and the St. Croix Rivers had from 500 to 1,000 settlers. The prohibition on grants effectively prevented the organization of local government, both town and county, and therefore the legal resolution of differences among settlers. Fearing the complete collapse of law and order in the region, and the emergence of groups similar to the regulators in North Carolina, Hutchinson thought it best to sanction the grant of Machias, the site of the largest settlement in the region. He acknowledged the Board's position that no settlers should be in the area, but, he noted, measures to eject the settlers would have had to originate in either the Massachusetts Council or House of Representatives, a move neither body would take. Hutchinson felt that unless Parliament took unilateral action and removed Maine from the jurisdiction of Massachusetts, he had to accept the reality of settlement and under the laws of the Bay Colony provide for civil governance.[42]

Hutchinson was trapped. As a royally appointed governor he answered to the Crown through the Board of Trade. As the governor of Massachusetts, he was responsible for civil governance. Settlement in eastern Maine put the two obligations at odds, although Hutchinson might have argued that the area was beyond his jurisdiction. In a manner similar to Bernard's, he defended his approval of the Machias grant in terms of the immediate exigencies to be met: for Bernard, in 1763, the benefit of settling British subjects in Maine; for Hutchinson, in 1770, the need to have some semblance of legally constituted government among downeast settlers to forestall unrest and create legitimacy. Hutchinson saw the short-term benefits of recognizing grants and establishing civil governance as having greater primacy than the long-term controversy between Whitehall and Boston over who had ultimate jurisdiction in eastern Maine. The Board of Trade, as it had done with Bernard, sent Hutchinson a strong reprimand. By signing the Machias grant, Hutchinson reinforced Massachusetts's control, which would subsequently influence the position of eastern Maine in the revolutionary conflict. As long as the settlers' petition stalled in the General Court, their discontent was focused there or diffused. Once the General Court and Hutchinson approved the Machias grant, the metropolitan government, and not the provincial government, became the barrier to clear land titles, and settlers directed their discontent explicitly at the Crown's refusal to approve the grant.

Hutchinson also reinforced New England patterns of social and political organization, perhaps most particularly the sense that one of the functions of the colony's government was to protect local and private interests against the intrusive and restrictive policies of the metropolitan government. He thought it best to approve the grant so that some institutions for the maintenance of public order could be established. His superiors in London thought otherwise, judging from their condemnation of his decision and their position on the Nova Scotia settlements. In Nova Scotia the Board of Trade blocked both legislative and executive action to allow autonomy at the local level, whether quasi-public proprietorships or incorporated town government. The Board's response to grants in the Territory of Sagadahoc indicates a similar vision for that region. But in Maine the Board confronted the Massachusetts government, much older and stronger than the Nova Scotia government and with vested rights and privileges that the younger colony did not have. In Boston the General Court had no intention of capitulating to the Board of Trade, as had the governor, council, and assembly in Nova Scotia. From the Board of Trade's perspective, the only immediate ploy for maintaining some control over settlements in Maine was to keep the governor from signing any grants passed by the House of Representatives and the Council. Withholding Crown approval blocked clear title to land and incorporation of the town, but it did not prevent the incorporation of the proprietorship that provided for the division of the land and also served to replicate and legitimate New England patterns of corporatism and local control.

Once Hutchinson signed the Machias grant, the grantees applied to a Massachusetts justice of the peace, Samuel Danforth, to issue them a warrant to call the first meeting of the proprietors. (As noted above, when settlers in Londonderry, Nova Scotia, had done likewise in 1767, the Council voided the warrant.) The Machias grantees did not immediately act to receive the Crown's approbation, a task that was not on their agenda when they first met on September 11, 1770. Rather they elected the customary proprietary officers: a clerk, a committee for calling future meetings, a collector of proprietary taxes, a treasurer, a committee to examine the expenses involved in getting the grant, and a committee of lot layers. They voted to guarantee the mill rights of the first sixteen settlers to Machias and passed a bylaw to confiscate and sell the property of proprietors who failed to pay proprietary taxes. Only at their second meeting, held on November 8, 1770, seven months after they received the grant, did they vote to hire an agent to obtain royal approval.[43]

The sequence of events is significant. First, the Massachusetts government did not itself seek royal approval. Rather the grantees had to assume the responsibility, and they sought it not as a group of individuals, in the way they had approached the General Court to receive the grant, but as a private corporation created by the General Court. The lack of royal approval did not keep a justice of the peace from issuing a warrant for the grantees to meet, elect officers, and vote to tax themselves. This part of the replication of New England society they treated as separate from the grant of land and not dependent on Crown sanction. The absence of royal approval blocked settlers from obtaining unencumbered title to property. But with a large number of resident proprietors, as were present in Machias, that absence only provided a minor block to orderly development. The proprietors proceeded to divide the land and define individual lots, thus avoiding or resolving disputes over property boundaries. Even without warrantable land titles, defined property boundaries allowed settlers to sell land on quitclaim deeds, in which the selling party relinquished all claims to the property, hence quitclaim, but could not guarantee the title to land necessary for a warranty deed. Hutchinson's signature had devolved corporate rights on the people at the local level that the Board of Trade had carefully guarded against in the Nova Scotia settlements.

The Machias proprietors most assuredly knew the difficulty they faced in obtaining the Crown's approval. Townships Four, Five, and Six, west of Machias, had been granted in 1762 and still lacked royal approval in 1770. The grantees to those townships had applied at least once for time extensions on their grants. One of the primary organizers for Township Six, Daniel Merritt, surveyed the marsh for the Machias proprietors, and they surely discussed the difficulty of obtaining royal approval of grants in the Territory of Sagadahoc.[44] Possibly, the Machias grantees made a decision to have their proprietorial affairs well established so that when they received news that the Crown refused to approve the grant, their affairs would have the legitimacy of execution, application, and custom. If custom could not be transferred from one colony to another, as the Liverpool settlers recognized in their petition protesting the appointment of a proprietors' committee, it could be reproduced within a colony, as the Machias settlers indicated by their course of action. In Liverpool settlers proceeded without the support of Halifax, whereas in Massachusetts, Boston clearly supported the downeast grantees.

George III never approved the Machias grant. The outbreak of fighting in 1775 and the revolutionaries' declaration of independence in 1776 eclipsed the controversy over land grants in eastern Maine. In January 1779 a group of men living in Machias petitioned the Massachusetts Council and House of Representatives to regrant the land and incorporate them "into a Town by the Name of Gatesborough," probably in honor of Horatio Gates, the general of the Continental Army that defeated the British army under General John Burgoyne at Saratoga, New York, in October 1777. By 1779, over eighty-one nongrantee heads of households lived in Machias and wished to be included in a new grant. The General Court took no action, probably because it was questionable whether Massachusetts and the United States would be able to hold the region east of the Penobscot River or whether it would fall to the British, following the June 1779 invasion of Penobscot Bay and the establishment of a British fort at Castine. As well, the British had a plan to make the area into a new loyalist colony of New Ireland.[45] In 1784, after the end of the war, the Machias proprietorship, on behalf of the original grantees, petitioned the General Court to have the grant confirmed and the inhabitants of the township incorporated as the Town of Machias, which the court finalized on June 25, 1784. In its confirmation of the grant, the General Court required that the proprietors allow "a reasonable quantity of … land" to nongrantee settlers, to compensate people who had settled in the township after the 1770 grant.[46]

The Revolution ended group grants in New England; Machias was the last one in Maine. Faced with a large war debt, the Commonwealth of Massachusetts initiated a program to sell Maine land to raise money to repay its loans. On October 28, 1783, the General Court appointed the Eastern Lands Committee to dispose of the unappropriated land in Lincoln County, Maine, by settling squatter rights and selling the vacant lands. The committee circulated a notice throughout Lincoln County for people with squatter claims to submit a statement to the committee either individually or as a group. During the late colonial and revolutionary era numerous settlements had developed in the Territory of Sagadahoc, and most people submitted their claims as part of a group petition, with individual claims tendered almost exclusively for specific islands along the coast.[47] These petitions, either explicitly or in tone, acknowledged the changes in land policy wrought by war and independence. But these settlers also knew that a group petition for a colonial-style grant was their best chance of persuading the government to give them more than 100 acres in squatter rights. Because most settlements did not have enough adult men to constitute a proprietorship, these petitions had a number of nonresident signatories.

Eighteen people petitioned for Bucks Harbor, a small peninsula adjoining Machias, and they included a detailed summary of their individual claims. Calculating that the whole peninsula would yield approximately 170 acres for each petitioner and noting that much of the land was rocky, broken, and unfit for cultivation, they asked for the whole to be granted to them in common so that they could divide it among themselves. The Eastern Lands Committee rejected the petition and included Bucks Harbor in the sale of Plantation Number 22, the deed of which named the five petitioners who resided in Bucks Harbor and stipulated that they be allowed 100 acres for every five Spanish milled dollars paid to the purchasers within six months' notice.[48] The claims of the other thirteen petitioners, many of them Machias residents, were not acknowledged.

Another sixty-one men, twenty-five of them settlers, petitioned for the land around the settlement at Chandler's River, what became the primary settlement of Plantation Number 22 (which encompassed present-day Beal's Island, Bucks Harbor, Jonesboro, Jonesport, and Rogue Bluffs). Because the tract included great sections of barren heath or wild blueberry land, the petitioners reasoned that the usable land would allow "but a moderate share" to each of them. But the Eastern Lands Committee sold this land, together with Bucks Harbor, as Plantation Number 22 for £6120:17:5 to eleven men from Boston, and the twenty-five settlers at Chandler's River received the same consideration for land as did the five settlers at Bucks Harbor. Significantly, the Chandler's River "squatters" claimed the marsh, the most valuable land in the township because it provided natural livestock fodder. Under a colonial-style proprietorship, the marsh would almost certainly have been equitably divided among the grantees. (See Chapter 3.) But with the postwar decision to sell land to speculators, and to limit "squatters" to 100 acres, they exacted their revenge by claiming and engrossing the most valuable land.[49]

Unlike colonial petitioners, postwar petitioners felt it necessary to justify their requests for extensive tracts of land. In both the Bucks Harbor and Chandler's River petitions the justification was the poorness of the land, a reasonable claim, although surveyors from Boston waxed eloquent about the region's agricultural prospects. Other petitioners mentioned their steadfast loyalty to the rebels' cause in the late war, hoping it would give them greater claim to the grant of a township. All emphasized the labor and money they had already expended in settling the land. The level of justification in land grant petitions had increased markedly from colonial petitions, because these postwar petitioners, mostly persons of modest means, knew that their best chances for a substantial grant lay in petitioning as a group.[50] Although these settlers did not gain the privilege of a township grant, they did have the right to meet to discuss plantation concerns, tax themselves for needs such as roads and a minister, and eventually to petition for incorporation as a town. One part of the colonial resettlement practice was lost after the war; however, the local rights of town government and self-regulation were retained. In this respect the corporate patterns of New England resettlement remained strong and intact.

* * *

When land-hungry New England soldiers settled on "some of the Lands they had Conquered" in Maine, they believed naively that the Anglo-French conflict over the area was the only significant barrier to settlement in the northeast. Similarly, New Englanders who settled in Nova Scotia (many of them on the former lands of the Acadians) did not initially realize the complexities of the conflicts over the region. The lands they entered remained a contested marchland between British and Native claims, between colonial ways and metropolitan ways, between an old colonial system and a new imperial one. In areas of settlement opened in the eighteenth century, whether in Nova Scotia, northern New England, or the backcountry from Vermont to Georgia, metropolitan authorities, colonial governments, and colonists quarreled over whether the form of local public spheres should be reproduced or recast, replicated to continue colonial customs or reformed to suit a changing empire. The issues drawn into the debates included what government would control an area, what the structures of authority would be, how local governments would be established, and how local officials would be chosen or appointed. As the Board of Trade knew, and contrary to what Governors Bernard or Hutchinson thought, the granting of land was a critical junction on the road toward establishing a new system or toward reproducing an old one.

Nova Scotia, conquered from and ceded by the French during the War of the Spanish Succession (1702–1713), was a relatively new colony by British American standards. Coming under British control after the development of the Crown-in-Parliament, the metropolitan government's remaking of land-granting practices elicited protests but not strenuous resistance from settlers. In the 1760s, most of Nova Scotia's 14,000 people were recent arrivals, and the assembly had first convened in 1758, too recently to have developed customary rights specific to the colony. Unencumbered by custom and financially beholden to Parliament, the metropolitan government, by changing a few rules and procedures in the land-granting process, could avoid in Nova Scotia many of the troublesome private interests and corporate forms characteristic of New England land-granting practices.

The distribution of land in severalty in Nova Scotia, rather than to grantees as tenants-in-common, not only eliminated the incorporation of the proprietorship and protected against nonsettler speculators, but it also allowed for both the retention of Crown land in townships and the creation of public spaces within them. (See Chapter 3.) By prohibiting proprietorships and by obliging colonial officials in Halifax to appoint proprietors' committees, the Board of Trade guaranteed that private corporations would not be created with the granting of townships and that local leaders would be acceptable to Halifax. The requirement that grantees settle in Nova Scotia technically eliminated speculators residing outside the colony. In New England, speculators, many of them merchants, often helped to fund the initial settlement of a township. They also acted as suppliers and creditors for the settlers. Machias grantee and agent Ichabod Jones, a Boston merchant, served in just such a capacity. In Nova Scotia, government subsidies for food and transportation helped to cover some costs that speculators might have covered. Halifax merchants filled the financial credit gap by establishing ties to Liverpool traders, and became politically and economically influential in the community. Through the Council, many Halifax merchants and government officials received individual grants in townships such as Liverpool, a significant caveat to the settlement requirement, but one that helped to reorient commerce and politics from New England port towns to Halifax.[51]

In Nova Scotia, there were in principle, although not always in practice, clear vertical linkages in the chain of authority from Crown-in-Parliament, to Board of Trade, to governor, to council and legislative assembly, to local government administered through a county court system with royally appointed officials. Autonomous local structures of authority, such as incorporated proprietorships (private/quasi-public) or incorporated town government (public), and which often fostered horizontal linkages at the expense of vertical ones, were not allowed. Significantly, throughout post-1783 British North America, the British incorporated only one municipality, the Loyalist-settled city of Saint John, New Brunswick. All other urban centers, including Halifax, Quebec, Montreal, Kingston, and York (later Toronto), were run through the county court system until the 1830s, an indication of how thoroughly the metropolitan government intended to minimize the number of incorporated entities that could undercut the centralized organization of authority.[52] Although the metropolitan and colonial governments could, with the stroke of the pen, or the lack thereof, severely restrict local rights in Nova Scotia, changing behavior could not be accomplished so speedily. As subsequent chapters show, Yankees in Nova Scotia maintained a significant degree of local autonomy, albeit without legal sanction. In many respects it was more intense and idiosyncratic than New England localism, precisely because it did not take its definition from statute law and colonywide practices, but derived it from transplanted culture and diverse local circumstances.

The Massachusetts colonial government, unlike Nova Scotia's, was not one tier in a hierarchy of authority linking the Machias grantees on the bottom with the Crown-in-Parliament on the top. Indeed, the people of Massachusetts, as in colonies established in the seventeenth century before the British constitutional development of the Crown-in-Parliament, argued passionately and militantly that they had constitutional relationships with the Crown that were independent of Parliament, an important characteristic distinguishing Massachusetts from Nova Scotia. In the 1760s, nothing so graphically illustrates the ambiguous relationship among constituent parts of royal government in Massachusetts as the requirement that the Machias grantees obtain the Crown's approbation of the township grant on their own. That requirement, based on the 1691 charter, put the Machias grantees, and the grantees of the other eastern townships, in the curious position of petitioning the Crown as a private corporation created by the Massachusetts government. By sanctioning private petitions to the Crown, the Massachusetts government facilitated the private interests of its residents more than it facilitated the interests of the metropolitan state, a function it had performed since its inception as the government of the Massachusetts Bay Company when it buttressed private Puritan interests against Charles I and his ministers. The Bay Colony's ingenuous strategy for maintaining autonomy from metropolitan interests, whether it be in resisting the ecclesiastical hierarchy of the Anglican Church or the political control of the Ministry and Parliament, was to give considerable power to congregations and local communities, power that was protected through the right of the Massachusetts government after 1691 to incorporate them. Much of the function of the Massachusetts colonial government was to shield its residents from the centralizing tendencies of the metropolitan government, an intrinsically adversarial role and one which was predicated on the notion that the interests of colonists and the interests of the British state were frequently oppositional rather than complementary.

The colonial New England practice of incorporating local groups, both public and private, engendered a deep commitment to this pattern of social and political structure. Group grants allowed many middling and probably some quite poor people access to land. A group had a voice strong enough to be heard in positions of power that an individual of modest circumstances lacked. Groups also gave individuals greater flexibility, for not every grantee had to settle for the terms of the grant to be met. The corporate structure reinforced private individual interest by protecting one's share of land even in one's absence, provided enough of the group settled. Group settlement also promised the more rapid extension of political rights through the incorporation of a town than did individual settlement. In New England political rights were extended through one's inclusion in a town. Thus to settle without benefit of a group that could soon be incorporated as a town and send a representative to the assembly was to choose to be disenfranchised for an indeterminate period of time. Most New Englanders avoided this situation. When the United States government opened the Northwest Territory for settlement, Thomas Jefferson rewrote the 1784 Northwest Ordinance in 1787 to include provisions for a territorial government and the establishment of state governments, done to attract New England settlers who were leery of resettling without clear promises of law and order and the protection and extension of political rights.[53]

Years before Parliament passed the Sugar Act (1764), which traditionally marks the rise in tensions between colonists and the British government, another power struggle had emerged over land distribution, probably the single greatest form of government largesse and patronage in the British overseas world. Throughout British North America, some of the first people to confront changes in colonial practices were settlers seeking land for new communities. In Nova Scotia, New Englanders found themselves under a new system of colonial government. But in many areas, from eastern Maine to the Carolina piedmont, colonists found themselves in power struggles between colonial governments and the metropolitan government over the granting of land and the right to define new areas of settlement.

2

Liverpool, Machias, and the North Atlantic Region: An Historical, Demographic, and Economic Profile

The mid-eighteenth-century sweep of Yankees into downeast Maine and Nova Scotia ushered in a new era in the 300-year history of European involvement in northeastern North America. John Cabot first claimed the region for the English in 1497. Subsequent adventurers coasted along its shoreline and nosed up its rivers. European fishers and whalers harvested the rich waters. Traders bartered European manufactures for furs with native peoples. French and British strategists jockeyed for dominance in the region. A few hardy, and sometimes foolhardy, people hazarded settlements in sheltered coves and harbors on the long and indented North Atlantic coast. On the fertile red soil along the Bay of Fundy and on the rocky Newfoundland shore, a few Europeans put down new roots. When New Englanders relocated to Liverpool and Machias, the region still had only scattered pockets of Euroamerican inhabitants, but settlement was a deceptive foil for a long and varied European presence in the area.[1]

The maritime fishery was the region's first and most persistent attraction for Europeans. When they learned of the abundant stocks of fish and large pods of whales is unknown, whether before or shortly after explorers brought back official reports of marine riches, but by the first decades of the sixteenth century, the journals and memoirs of adventurers began to chronicle a multicultural world of Basque, Portuguese, French, and English fishers and native peoples. Ships sailed west in the spring and returned to Europe in the fall with their cargoes of fish. Large vessels, most notably those of the French, could fish miles offshore on the Grand Banks; their crews cleaned and packed cod layered with generous quantities of salt in barrels, and when they had filled a ship's hold they would sail for Europe never having made landfall. Salt-poor fishers, especially the English, worked from shore where they could dry their lightly salted fish on flakes, or wooden drying racks. During the sixteenth century the odd European may have wintered in Newfoundland, but most sailed eastward in the fall. On the Labrador coast a few sixteenth-century Basque whalers wintered at the large facilities from which they hunted whales and where they rendered whale blubber to oil. In the early seventeenth century the migratory fishery developed a sedentary component. More fishers wintered over in Newfoundland, some without official approval, others the human remnants of failed colonial ventures by English promoters. A few English crews ventured southward down the coast and established fishing stations on the coasts of Maine, New Hampshire, and Massachusetts.[2]

In the early seventeenth century when the English manifested a vigorous interest in founding colonies, seven groups attempted settlements in New-foundland only to learn that the winters were much longer and harsher than in England, Scotland, or Ireland, despite the similarity in latitude. The French, Scots, and English all planted colonies in what is present-day Maine, New Brunswick, and Nova Scotia, inaugurating a prolonged international struggle for control of the region. The French king, Henri IV, granted Pierre Du Gua, Sieur de Monts, a patent in 1603 to colonize Acadia, a region between forty and forty-six degrees north latitude. Wintering the first year on an island in the St. Croix River, he moved the settlement to Port Royal (later Annapolis Royal) where it survived for three years, was abandoned for three years, and then reestablished in 1610. De Monts's French patent conflicted with the 1606 grant by James I of England to the Virginia Company for land extending from thirty-eight to forty-five degrees latitude, the northern part of which came under the control of the Plymouth branch of the company and its primary promoter Sir Ferdinando Gorges. The same year that Jamestown, Virginia, was established, Gorges attempted a settlement at Sagadahoc, Maine, but the lack of trade goods, the death of the head of the colonizing party, and, not least, bad relations with the local natives doomed the venture. In 1613 a French Jesuit settlement on Mount Desert Island in the Penobscot Bay lasted a few brief weeks before being destroyed by attacking Englishmen from Virginia. In 1621 Sir William Alexander, a Scot and senior royal official, received a grant of land for a colony to be known as New Scotland, or the latinized version, Nova Scotia, which included present-day Nova Scotia, New Brunswick, and Prince Edward Island. He sent out one colonizing party in 1628 that failed within the year, a second lasted from 1629 to 1632.[3]

Despite this early interest in the land along the northwest Atlantic, little permanent settlement occurred in the region. Settlers found the winters long and cold and the summers short and mild, often too cool to bring grain crops

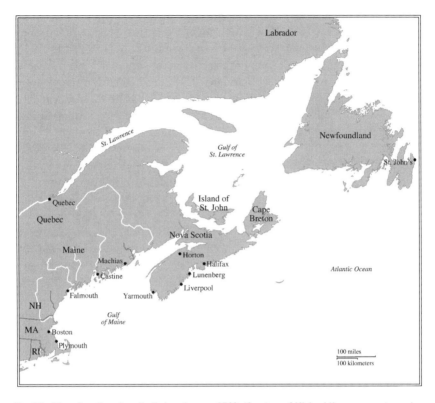

Fig. 2.1 Map of northeastern North America, ca. 1763. (Courtesy of Michael Hermann, cartographer, and the University of Maine Canadian-American Center Cartography.)

to ripeness. For the Natives living on the Atlantic littoral, central Maine marked a break between horticultural groups to the south with their maize, squash, and bean crops and the hunter-gatherers to the north. For Europeans this meant that the Natives' winter stores of crops that sustained so many colonists further south were not available in the northerly latitudes. A few French settlers along the Bay of Fundy adapted their agricultural practices to the environment and developed into a society known as Acadians, French-descended colonists who were culturally distinct from the French Canadians along the St. Lawrence River. They dyked the marsh along the Fundy shore to reclaim rich farmland from the sea, and on it they raised wheat, herded livestock, and planted orchards.[4]

Farther south the English planted what became larger and more stable colonies. The independent English who fished along the southern New England coast greeted the Pilgrims when they arrived in 1620. The Plymouth Colony, with its major settlements in the Cape Cod region, explored up the coast and stationed fur traders at Machias in 1633 only to be pushed out by the French from Acadia. In 1629, a vanguard of Puritans settled at Salem, Massachusetts; the following year John Winthrop, governor of the Massachusetts Bay Company, arrived with a larger group of Puritans at Boston and formally established what was to become one of the most successful and populous English colonies on the eastern seaboard. Religious dissidents hived off from the Bay Colony and began the colonies of Rhode Island and Connecticut. The Puritans had finally produced English settlements in North America that could persist, reproduce themselves, and exploit the riches of the North Atlantic. Significantly, their success, marked among other ways by the production of agricultural surpluses, enhanced the viability of settlements further north. New England fishermen-traders, joined later by traders from the mid-Atlantic colonies, traded agricultural and timber products for fish with settlers in Newfoundland.[5]

Colonists nudged settlement up the coast of Maine, chancing scattered fishing and farming communities. Extensive expansion was inhibited not so much by the natural environment, to which Europeans were learning to adapt, but by the political environment. Conflicts among the English, Natives, and French often found expression through the destruction of remote settlements. Beginning in 1675 with the Anglo-Indian conflict, King Philip's War (1675–1676), and followed by two Anglo-French conflicts, the Nine Years' War (1689–1697) and the War of the Spanish Succession (1702–1713), English settlements in Maine were vulnerable to attacks by indigenous nations, often in alliance with the French. In turn, French settlements in Acadia suffered attacks by the English. Between 1689 and 1713 only Kittery, York, and Wells in Maine remained continuously inhabited.[6] While the Natives kept English settlement confined to the southern corner of Maine, the British, with the help of colonists from Massachusetts, captured Port Royal, Acadia, in 1710, and in 1713 the French formally ceded the colony. Most of the French-speaking Catholic Acadians declined the French invitation to relocate to either Ile Royale or Canada and remained on their farms along the Bay of Fundy.[7]

Strategically the area from Maine to Newfoundland remained vital to both the French and the British. Jutting into the Atlantic, Nova Scotia lay on the path between northern Europe and New England, making it one of the first and the last landfalls on the northern shipping route between Europe and North America. Ships headed from England to New England came down around Newfoundland and Nova Scotia before sailing into the ports of Portsmouth, Boston, or Salem. Europeans headed to the West Indies caught the southwesterly trade winds that blew them along the Iberian coast then west into the Caribbean; to return they continued the trade winds circuit, sailing to thirty or forty degrees north latitude before turning east, bringing them within a couple of hundred leagues of Nova Scotia. Between Newfoundland on the north and Cape Breton on the south lay the entrance into the Gulf of

St. Lawrence, at the western end of which the French had planted the colony of Canada. The harbors along the south coast of Nova Scotia attracted sailors during storms or freezing weather when other North Atlantic harbors were ice-locked. For these strategic reasons Nova Scotia and the contiguous areas of Maine and Cape Breton were important to the French and the British in their attempts to ensure access to the lucrative fishery, forge alliance with Natives, and provide security for their more populous colonies.[8]

With the Treaty of Utrecht in 1713, France conceded British claims to New-foundland, although they retained exclusive seasonal shore rights on the north and west sides of the island. France also ceded Acadia/Nova Scotia to Great Britain, but retained Cape Breton and Ile Saint Jean, which they reorganized as the jurisdiction of Ile Royale, a part of the larger jurisdiction of New France. They built fortress Louisbourg on the southeast coast of Cape Breton, where they reestablished their fishery, carried on a brisk trade, and maintained naval facilities to protect their American territories, stretching from Canada and Cape Breton to the French Antilles and Louisiana. Across the Gut of Canso separating Cape Breton Island from peninsular Nova Scotia, New Englanders built Canso, a fishing settlement and one of the largest concentrations of English-speaking people in the northern maritime region. The British main-tained a small administrative center at Annapolis Royal (formerly Port Royal) on the Bay of Fundy.

The 1720s and 1730s, especially after the signing of treaties in the 1720s between the British and the Wabanaki, Mi'kmaq, and Wulstukwiuk, were years of relative peace in the area, and it experienced significant population growth and expansion of the Acadian population.[9] With the outbreak of fighting in the Caribbean between the British and Spanish in 1739, tensions increased throughout the Atlantic basin. With the entry of the French into the War of the Austrian Succession in 1744, New Englanders, under the leadership of Governor William Shirley of Massachusetts, seized the initiative and launched an attack against Louisbourg and took it, only to watch the British return it to the French in exchange for Madras in India in the Treaty of Aix-la-Chapelle in 1748. That same year the British government decided to move the government of Nova Scotia from Annapolis Royal around the coast to Chebucto Bay where it established Halifax, the British counterpoise to Louisbourg.[10]

Long-standing boundary disputes complicated the tensions in the northeast. The Treaty of Utrecht had left the mainland boundaries of Acadia/Nova Scotia, Canada, and Maine ill defined and hence contested. The French would only concede peninsular Nova Scotia as Acadia; land on the west side of the Bay of Fundy (now New Brunswick and parts of Maine) they claimed as part of their St. Lawrence colony of Canada. To solidify that claim, they rein-forced alliances with the Mi'kmaq, Wulstukwiuk, and Wabanaki nations with gifts and missionary priests. As tensions mounted in the 1750s, the French built Fort Beauséjour on the isthmus connecting peninsular Nova Scotia to the mainland just to the west of Missiquash River, a small stream which they claimed as the boundary between British-held Nova Scotia and French-held Canada. On the other side of the river the British built Fort Lawrence.[11]

During the first decades of the eighteenth century the French-speaking Acadians with their villages along the Bay of Fundy had prospered, grown, and expanded northward along the shores of the bay. By 1750 they numbered around 15,000 people. Most lived in uncontested British territory, but only in 1729 and 1730 had they agreed with Governor Richard Philipps to swear an oath of allegiance to the British crown. They subsequently argued that they had agreed orally with Philipps that they would not bear arms and favored neither the French nor the British in the international struggle over control of the region. Finally in 1755, British regulars, reinforced with New England troops, took Fort Beauséjour. With British and French tensions smoldering in a number of places in North America and the Caribbean, Governor Charles Lawrence of Nova Scotia decided that the Acadians posed an intolerable risk to British security and ordered them deported. Herded onto New England–owned vessels hired for the task, the Acadians saw their homes and barns burned and their livestock scattered or confiscated. They disembarked in British port towns from Portsmouth to Savannah. A significant number eluded expulsion by escaping into the woods and reestablishing communities in more remote areas in Nova Scotia, although many were caught up in the 1758 expulsion. After the end of the war, a large number sought new homes in Louisiana, by then Spanish territory, where they became known as the Cajuns. And many thousands gradually returned to the Maritime colonies.[12]

The Seven Years' War militarily resolved conflicting French and British claims on the continent. In the north, France retained only the islands of St. Pierre and Miquelon lying off the southern coast of Newfoundland. It relinquished all claims to mainland Nova Scotia and ceded Canada, the trans-Appalachian West, and a number of colonies in the Caribbean to the British. In 1762, France gave New Orleans and Louisiana west of the Mississippi River to Spain. The end of the prolonged French and British contests in northeastern North America unleashed a flood of expansion into Nova Scotia and northern New England, to which the Liverpool and Machias settlers were party.[13]

British policy in Nova Scotia, determined by the Board of Trade and the colonial government, sometimes together, sometimes in opposition, shaped the province's demographic character. In 1749, Parliament subsidized the settlement of approximately 2,500 British subjects in Halifax, joined over the next five years by 2,500 German, Swiss, and French Protestants, many of whom went down the South Shore and settled Lunenburg and the surrounding coastal area. From 1755 to 1763 the Nova Scotia government reduced the population of the colony by deporting approximately 15,000 Acadians. In 1758 and 1759 Governor Lawrence issued his proclamations inviting New Englanders to settle in the colony, in particular on the former Acadian lands, and from 1760 to 1765 approximately 7,000 accepted his invitation.

Census figures for assessing the scale and character of population changes for Nova Scotia are scarce, but the few existing ones give a skeletal, if not a fully fleshed out, demographic picture. The 1767 census provides the most complete early analysis of the colony's population; at 13,374 souls Nova Scotia had still not regained the population that it had shortly before the deportation of the Acadians. (See Table 2.1.[14]) "Americans," mainly of New England origin, had supplanted the Acadians as the largest single ethnic group in the colony, although the Acadians did represent nearly 10 percent of the enumerated population. The Irish were the second-largest group, although they were split between Irish Catholics, primarily men working in the fishery, and Irish Protestants, primarily families with farms. The numbers of English and Scots were quite small, although the latter would become more prominent in the late eighteenth and early nineteenth centuries.

The effects of war and its aftermath in North America once again reconfigured Nova Scotia's population when in 1783 the British evacuated Loyalists from New York, Charleston, and St. Augustine and they sought new economic, political, and social niches in the reduced British Empire. Approximately 40,000 Loyalists landed in the northeast Maritime colonies: 20,000 settled in peninsular Nova Scotia; 15,000 in the St. John Valley; and another 5,000 scattered throughout the rest of maritime British North America. Many of the Loyalists remained unsettled for a number of years as they sought to make new lives for themselves. This confluence of people prompted the British to create the separate Loyalist colony of New Brunswick in 1784 from the western portion of Nova Scotia. That same year Cape Breton became an independent colony, which it remained until rejoined to Nova Scotia in 1820. Island of St. John, renamed Prince Edward Island in 1799, had been a separate colony since 1769.[15]

In 1817 the Earl of Dalhousie ordered a census of Nova Scotia to be taken; summary results showed 82,053 inhabitants in the colony. A more thorough

TABLE 2.1 Population of Nova Scotia by Ethnicity, 1767

Ethnicity	Population	Percent (%)
English	912	6.8
Scottish	173	1.3
Irish	2,165	16.2
American	6,913	51.7
German and other foreigners	1,946	14.5
Acadians	1,265	9.5
Total	13,374	

census ten years later documented a population increase of 50,000 persons over the preceding decade, 12,760 of whom were from reannexed Cape Breton. Over the next twenty-five years the colony's population more than doubled to over 250,000, making a nineteenfold increase from 1767 to 1851. (See Table 2.2.)

Population in Liverpool and surrounding Queens County grew, but not as fast as in Nova Scotia in general. The population of the colony increased eightfold during the years 1767 to 1827, whereas Liverpool's increased only fourfold. The slower growth rate in Liverpool is partly attributable to its growth in the early 1760s. By 1767 with 634 inhabitants, Liverpool tied Horton as the third- and fourth-largest settlements in Nova Scotia, after Halifax and environs with 3,022 inhabitants and Lunenburg with 1,468. Situated on the rocky Atlantic shore, Liverpool more quickly reached its physical potential for absorbing people than did areas with greater agricultural potential or that had no white settlers until the end of the eighteenth or beginning of the nineteenth centuries. The expansion of the local timber industry in the wake of the Napoleonic Wars encouraged the early-nineteenth-century population growth that brought Liverpool's population to 3,262 by 1827.[16]

Across the Bay of Fundy and the Gulf of Maine, the population of the District of Maine ballooned. Before 1760 settlement in the district had eddied along the southern coast and along the lower reaches of the Kennebec, Piscataqua, Saco, and Presumpscot River valleys. In 1765 the population of Maine was 21,817. By 1776, Lincoln County alone, which stretched from the Androscoggin River to the St. Croix River, had 15,546 people. From 1765 to 1830 Maine's population increased eighteenfold, a greater increase than Nova Scotia's but comparable in timing. Machias, like Liverpool, was one of the largest early settlements in its local area. The population data for early Machias are sketchy, partly because it was unincorporated until 1784. The 1771 commission sent by Governor Hutchinson to report on the "illegal" settlements in eastern Maine estimated that Machias had 150 males over sixteen years of age and upwards of sixty families. Using an estimated family size of five, there would have been about 300 inhabitants in Machias in 1771. Ten years later a 1781 enumeration of Lincoln County done for the Continental Congress listed 7,311 inabitants living in unincorporated settlements; Machias

TABLE 2.2 Population Growth in Nova Scotia, 1767–1851

Year	Nova Scotia	Queens County	Liverpool	Queens without Liverpool
1767	13,374	—	634	—
1787	—	1,434	1,014	420
1817	82,053	3,098	—	—
1827	123,848	4,225	3,262	963
1851	276,117	—	—	—

was the largest with 626 inhabitants. The next-largest settlement, Newcastle, had 582 inhabitants.[17]

After the commencement of decennial U.S. censuses in 1790 population figures for Machias become more regular and reliable. Machias, like Liverpool, grew more slowly than the surrounding area, in this case Washington County, and the town grew at about the same rate as the state, except for the decade from 1790 to 1800 when the state grew faster. (See Table 2.3.) Washington County, of which Machias is the county seat, grew particularly rapidly. It is important to note, however (and this is a point that is returned to in a discussion of the structure of government in Nova Scotia and Massachusetts), Washington County was both demographically and spatially much larger than Queens County, and proportionately much larger than Machias as compared to Queens County and Liverpool. In 1827 Liverpool accounted for 77 percent of the population of Queens County; in 1830 Machias, including East Machias and Machiasport, which had been separately incorporated in 1826, accounted for only 13 percent of the population of Washington County.

The seventeenth- and eighteenth-century political instability along the North Atlantic littoral precluded Europeans from making a discerning assessment of the region's economic assets. In unknown ratios, it had three resources that people wanted and for which they would resettle: timber, fish, and farmland. Knowledge of the last was particularly marginal, as was much of the land itself. Maine and the Maritimes did have some areas that satisfied farmers looking for arable land. In Nova Scotia the lands in the Minas Basin and Annapolis Valley gave a comfortable living first to the Acadians and then to the descendants of New Englanders and Loyalists who settled there in the 1760s and 1780s. Along the Northumberland Strait and on Prince Edward Island, Scottish immigrants found deep fertile land. Loyalists established viable farms up the St. John Valley in New Brunswick.[18] Along the coast of Maine and up the river valleys, the land once cleared could, with attention, produce enough for a family and some surplus for market. Many hoped, and some believed, that Maine, Nova Scotia, and New Brunswick would become a prosperous agricultural region and that the latter two as part of the remade British Empire would be able to supplant the New England and Mid-Atlantic states in

TABLE 2.3 Population of Maine, Washington County, and Machias, 1790–1830

Year	Machias[a]	Increase (%)	Washington County	Increase (%)	Maine	Increase (%)
1790	818	—	2,759	—	96,540	—
1800	1,014	24.0	4,436	60.8	151,719	57.2
1810	1,570	54.8	7,870	77.4	228,705	50.7
1820	2,033	29.5	12,744	61.9	298,335	30.4
1830	2,779	36.7	21,294	67.1	399,437	33.9

[a]This figure includes the populations of East Machias and Machiasport, which were divided off from Machias in 1826.

the provisioning trade to the West Indies. Many people expected that farming would become the region's primary economic pursuit, in part because fishing and timber were believed to create unstable social environments and were to be tolerated out of economic necessity but not encouraged. But nature had only selectively endowed the northeast with arable land, and it was not in abundance at either Machias or Liverpool.[19]

Liverpool's agricultural shortcomings had never disguised themselves. When surveyor general Charles Morris visited the region in 1761 he noted that "the Township of Liverpool affords little for the Sythe or Sickle being in general an assemblage of Rocky Substances with few intervening spots for Pasture or Garden." Some Liverpool residents maintained kitchen gardens, growing beans, potatoes, turnips, peas, cucumbers, pumpkins, squash, and cabbage. Simeon Perkins, Liverpool merchant and magistrate, acknowledged that the land was "hard and rocky" but nevertheless thought that all residents should apply greater effort to raising kitchen crops. After a long winter in 1773 townspeople took their salt supplies for the fishery to neighboring communities to trade for provisions, prompting Perkins to complain in his diary that "We do not raise half a supply of potatoes, and roots, and very little corn. It is enough to discourage anyone from being among these people, even if a fortune was to be made. Three quarters of the inhabitants are out of bread and meat, and not one basket of grain to be sold." But the lack of arable soil made even gardening a challenge. On June 19, 1780, after nearly two decades in Liverpool, Perkins recorded in his diary that he had seen some of the best land in the township, with topsoil nearly two feet deep. He estimated the extent of the land to be four or five acres, not enough to support a family much less produce a surplus.[20]

Although Liverpool's agricultural potential was manifestly marginal, Machias's was not. The 1771 commission that reported to Governor Hutchinson on the settlements in eastern Maine thought that "[t]he quality of the Land at Machias is very good, capable of making extraordinary Farms, from the produce whereof the Grantees may live very comfortably and have a surplusage for market," a prospectus that actual settlers might have disputed. The land down the coast at Gouldsboro the committee "thought not very extraordinary, but we were informed that that was the worst of the Land." The post-Revolution land petitions submitted to the Eastern Lands Committee of the Massachusetts Assembly suggest a more realistic assessment, notwithstanding petitioners' interest in building plausible cases for large grants of land. The sixty-one petitioners for Chandler's River, now Jonesboro, a settlement neighboring Machias, argued that the four-to-five-mile-wide and ten-mile-deep tract of land they asked for "contains a great proportion of barren heath, unfit for cultivation or any other use & there would remain but a moderate share of good land to each of us."[21] Wild blueberries, that only became a vendable commodity at the end of the nineteenth century when refrigeration, steam transportation, and canning made urban markets viable, covered the heath. Despite reports of poor land, a perception of agricultural potential encouraged postwar speculators to invest in downeast lands. William Bingham, reputedly the richest man in the United States, bought three million acres in Maine, a million acres of it in townships between the Penobscot and St. Croix Rivers, despite the counsel of Machias lawyer Phineas Bruce, who cautioned Bingham's agent that the land was good for grazing but not to bank too much on it. Bingham subsequently had great difficulty disposing of it.[22]

The farming travails of Caleb Coolidge, a late-eighteenth-century settler at Chandler's River, provide poignant testimony to the difficulty of successful downeast farming. In the fall of 1788, Coolidge left Boston to establish a farm in Plantation Number 22, which his uncle Caleb Davis had purchased along with other Boston merchants. Upon arriving at the Chandler's River settlement Caleb wrote his uncle informing him, rather judgmentally, that there was scarcely a farmer in the area; all of the old inhabitants were involved in the lumber trade, and few folks tried to grow anything but potatoes. Caleb had left Boston intending to plant wheat his first spring in Maine but found he would not have his land cleared until the spring of 1790. Over the next six years he learned through hard work, hard luck, and hungry days that farming in downeast Maine was a far more precarious enterprise than he could have imagined. By the spring of 1791 he had begun fishing and digging clams to feed his family, causing him to reflect that he could have supported them more comfortably as a laborer in Boston. Potatoes became the staple of his family's fields and table. Trying to make ends meet, Caleb found himself enmeshed in the timber trade. Experience notwithstanding, he pursued his original vision of being a farmer with grains as his major crop. Rye and wheat grew indifferently, some years not ripening, other years barely returning the seed. By 1793 he was complaining to his uncle that he had cleared some land three times, but without livestock to graze it or seed to plant it, it grew back in scrubby raspberry bushes and cherry trees, both more difficult to clear than the original forest and neither with any market value. During the six years he wrote to his uncle, potatoes were Coolidge's only agricultural success.[23]

Fish and timber for the export market, not farm products, were the economic mainstays of both Liverpool and Machias. The men who first settled Machias came with a sawmill in their boat. Locating the mill on the West Machias falls, which cascaded to the tide line and ocean-bound shipping, other lumbermen soon joined them and sited mills on the West, Middle, and East Machias Rivers. By 1794 seventeen sawmills cut approximately three million feet of boards per year, most of it shipped to wood-poor urban centers further south. John Cooper, county sheriff, contended, as had Caleb Coolidge, that people's obsession with the lumber industry made them neglect agriculture. He noted that the greatest amount of land had been cleared during the American Revolution when the export market for lumber nearly stopped. With no money to import food, people had had to clear land to grow their own. The "partiality for mills and lumber has been, and still is," Cooper argued, "the bane of Machias and no inconsiderable part of the eastern country." Inveigh as he might against Downeasters' economic proclivities, poor soil, miles of forests, and an international demand for lumber meant peoples' livelihoods were not destined to change.[24]

The 1786 state valuation for Machias reflected the "partiality for mills and lumber" and ancillary mercantile activity. Machias had one shop for every 5.4 houses and one mill for every 13, but only 3.7 acres of tilled ground for every house. With 818 residents in 1790, that would be only .24 acres of tilled land per person.[25] (See Table 2.4.) For the 1820 census, enumerators collected economic statistics to measure the nation's agricultural, manufacturing, and commercial strength. In Maine, Washington County had one of the two weakest agricultural sectors in the state. County residents tilled only .17 acres per person, less than at the end of the eighteenth century. On that land, they grew .81 bushels of grain per person, including Indian corn, wheat, rye, oats, and barley, whereas the average for the state was 3.13 bushels. In all areas of agriculture, people in Washington County grew fewer crops, tilled less ground, raised less livestock, and built fewer barns than almost any other place in Maine, except for the raising of oxen, which were the primary draft animals in the timber industry. (See Table 2.5.) Machias and Washington County's strength lay in the timber industry and the attendant milling and commercial activity. In 1820, there were 196 people for every sawmill, and 1,026 people for every warehouse, compared to 400 and 1,704 people, respectively, for the rest of the state. The sawmills were also among the most capitalized in the state with the largest valued at $450, one-third more than the highest-valued mill in any other county. In other manufacturing areas, however, the county was weak. It had fewer tanneries and carding machines than the state in general and no distilleries, potash works, textile factories, or bakehouses.[26]

TABLE 2.4 Economic Profile of Machias, 1786[a]

Buildings	No.	Moveables	No.	Land (acres)	No.	Livestock	No.
Houses	65	Trading stock	£150	Tilled	200	Horses	25
Barns	30	Vessels (tons)	150	Mowed	340	Colts	6
Mills	5	Silver plate	£20	Fresh marsh	100	Oxen	120
Shops	12	Cash	£8	Salt marsh	40	Neat cattle	140
Warehouses	2	Debts due	£150	Pasture	230	Cows	150
				Woods	18,000	Sheep	160
						Swine	75

[a]Number of polls (men between 16 and 60): 110.

TABLE 2.5 Agricultural Profiles of Machias, Washington County, and Maine, 1820

	Machias		Washington County		Maine	
	Number	Ratio[a]	Number	Ratio[a]	Number	Ratio[a]
Population	2,033	—	12,744	—	298,335	—
Acres pasture	1,838	.9/1	8,065	.63/1	272,717	.91/1
Acres tilled	344	.17/1	2,350	.18/1	78,964	.26/1
Acres mowed	2,058	1.01/1	8,761	.69/1	301,394	1.01/1
Grains, bushels	1,637	.81/1	12,072	.95/1	933,650	3.13/1
Hay, tons	1,775	.87/1	8,151	.64/1	240,741	.81/1
Barns	173	.09/1	903	.07/1	31,019	.10/1
Horses	—	—	184	.01/1	17,849	.06/1
Oxen	—	—	1,467	.12/1	18,224	.06/1
Cows	—	—	2,666	.21/1	95,091	.32/1
Swine	—	—	2,211	.17/1	66,639	.22/1

[a]Ratio is number/person.

Liverpool and Queens County also had weak agricultural and strong resource extractive sectors, especially fishing. Table 2.6, based on the 1767 census for Nova Scotia, compares two towns settled by New Englanders: Liverpool, the largest of the fishing-oriented South Shore communities, and Horton, the largest of the Minas Basin farming communities established on former Acadian land. Liverpool had very little livestock. The animals it did have served functions that a more industrialized society would make unnecessary. Oxen were used for sledding logs out of the woods to the sawmills. Cows provided fresh milk before rail or steamships and refrigeration made it possible to transport milk over significant distances. Sheep could be pastured on rocky soil. And swine could be fed fish offal, which outsiders reported gave the pork a fishy flavor. Horses were an elite item, even if they were used as draft animals on occasion, and there was only one for every 80 people in Liverpool.

Horton, by comparison, had a large number of livestock, 2,232 head combined or 3.5 animals per person. Liverpool had only a total of 396 head of livestock, or approximately one animal for every two people. Liverpool's residents, like Downeasters in Machias, scarcely bothered to plant grains, harvesting only 63 bushels in 1766, whereas Yankees in Horton produced almost thirteen bushels of grain for every man, woman, and child. If Liverpool's Yankees did not plow the land, they did plow the seas and harvest the forests and shipped them to market in their own ships. They cured 7.5 barrels of fish per person and cut 528 board feet of lumber for every resident.

The agricultural profile of Queens County in 1827, as shown in Table 2.7, is very similar to the eighteenth-century pattern, except that agricultural production and the number of livestock had increased significantly throughout Nova Scotia since the late eighteenth century.[27] Compared to the rest of Nova Scotia, Queens County was agriculturally weak, although stronger than Washington County, Maine. Queens County, for example, produced 1.14 bushels of grain per person compared to .95 for Washington County. Indeed,

TABLE 2.6 Economic Profiles of Liverpool, Horton, and Nova Scotia, 1767

	Liverpool		Horton		Nova Scotia	
	Number	Ratio[a]	Number	Ratio[b]	Number	Ratio[b]
Population	634	—	634	—	13,374	—
Horses	8	.01/1	148	.23/1	1,237	.09/1
Bulls and oxen	36	.06/1	217	.34/1	2,299	.17/1
Cows	62	.1/1	393	.62/1	4,861	.36/1
Neat cattle	60	.09/1	568	.9/1	5,502	.41/1
Sheep	105	.17/1	560	.88/1	7,843	.59/1
Swine	125	.2/1	346	.54/1	3,479	.26/1
Grains, bushels	63	.1/1	8,197	12.9/1	67,716	5.1/1
Fish, barrels	4,762	7.5/1	207	.33/1	63,510	4.74/1
Oil, barrels	34	.05/1	2	—	639.5	0.05/1
Board ft. lumber	335,000	528/1	100,000	158/1	1,271,000	95/1
Fishing vessels	23	.04/1	7	.01/1	367	.03/1
Trading vessels	15	.02/1	1	—	122	.01/1

[a]Ratio is number/population.
[b]Ratio is number/person.

Nova Scotia generally had higher agricultural production per person than Maine. It harvested 4.89 bushels of grain per person compared to 3.13 in Maine. Nova Scotians, on average, also had significantly more livestock than did Mainers. The total number of horses, cattle, and swine in Maine and Nova Scotia in 1820 and 1827, respectively, was 197,803 and 195,281, or 66 and 1.6 animals per person, respectively.

The weak agricultural and strong export-oriented resource economies of Liverpool and Machias were the most manifest signs that these towns were closely tied to the Atlantic economy and its networks. From the early sixteenth century, Europeans in the region depended on imported food supplies, first from Europe and later from more southerly colonies. The long centuries of international competition for the marine resources and for control of the territory, and the region's use as a buffer and war zone between the more

TABLE 2.7 Economic Profiles of Nova Scotia and Queens County, 1827

	Nova Scotia		Queens County	
	Number	Ratio[a]	Number	Ratio[a]
Population	123,848	—	4,225	—
Acres cultivated	1,292,009	10.43/1	5,630	1.33/1
Wheat, bushels	152,861	1.23/1	1,362	.32/1
Other grains, bushels	449,626	3.63/1	3,476	.82/1
Potatoes, bushels	3,298,220	26.63/1	52,817	12.5/1
Hay, tons	163,218	.32/1	3,577	.85/1
Horses	12,951	.10/1	163	.04/1
Horned cattle	110,848	.90/1	2,436	.58/1
Sheep	173,731	1.40/1	2,737	.65/1
Swine	71,482	.58/1	1,941	.46/1

[a]Ratio is number/person.

populous colonies of the French and the British, made it a frequent bargaining chip in European diplomatic circles. War and international swapping stunted colonial political developments, subordinating them to metropolitan designs and dictates. While British colonies further south refined and elaborated their internal political institutions, from central Maine to Newfoundland European-derived political institutions remained weak and idiosyncratic or nonexistent. After the British takeover of Nova Scotia in 1713, it had a governor and council, but not until 1758 did it have an assembly. The British established governments for Prince Edward Island, New Brunswick, and Cape Breton as those colonies were carved off Nova Scotia. Newfoundland, however, had no year-round governor until 1824. In central and eastern Maine, disputes over land effectively blocked the establishment of town government into the nineteenth century.

In the mid eighteenth century the political life of northeastern British America was very plastic, and conflicts arose as people tried to mold its form. Beginning with Nova Scotia, the colony was given a government like that of other colonies, to paraphrase Governor Lawrence. But the colonial government of Nova Scotia, established *after* rather than before the British metropolitan state had grown very powerful, would have a very different relationship with the Crown and Parliament than would the governments of older colonies with political institutions and practices rooted in decades of custom and long usage.[28] As metropolitan officials tried to tighten the reins on empire and people started to resist the bridling, their footing was firmest where political precedent existed, even if it was on the fringe of Massachusetts's jurisdiction. But in Nova Scotia, a model for a new imperial constitution would take shape and change the way people thought about how government affected their lives in large and small ways.

3
Dividing the Land

When New Englanders settled Liverpool and Machias, the two townships were unsurveyed tracts of land. Nova Scotia's surveyor general, Charles Morris, had defined the perimeters of the townships that the government proposed to settle with New Englanders. Liverpool's western edge began "four Miles West of the Western Head of the Entrance into Port Senior [Liverpool harbor]" and ran north-northwest fourteen miles into the interior of the peninsula. A parallel eastern boundary began "One Mile East of the Eastern Point of the Harbour of … Port Metway," and likewise ran fourteen miles into the interior. The northern boundary connected the east and west termini; the Atlantic Ocean washed the township's southern edge. More or less, it contained 100,000 acres to be divided into two hundred shares of five hundred acres each. Machias's boundaries, defined by the petitioners in their request for a township grant, were similarly vague. The township lay eight to ten leagues west of the St. Croix River, the boundary between Nova Scotia (later New Brunswick) and Massachusetts (later Maine); this detail was included in the description to verify that the township was within the jurisdiction of Massachusetts. Ten-mile-long north–south boundaries and eight-mile-wide east–west boundaries were referenced from a single point: "a dry Rock at a place called the Eastern Bay near the House of Mr. Samuel Holmes." From the east the Machias Bay cut through the middle of the eight-square-mile rectangle; into the bay flowed the West, Middle, and East Machias Rivers. The share for each Machias grantee, factoring out water, would be approximately 500 acres.[1]

Both townships would need to be surveyed and divided into lots before settlers could be confident about the locations and limits of their shares, a responsibility the grantees had to undertake. The task might have occasioned discord as unwieldy groups of 80 and 164 grantees distributed thousands of acres of land among themselves. But in neither Machias nor Liverpool did serious differences of opinion arise as the grantees in each initiated the distribution of land in very similar ways. By the 1760s, the self-governing proprietorship, which surveyed and divided the land of new townships, or the undivided land of old townships, was such an accepted institution in New England that its form and function needed little or no articulation in the grants. A basic consensus on the process of land allocation had rooted itself deeply in New England culture and informed the behavior of settlers of Yankee extraction throughout northern New England and Nova Scotia, as well as the colonial governments of the region.[2]

Holding together that consensus was a core set of values about the relationship of land to social structure, to community formation, to individual competence, to economic achievement, and to political rights.[3] Some values reinforced the individual, some the group, some enhanced private rights, and some the public domain. Yankees shared values about the place of land in society in their generalities, if not in all their particular applications. Yet, in the particularities lay the scope for change. Small modifications in how governments granted and distributed land, and in how they allowed settlers to distribute land among themselves, had far-reaching repercussions on how settlements developed, on how wealth and power—from the individual to the metropolitan government—were allocated and maintained, on how jurisdictions were established, and on how the public sphere at the local level was shaped and controlled.

In Nova Scotia, the colonial government and the Board of Trade were making those small changes, first with the initial grants and then with legislation and executive orders. They granted land in severalty shares of 500 acres, they prohibited the grantees from acting as tenants-in-common and forming a local corporation, they appointed proprietors' committees to oversee the distribution of the land. Yet against these bureaucratic changes, which were piecemeal and had weak mechanisms of enforcement, the practical need to divide the land remained. In the absence of day-to-day government oversight, Liverpool residents incorporated many New England practices into the spirit, if not the letter, of Nova Scotia policy.

Settlers in Liverpool and Machias knew how to proceed when dividing the thousands of acres granted to them. They petitioned a justice of the peace for permission to call meetings. They elected officers, appointed committees to survey the land, established procedures for setting aside land for roads, and made inquiries about hiring a minister. In both townships, the proprietors initially organized themselves as though they were a private corporation with quasi-public functions. With the establishment of town government in Machias, the proprietors became solely concerned with their private corporate interests. In Liverpool the opposite occurred. The Crown disallowed provincial legislation from 1759 that would have allowed grantees to hold land in common and function as a corporation.[4] With the suppression of the private corporate rights of proprietors, their role in the township, especially in the absence of town government, became increasingly concerned with managing undivided and public lands.

To analyze how two groups of settlers, beginning with very similar ideas and procedures about the distribution of land, could develop different structures and functions, this chapter analyzes four aspects of land distribution and institutional structures: one, the standards and procedures for determining proprietary membership, and hence access to a portion of land; two, the procedures by which the proprietors distributed land among themselves; three, the ancillary township developments they supported; and four, the eventual disappearance of the institution of the proprietorship. Small differences in land distribution in the two towns produced large consequences. In Liverpool, a public interest in land emerged, whereas in Machias the ownership of land was privatized. In the distribution of land one can discern the redefinition of public and private responsibilities, as well as corporate and individual rights, that lay at the center of many of the imperial controversies of the eighteenth century.

* * *

The actual membership of the Liverpool proprietorship reflected a compromise between Nova Scotia policy and New England practice rather than an adherence to either. Group grants were an efficient way to establish new settlements and distribute land, as the British government repeatedly acknowledged. Between 1749 and 1773, the Board of Trade instructed governors in Nova Scotia, Quebec, East Florida, and West Florida to lay out land in townships. After the American Revolution, the governments of Nova Scotia, New Brunswick, Lower Canada, and Upper Canada surveyed land in townships as part of the distribution of land to Loyalists. Similarly, the United States government laid out townships in the Northwest Territory.[5] Thus the Nova Scotia government had to curtail the rights of the grantees to keep proprietorships from arising, while still enabling settlers to divide the township lands. Liverpool's grant, and the other township grants issued in 1759 and 1760, created a modified system of land distribution based on severalty ownership of land in shares fixed at 500 acres, combined with a settlement requirement. Unlike other colonial systems of land distribution based on severalty ownership where colonists registered their claims directly with county courts (for example, in Virginia), in Nova Scotia the system was adapted to the New England practice of group grants with the division and recording of land distributions happening at the level of the township. An appointed proprietors' committee was to be a temporary instrument of the colonial government that operated at the township level to distribute land to individual settlers. The proprietors did not jointly own the undivided land, as did proprietors in New England. Rather they had a claim to their individual share, and served as stewards of a township's undivided land, thereby serving both private and public interests.

The Nova Scotia requirement that grantees validate their right to a land share through settlement, a mechanism to staunch speculation, meant that the shares of grantees who did not move to Liverpool became available for non-grantee settlers. The 1759 grant named 164 men, but extant records show that only 39 ever came to the township, leaving 125 shares of unclaimed land. Liverpool's population grew rapidly, suggesting that some of the original grantees sent family members or associates in their stead, relinquishing their own claim yet making it available to others. In New England, tenancy-in-common protected the rights of nonsettler grantees, if a critical mass of grantees did settle, but it was a practice that could not be sustained in Liverpool or the other Nova Scotia townships settled by New Englanders. Charles Morris, surveyor general of Nova Scotia, traveled around the province checking on the progress of the settlements. In 1761 he reported that Liverpool had 90 families, or 504 inhabitants. In a group this large, the absence of a few grantees, although not more than 100, could have been disguised and their shares protected.[6]

The settler grantees in Liverpool, who initially organized the proprietors, honored the spirit of severalty division mandated by the grant, and chose to divide the land among only settlers, both grantee and nongrantee. At the first proprietors' meeting, they voted "That all those People whose names are not Included in the Grant, and have Since Signed With us, (Minors Excepted), Have an Equal Share, and be accepted as Proprietors, with those whose names are Mentioned in the Grant." At the next meeting, to clarify their intentions, they inserted "and are now Present" after "(Minors Excepted)," thereby empha-sizing that residency in the township was the chief criterion for a share of land, rather than simply a right to property based on the grant. In Liverpool, proprietor equaled settler; in New England, proprietor equaled grantee.[7]

By making all adult male settlers proprietors, the settler grantees resolved the legal and practical problems of absentee grantees. Surveying and dividing land incurred significant expenses that had to be borne by the proprietors. By excluding nonsettlers from land divisions, settler grantees had no need to collect money from them for proprietary expenses. In turn, by defining all adult male settlers as grantees, all settlers could be brought under the propri-etary umbrella, and everyone could be assessed for settlement expenses. In Liverpool, cultural customs and local acceptance, not statute law, allowed the proprietors to assess themselves for expenses. In New England, proprietors could tax themselves for proprietary expenses, but could not tax nonmembers. The inclusion of all adult male settlers in the division of lands allowed for townshipwide assessments, a Liverpool innovation that straddled the line between the extralegal and the illegal.

A community dependent on the fishery needed a substantial labor force to work on the ships. By 1761 seventeen fishing schooners sailed from Liverpool harbor; by 1767 there were twenty-three, along with fifteen trading vessels. In a relatively isolated settlement, the labor force had to be drawn largely from within the community, and therefore had to be bound to it. Land provided a powerful tie. Significantly, at their first meeting, the proprietors voted "That all Single Men, being of Age, shall have a whole share in the Fish Lotts." Laid out along the shore of the harbor and rivers, the fish lots provided access to the seasonal runs of salmon and alewives, land on which to erect flakes to dry fish, or water frontage for wharves, making these lots among the most valuable land in the township. A fish lot vested all men in Liverpool's maritime economy, rather than letting a select few monopolize the shorefront.[8]

Distributing land only to settlers, regardless of whether they were listed in the grant, resolved the problem of absentee grantees, but those who came did not always stay and thus forfeited their claims. Transiency complicated the monitoring of land allocation and proprietary membership. There are several touchstones for assessing the proprietors of Liverpool: the initial 1759 grant, a 1761 township census by head of household, the 1764 grant superseding the 1759 grant and confirming the title to actual settlers, the 1771 supplemental grant, the 1784 proprietors' report to the government, and the proprietors' land allotment book. Together they provide a fairly detailed picture of population fluidity in the early settlement of Liverpool.[9]

Most of the original grantees never went to Liverpool. Of the 164 names on the 1759 grant, 39 appear in the proprietors' allotment book, and only 31 of those 39 grantees had their share of land confirmed in the 1764 grant. Thus, 125 men did not claim their shares, whereas another 8 claimed and then forfeited theirs by leaving the settlement. The names of another 51 men are found only in the allotment book. Presumably they came sometime between 1759 and 1764, but did not stay long enough to be enumerated in the first grant or on the 1761 census. Most of those 51 men received a fish lot, a town lot, or both, the first land distributions made in Liverpool. A few of them received divisions of 5, 12, or 30 acres. Two of the 51 men received up to 250 acres, the largest amount distributed through proprietors' draws. Grantees willing to pay for a survey could claim a 200-acre lot. In most cases, the allotment book indicates that the 51 grantees forfeited the land when they left Liverpool, although they may have sold their town and fish lots to pay debts. The names of another 33 men are found in the allotment book and on the 1761 census, but not on the 1759 or 1764 grants. Like the men whose names are found only in the allotment book, these 33 men received some division of land that they forfeited upon departure. Most of them were single, although 10 headed a household of two or more. Thus from 1760 to 1764, 92 men (an average of 23 a year) resided in Liverpool long enough to be recorded in the proprietors' allotment book, but not long enough to have their claims confirmed in the 1764 grant.

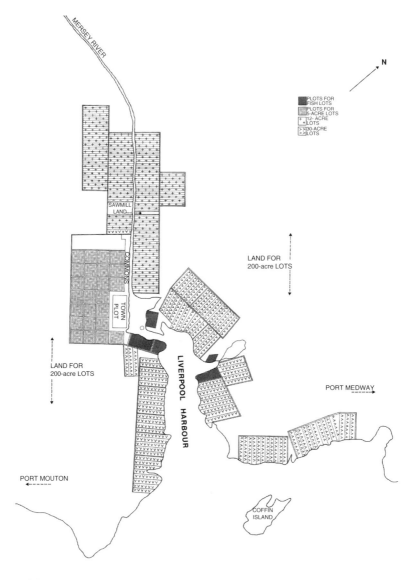

Fig. 3.1 Land divisions in Liverpool, ca. 1770. (Courtesy of the author.)

In 1764, the proprietors' committee relinquished the original grant, and the government issued a new one to the 142 heads of households who had settled in Liverpool. This group represented a solid community core. Of the 142 grantee names in the 1764 grant, 117 were listed in the 1761 census and therefore had been in the township at least three years. All 142 grantees are in the proprietors' allotment book. In 1771, the government issued a grant addendum giving shares to 15 men, whom the proprietors admitted at a December 2, 1770 meeting. In 1784, the proprietors' committee reported to the government that at the December 1770 meeting, it admitted another 10 men, who "were designed to have been inserted in the Last Grant [1771], but being either Absent, or not able to raise the money to pay their proportion of the Expence, they were Ommitted." By Liverpool standards they were proprietors, having "Built & made Improvements … & done all the dutys of Proprietors." By 1784, the government had recognized 157 proprietors in the combined 1764 grant and 1771 addendum. An additional 10 men had been recognized as grantees by the proprietors. The 1784 report noted that 40 settlers had left the township, which is an attrition rate of approximately 25 percent over the previous twenty years. Twenty-six of those 40 had made some improvements on their land, but "by reason of Poverty, and the Difficultys of Living in a New Settlement, were in debt & obliged to Sell their Houses & parts of their Lands, or had them taken away by Execution & Sold at Auction." Fourteen had made no improvements.[10]

Those people committed to staying in Liverpool monitored the comings and goings of prospective settlers and the allocation of land. Legally, the shares of the nonsettler grantees reverted to the Crown, but the localized process of land distribution meant that the reallocation of forfeited shares came under the stewardship of the Liverpool proprietors' committee. The settlers could not use the forfeited shares to aggrandize their own holdings, except to grant shares to sons. However, they could and did exert considerable local control in the distribution of land. The proprietors' records show that the committee appointed by the government in 1761 negotiated for the reissuance of the grant in 1764 and oversaw the admittance of new settlers. The proprietors' records and the 1784 report, however, indicate that all the landowners (and not just the appointed committee members) could attend committee meetings, a practice that went beyond officially sanctioned practice. Over the decades, Liverpool's proprietors came to be served by a standing committee, later known as trustees, and they would occasionally call town meetings. As members died or stepped down, the committee selected its own replacements, even though the government in Halifax had appointed the original committee. The Liverpool proprietors transformed themselves from an exclusive group charged solely with the distribution of the land to an inclusive group serving multiple interests, including the Crown's interest in ungranted land, the property owners' interest in the undivided land, and the local public interest in public lands in the township.[11]

The membership of the Machias proprietorship evolved very differently from Liverpool's. By 1770, when the Massachusetts General Court granted the township, some settlers had been in Machias for seven years. Settlement began in 1763 and grew quickly for the first three or four years. The first indication of the composition of Machias's residents is the 1767 power of attorney given to Boston merchant Ichabod Jones to act on behalf of the settlers in acquiring a grant. Eighty-two names are on that document, including Jones's; evidence from militia, proprietor, and town records indicate that most were settlers in Machias. The 1769 petition, which resulted in the 1770 grant, had eighty names. In the 1773 proprietors' draw for the marsh lot there were eighty shares. From the writing of the power of attorney in 1767 to the 1773 proprietors' draw, there were almost no name changes, indicating a stable settler base.[12]

Unlike the Liverpool grant, the Machias grant neither required that the grantees themselves settle nor stated how many acres a share represented. Rather the grant entitled each proprietor to one-eightieth part of all land in Machias township, giving them little incentive to add new proprietors and thereby reduce their portion of the whole. In 1781, an unnamed person requested that the proprietors discuss whether to expand their membership. No recorded minute indicates whether the proprietors discussed it. With the exception of a proposal to give 100 acres to anyone who would agree to serve a term as a schoolteacher, which the proprietors dismissed without recording a reason, their minutes contain no further mention of new members until 1784.[13]

At the end of the Revolution, the Machias proprietors sent James Avery to Boston as their agent to petition the Massachusetts legislature to confirm the grant (which the Crown had never approved) and to incorporate Machias's residents as a town, which the legislature did in 1784. The legislation made two stipulations modifying the 1770 grant. It required the proprietors to set aside a public share to benefit Harvard College, in addition to shares already allotted for schools and the ministry. Second, and more significantly, the General Court required the proprietors to give a "reasonable quantity of … land" to any nongrantee settler within the township who had not already had some land "assigned and confirmed to him."[14]

At the August 16, 1784 meeting, the proprietors dealt with the first nonproprietor claims. They granted land to thirteen men; eleven received 125 acres, one 150 acres, and one 250 acres. The heirs of one deceased settler received an unspecified amount of land, including mill rights. These one-time grants did not include a future interest in the township's undivided lands. Most "squatter" settlers had located close to water, so that the proprietors allowed them 50 rods (825 feet) of water frontage with parallel lines running back until the designated number of acres came within the property boundaries, provided the lot did not interfere with the lot of an original grantee. In all cases the recipient was to pay "his proportion of all the charges that the original grantees are subject to pay for obtaining the grant of said Township or in bringing forward the settlement of the same." They also had to pay for their own property boundaries to be surveyed. At the same meeting the proprietors admitted another nine men as proprietors with a right to a full share. James Avery received a share for serving as the proprietors' agent in Boston after the war. The other eight shares reflect the fervent attachment of Machias residents to American independence. For distinguished service and leadership during the American Revolution, the three O'Brien brothers, George Stillman, Stephen Smith, James N. Shannon, Peter Talbot, and David Longfellow all received a share. The only caveats attached to these shares were that they did not include mill rights or divisions of the already distributed marshlands. All shares carried obligations to pay a portion of the proprietary costs.[15] The addition of nine proprietors in 1784 brought the total number of shares, including those for Harvard College, the support of schools, and the ministry, to ninety-one.

For another fifteen years the Machias proprietors continued to receive the odd request for township lands, but they gave land to only three men. In 1787 they granted 100-acre lots to William Albee and Dr. Parker Clarke, provided they settled upon and improved them. Clarke had fought in the short-lived rebellion in Nova Scotia, and was one of only two people in Nova Scotia tried and convicted for treason in conjunction with the American Revolution. Before his date to hang, he escaped and fled to Maine. It is not clear if the Machias proprietors gave him land in recognition of his support for the revolutionary cause or to encourage him to settle in the town and provide medical services.[16] After repeated requests, Francis Milton received 120 acres in 1799 on grounds that he had been a squatter since before 1784, the last acreage granted to a nonproprietor. The records are silent as to why the proprietors took fifteen years to acknowledge his claim.[17]

Proprietors could transfer all or part of their shares through sale or inheritance. Some proprietors sold their rights very quickly. In 1773, James Dillaway sold his proprietor's right for £3:12:0 to John Coffin Jones, a Boston merchant and one of the township's absentee proprietors. In 1774, Abiel Sprague, yeoman, sold a 250-acre lot with a house and fence to Abraham Clark, a blacksmith. He included in the sale his proprietor's right. The Machias proprietors did not maintain a record of these transfers. Their records include a list of the original proprietors and land divisions, the only public record of the lot locations. When land was sold or transferred, the transaction was recorded in the county registry of deeds. All records of shares in the proprietors' book continued to carry the name of the original grantee. The proprietors' assessments for expenses in 1799, 1807, and 1821 were entered under the names of the original proprietors with the present owners, if known, listed on the side. A name analysis by last name indicates that by 1799 thirty-six shares had changed hands by sale; by 1807 the number had risen to forty-one and by 1821 to fifty-four. These transfers do not include inheritances.[18]

The composition of the Machias proprietors conformed to colonial New England practice, with the exception of the 1784 additions and the land given to squatters. The initial grant made the proprietorship an exclusive group that owned the undivided lands. In Liverpool, governmental policy defined proprietors first as grantees who settled, and then as settlers who became grantees. Rather than jointly owning the undivided township lands, Liverpool's proprietors acted as stewards in its distribution to individual settlers and in protection of the Crown's interest in ungranted shares.

* * *

Defining who could be a proprietor was the single most important determinant in preparing for the division of township lands. Other considerations, however, influenced land distribution. No grantee received a single tract of land, either 500 acres in Liverpool or one-eightieth of Machias. (Indeed, the Machias proprietors could not have admitted new proprietors or honored squatter rights if they had divided the land in large tracts upon receiving the grant in 1770.) A number of factors militated against dividing the land in large tracts. First, families would have been scattered across the landscape with nearly a mile between homes. (A square mile of land is 640 acres.) Second, some grantees would have engrossed the best land, whether valuable bottomland or water frontage, while others received poorer land. To ensure the equitable distribution of the most valuable lands, proprietorships in New England had traditionally assessed the varieties of land, divided types of land in equitable portions, and then drew for lots. Third, by distributing only the most valuable land first, survey costs could be delayed. And fourth, equitable distribution of the best lands helped to ensure the success of a settlement.[19]

Before significant distributions of land could be made, claims that preexisted a grant had to be honored or extinguished. In Liverpool, few settlers had preexisting claims. Samuel Freeman had taken up land along the river, which the proprietors allocated to him as his fish lot. They allowed Captain Silvanus Cobb "being here Sometime … a Spott to build a Store and Wharf."[20] Beyond these two cases, the proprietors acknowledged no claims to specific pieces of land, largely because the granting of the township (1759) and the initiation of organized land distribution (1760) were only a year apart.

In Machias, during the years between the initial settlement in 1763 and the grant in 1770, many eventual grantees had improved land, an investment of labor that they wanted secured with title. The most valuable claims were those with capitalized improvements, in particular the mill privileges. At the first meeting the proprietors voted "That the first sixteen settlers or builders of the first saw mill, unmolested enjoy their lots called mill lots, each lot containing seven rods front & extending to the marsh back not exceeding half a mile together with Mill privileges." Locally known as "seven acre lots," they became the nucleus of settlement at the West Falls. Settlers erected at least five other mills, two more on the West Falls, one on the East Falls, one on the Middle River, and one on the stream feeding out of Gardner's Lake on the east side of the township. Ownership of these mill privileges was acknowledged along with a vote "That each proprietor be quieted in the improvements he has made and settled upon and possess one hundred rods front marsh excluded, if it is to be had without disposing one another in the improvements they have made, together with the mill privileges they now enjoy; said lots to extend back so far as to contain the quantity of Two hundred and fifty acres to each first division lot." Significantly, the valuable marshlands were excluded from considerations of preexisting claims, but unlike the mill privileges, the long-term value was in the natural condition of the land, not in capitalized improvements.[21]

None of Liverpool's mills predated the granting and settlement of the township. Consequently, the proprietors could, without challenge, assert a right to grant and monitor mill privileges, in which they shared a mutual interest; sawmills produced building materials and gristmills ground grain for bread. Mill sites also represented wealth: in the land itself, in the capital investment in the mill, and in the income a mill might generate. At the first proprietors' meeting, they discussed "what is Necessary to be done in regard to the building of Saw mills & Grist mills," reflecting their importance to the settlement's viability. One group of settlers proposed building a sawmill; the proprietors gave them the mill site and sixteen adjoining acres, provided they keep "a Convenient Place for Landing." Another four men received privileges to Mill Brook and the right "to flow [i.e., flood] as much Land as they shall think Necessary, together with four Acres of Land," a site the proprietors intended for the gristmill. In the next few years, the proprietors granted sawmill privileges to three other settlers.[22]

Liverpool's export trade in lumber, most of it destined for West Indian markets, made sawmills attractive investments, and the proprietors had no difficulty finding men to build and maintain them. A gristmill in an agriculturally marginal settlement, in contrast, offered few investment advantages. On March 28, 1768, the proprietors' committee appointed an ad hoc committee "to Regulate the Affairs of the Grist mill, and Brook in said town, in Behalf of said town." In its May report, the committee determined that the absence of "any Conditions, or Consideration" in the earlier grant of the Mill Brook made it "Void in its own Nature" and justified putting the "said Brook … in the Hands, and at the Disposall of the Propriety." Very probably, the recipients of the gristmill site either did not maintain a mill or used the site for a sawmill. The committee clarified the proprietors' position by establishing the conditions for the gristmill privilege. The "owners of the Grist Mill [must] … Carefully Stop the water, and Keep a Mill in Good order, and Grind for a Sixteenth Part, and Give Good Attendance on said Mill, three days in a week, viz. Mondays, Wednesdays, and Saturdays." If the previous recipients of the gristmill privilege were willing to meet those conditions, then they could have the use of the site, otherwise it would "Return to the Propriety." On June 14, 1768, Joseph Collins, Jonathan Crowel, and William Freeman accepted the conditions.[23]

In the committee's judgment, the public interest in a gristmill took precedence over any private claim. The committee's recommendation that violations of the terms for operating a gristmill would automatically return the mill to proprietary stewardship was predicated on the assumption that the proprietary would continue to exist. It was a grand assumption for an entity that was not to exist in Nova Scotia except as a committee to divide the townships' undivided lands. In practice, however, the proprietorship existed as a public institution and Liverpool's leaders used it to shape the commonweal as they saw fit. At least twice the proprietors invoked the conditions established by the committee in 1768 to regrant the gristmill privileges, once in 1777 and again in 1785.[24] By these latter dates, if not by 1768, it was clear to all that the government in Halifax, not to mention Whitehall, would not allow town government. In Liverpool, the quasi-public responsibilities of New England–style proprietorships reconfigured themselves into truly public functions in the absence of town government, in the presence of need, and through the compulsion of culture. As discussed later, the grist mill privilege was not the only property that Liverpool's proprietors retained for public use and under proprietary oversight.

In Machias, the proprietors excluded marshlands from preexisting claims. With three rivers and a saltwater harbor, Machias was blessed with extensive water frontage, much of it marsh. Settlers had claims aplenty for it, but as a natural source of livestock fodder, it was very valuable land, and needed to be divided equitably among all grantees. The proprietors had the marsh surveyed at proprietary expense, and on July 22, 1773, they drew for shares, one for high marsh and one for low marsh, or marsh and thatch, as surveyor Daniel Merritt called them. The high marsh generally occurred in low-lying areas bounded by fresh water. The thatch or low marsh grew in salt or brackish water. Machias had 572 acres of marsh: 181 acres were thatch and 391 acres were high marsh. (In comparison, Liverpool had approximately 80 acres of marshland.)[25] One dispute arose when the proprietors surveyed the marsh. Two lot layers halted their survey when Japheth Hill, Samuel Hill, and some others threatened them, swearing "that they would knock the first man down that entered upon the marsh (upon any such business) [i.e., surveying] and that if any man should presume to bring any compass & chain & make any use of them, they would destroy them." Upon hearing of the incident, the proprietors voted to have the lot layers finish staking out the marsh lots, but any proprietor whose first division of upland adjoined marsh could have the contiguous marsh. All other proprietors received their marsh share through the draw on July 22, 1773. Fresh marsh lots were 4 acres and 55 square rods, and thatch lots were 2 acres and 13 square rods.[26] The small size of these lots, especially when compared to the 250-acre upland lots, illustrates the importance of this relatively scarce resource and the need to keep a few settlers from monopolizing it.

In Liverpool, the most valuable lands were the fish lots, and in the interest of equity, the proprietors surveyed and distributed them first. Indeed, a committee had been struck to lay them out before the first official meeting, when the proprietors voted to approve the committee's report. The proprietors also completed the survey and division of the town lots, which Nova Scotia's surveyor general, Charles Morris, had plotted. Designed for a compact nucleated village, the town site included a road 102 feet wide that was to be used "as a common" with 40-foot-wide streets running down to the water. These streets bear eighteenth-century names, such as King, Queen, Wolfe, Amherst, and Lawrence, but the major business and residential section of town did not develop on the town plot but rather on the fish lots in plot B where the harbor narrows. The Liverpool settlers explained in a memorial to Halifax that they found it "absolutely necessary that they should settle themselves [as] Contiguous as possible, and therefore a vote was passed in a Legal Meeting that any persons who was desirous of building might erect a house on the Land Adjoining the river below the Main Street."[27] James Monro, an itinerant minister to Liverpool in 1795, described the results of the settlers' efforts three decades after the town's founding.

> There are two good Meeting Houses in the Town near to one another. … Both Meeting Houses indeed are commodious and considerably elegant. Their dwelling Houses are also neat and commodious in general, and their ware Houses preferable to any in the province, at least to any I have seen. Their Churches, Dwelling Houses, and Ware Houses are painted in common with red or yellow paint which makes them look better and more durable.[28]

* * *

During their first summer in Liverpool, the proprietors planned for the settlement's maritime orientation. Settlers had "the Liberty to Erect Store houses by the Water Side." A committee laid out a common shipyard and set aside 18 acres near the water for "Erecting Fish Flakes" (wooden racks) for drying fish. They gave 100 acres of timberland to the sawmill operators so they could legally take wood. Idealistic esoterica also crept into the first summer's plans. The proprietors commissioned Mr. Benjamin Leigh of Halifax to design a town arms depicting a codfish, a salmon, a pine tree, and a sheaf of wheat.[29] The first three symbols gave a fair representation of the settlement's economic underpinnings; the fourth was wishful thinking. Anthony Lockwood, describing Liverpool in the early nineteenth century, noted that "it is not easy to conceive a place where nature has done less to favor man." One observer counseled understanding the natural landscape within its socioeconomic context.

> The southern shores of Nova Scotia, to the eye of a stranger, exhibit an unfavourable appearance, being in general broken and stony; but the innumerable islands along its coasts, coves, and harbours, though generally composed of rocky substances, appear by nature designed for the drying of fish, and are clothed with materials for flakes and stages, and there is sufficient for pastures and gardens to serve the purposes of fishermen.[30]

Liverpool scarcely had "land sufficient for pastures and gardens," and dividing the few meager patches taxed the proprietors. At their first meeting on July 1, 1760, they voted to lay out 100-acre farm lots, superseded the next week by a vote to distribute 5-acre lots, which were laid out around the town plot. The 100-acre plots remained an unsurveyed idea. The next summer eleven proprietors revisited the problem of "how Large to Lay out the Farm Lotts," although during their first year, the settlers surely discovered that Liverpool scarcely contained the first 100-acre tract suitable for a farm, much less one for each proprietor. With an eye toward both equity and the natural barrenness of the land, the proprietors' committee decided to distribute 90 acres to each proprietor, but in three 30-acre lots. Along the lower shore they surveyed and distributed the first 30-acre lots, but never laid out the other two allotments.[31] During the first decade of settlement, the land distributions in Liverpool included a fish lot, a town lot, a marsh lot, a 5-acre lot, a 12-acre lot, a 30-acre lot, and an optional 200-acre lot, the latter intended as a wood lot. Per share they added up to approximately 250 acres, the most any one grantee received through the proprietors' draws.

The names of 265 men appear in the proprietors' allotment book for Liverpool. Of these 265, approximately 80 men received some allotment of land that was subsequently forfeited, most receiving a fish lot, a town lot, a 5-acre lot, a 12-acre lot, or some combination of the four. A few received a 30-acre lot. Approximately 185 men, most of them permanent settlers, acquired land to which they received firm title. The total amount of land distributed among those 185 (plus three shares, one each for the glebe lands, the school lands, and a share for the first settled Anglican minister) was 36,500 acres or approximately 200 acres per man, 300 acres short of the 500 acres per share. These allotments left approximately 63,500 acres, or two-thirds of the township's land undivided.

The Liverpool proprietors maintained a legal fiction about the distribution of the land. In their 1784 report to the government on the status of the proprietors and their landholdings, they reported that 132 of the 172 grantees were still in the township, but provided no elaboration of their holdings. They gave a more detailed breakdown of the holdings of the 40 grantees no longer in the township, including the land sold. The report implies that the proprietors' committee had distributed a full share of 500 acres to each of these men. Of the 17,657 acres listed as unsold, at least 12,000 acres were part of the unsurveyed and undivided land. Locally the proprietors knew that two-thirds of the land was undivided. For government records, all the land was allocated.[32]

Most of Liverpool's land simply did not warrant immediate surveying. In 1784, Charles Morris asked Samuel Hunt, then deputy surveyor for Queens County, to lay out 200 acres at Little Port Joli, down the coast from Liverpool, for John Thomas, Esq., newly appointed sheriff for Queens County. On the survey submitted to Morris, Hunt explained that he "Indeavord to Describe the Lying or Situation of ye Above 200 acres, as to the Upland it is Miserable Except about four or five acres Produces Nothing but Small Fir poles Growing on a bed of Rocks. Their is some Skirts of Salt Meadow though Indifferent in Quallity, thre Small Islands in the Pond but of Very Little worth, as to Timber there is none." Most of the undivided land in Liverpool was timbered, which few people needed until the early nineteenth century when the international timber trade expanded. People with a claim to undivided land would ask the proprietors' committee for a parcel to be surveyed, a fairly routine request throughout the nineteenth century. For over 200 years the proprietors' committee oversaw the public land and monitored the surveying and distribution of the remaining undivided land. The proprietors' trustees were finally disbanded in 1978 when the last three trustees signed a deed giving any remaining land to the Municipality of Queens.[33]

In Machias, the distribution of undivided lands and the eventual end of the proprietorship happened far earlier, and after the proprietorship no longer had any public functions. The distribution of marsh lots, the acknowledgment of mill rights, and the allotment of 250 acres where grantees had settled resolved the initial land needs of Machias's grantees. The proprietors distributed additional land on September 8, 1800, when they drew lots for fresh meadow. Eight years later, they made their last draw on the township lands, this time for upland lots of 100 acres, but this distribution did not exhaust all the undivided land. Over the next twenty-six years, the proprietors' committee sold small parcels to various people. Then at a meeting on October 18, 1834, the proprietors voted "to sell and dispose of the remaining and undivided lands at private or public sale in order to close the concerns of the corporation or proprietary." Within a year a committee had arranged for the sale of the remaining lands. Some people purchased small tracts. But one group of buyers, headed by Samuel S. Lewis, purchased a tract for $10,000, which became the principal holding of the Boston and Eastern Mill and Land Company. That land sale effectively liquidated the proprietorship's land holdings and it then proceeded to terminate its existence. By December 24, 1835, it had settled outstanding accounts and began shareholder distributions totaling $9,438.97. Within a few weeks, most proprietors claimed their dividends; the last dividend was claimed on October 16, 1839, ending the corporation's seven-decade existence.[34]

* * *

In the late seventeenth century, New England governments created proprietorships so that groups could legally hold land in common and distribute it to members. Proprietorships also helped to make townships desirable places to settle. As the first organized group in a new township, the proprietors traditionally established the basis of a community's infrastructure. In both Machias and Liverpool, the proprietors built the first meetinghouse, hired the first minister, taxed themselves for his support, and surveyed and built the first roads. Machias's proprietors elected surveyors of lumber in 1770 to control the quality of the settlement's economic lifeblood. They also built two livestock pounds, one each at the East and West River settlements. Drawing on a common heritage and responding to the social needs of their respective communities, the proprietors of Liverpool and Machias established the institutional foundations for community development as understood by New Englanders.[35]

The incorporation of the Town of Machias in 1784, upon the petition of the proprietors, shifted the proprietary's public functions to the town. The town assumed the support of the minister. Surveyors of lumber became town officers. The building and maintenance of roads became a town responsibility, although the proprietors provided road easements in land divisions so that the town would not have to purchase them. This transfer of responsibilities to the town divested the Machias proprietorship of its quasi-public functions and left it with the management of its commonly held private land. When it no longer had land to manage, it ceased to exist, as had proprietorships throughout New England.

The Liverpool proprietorship never went through that transformation. It never had a positive, legal corporate definition. The extralegal definition that did emerge included elements of New England practice and accommodations to Nova Scotian policy. The Nova Scotian prohibition on town governments meant that Liverpool's proprietors could not shift the public responsibilities they assumed at the time of settlement to a town government the way the Machias proprietors had. Rather the proprietors' committee continued to oversee a range of public needs associated with the maintenance of public lands. It did lose some public tasks. When dissension arose in the church, religion became privately maintained. Most, but not all, road building and maintenance became county and provincial business. In 1796, they voted to appropriate half a fish lot for a highway.[36]

Underlying these changes in Liverpool was also a fundamental difference in the initial terms of land ownership in Nova Scotia and Massachusetts. In Machias, the proprietorship owned the undivided land. In Liverpool, the proprietors held the land in public trust, first for the Crown to be distributed to settlers and then for the settlers. Land designated for community or public purposes remained under the proprietors' control. Liverpool's proprietors' committee remained active in overseeing the distribution of undivided lands into the late twentieth century. They could not have done as the Machias proprietors did and sell the remaining undivided land, divide the money and terminate their existence, for quite literally they never owned the land they administered. Rather they had been trustees or stewards of the land held in severalty, but undivided. They also defined some land as common or public, for use by all the residents of the townships.

On issues concerning "common" or "public" lands, the Liverpool proprietors' committee remained actively in control. They continued to regulate the land set aside for shipbuilding. In 1796, the proprietors voted that unallocated land on "Ship Yard Point … Shall be, and Remain as a Common." At the same meeting, they decided that the eight town lots left in the town center for a parade be designated a public common, with the proviso that John and Jacob Peach, then using part of the land, could continue to use it for the remainder of their natural lives. In 1855, the proprietors leased land for a shipyard to Freeman Tupper of Milton, the settlement at the falls. In 1763, the provincial government reserved Bear or Coffin Island on the Atlantic edge of the Liverpool harbor as common land to be used for curing fish. With the 1764 grant, the island came under the control of the Liverpool proprietors who rented it and used the revenues for public purposes. Until 1782 they applied the money toward the minister's salary. After that they allocated the money for sundry purposes: to pay the proprietors' clerk, to help build a bridge in town, to purchase standard weights and measures for the community, and to pay for clearing parts of the island. On September 20, 1866, the proprietors' committee went to the island "for the purpose of ascertaining whether encroachments were being made on the said Island in regard to Cutting down, and destroying Wood and carrying off Ballast." They discovered the sea was eroding the south, or seaward, side of the island near the lighthouse, and decided to recommend to the provincial government, which maintained and staffed the lighthouse, that it should take anti-erosion measures. At the conclusion of their tour they "visited the Light House and Out buildings, found them all in good Order, and after enjoying a good Dinner at the House of Mr. Thos. Eaton, the Keeper, left for home."[37]

These acts of the Liverpool proprietors' committee indicate the extent to which it had evolved to become a local public institution. At some point in the late eighteenth or early nineteenth century, members of the committee began serving for life. When a member died, moved away, or retired, the remaining members chose a replacement. It became irrelevant whether the new member was an original proprietor or the descendant of one; being a "principal gentleman" of the town became the chief criterion for being on the committee. At a 1837 meeting to decide how to spend £18.13.7, derived largely from the rent of common lands and Coffin Island, the proprietors' committee decided to allow all freeholders a vote. They chose to use the money to open a road to the peat bog, and voted down proposals to fence the burying ground, complete a road to the West Falls, or loan the money for a year at interest. A proposal to apply the money to the purchase of a fire engine was rescinded.

The 1837 townshipwide meeting in Liverpool contrasts sharply with the 1834 meeting of the Machias proprietors when they decided to sell the remaining undivided township land and divide the proceeds among themselves. The proprietors' committee in Liverpool, in the absence of town government, had assumed a number of public responsibilities associated with the management of land. In Machias the proprietors met sporadically and

Fig. 3.2 Wash drawing of the lighthouse on Coffin Island, 1817, from the J. E. Woolford album, "Sketches of Nova Scotia." (Courtesy of the Nova Scotia Museum, Halifax, Canada; History Collection, 78.45.74.)

elected a committee to manage their private affairs, but by the 1820s and 1830s the committee's primary purpose was to divest the proprietors of their commonly held property. The Machias proprietors had long since divorced their interests from the public or common interests of the townspeople. The legacy of the proprietorship persisted well into the nineteenth century in both Liverpool and Machias, although with substantially different implications. Under the pressure of changes in imperial policy, the proprietorship in Liverpool, compared to that of Machias, ultimately encouraged the growth of a local public sphere and a weakening of private corporate identity.

In post-1783 British North America and New England the institution of the proprietorship fell into disuse, and its persistence in towns like Machias and Liverpool was a vestige of earlier practices. The British continued to use group grants to distribute land to Loyalists in Nova Scotia, New Brunswick, Lower Canada, and Upper Canada, but with careful controls to keep groups from holding the lands in common.[38] In postrevolutionary New England, only Massachusetts had substantial amounts of public land for new settlements, but like all states, it had incurred an enormous war debt, which it hoped to relieve by selling the unsettled lands of Maine. The decision to sell, rather than grant, land effectively terminated the use of group grants.

Although land proprietorships were local institutions, imperial, provincial, and then national forces effected their adaptations and eventual demise. The Machias proprietorship reflected a seventeenth-century New England practice to use private agents to fund and manage expansion. In Massachusetts, and the United States more generally, that practice continued, although increasingly it involved the incorporation of groups who were willing to build roads, purchase western lands, or invest in manufacturing.[39] That practice of empowering private agents was itself derivative of the decision of the English crown to delegate the responsibility of overseas expansion to individuals and groups, such as the Massachusetts Bay Company, the Carolina proprietors, or the Hudson's Bay Company. In the late seventeenth century, the Privy Council increasingly discouraged the practice, which it could do most effectively in new areas of overseas expansion. The Liverpool proprietorship reflects that development, so that the grantees were given no legislatively sanctioned powers. While the metropolitan government effectively proscribed unwanted institutions all the way down to the local level in Nova Scotia, it was less effective in prescribing alternatives. Consequently, in Liverpool the proprietors' committee honored the proscription, yet responded to local needs. The result was a curious hybrid of loyalty to the imperial system and idiosyncratic localism.

4

Choosing Sides: Liverpool and Machias and the Imperial Conflict

Machias and Liverpool were still struggling settlements when fighting broke out between British troops and Massachusetts militia units at Lexington and Concord on April 19, 1775. Soon thirteen united colonies were in armed revolt, and people throughout British America had to decide how they would respond to the escalation of the conflict. In Machias, the last major Massachusetts settlement before the border with Nova Scotia, settlers fought on the side of Massachusetts and the Continental Congress, thereby helping to hold the region between the Penobscot and St. Croix Rivers as part of the United States. In Liverpool, people tried to remain observers of the conflict. The government in Halifax suspected most of them of rebel tendencies, a few did return to New England to assist the revolutionaries, but the majority remained loyal to the King and Empire. In both Liverpool and Machias, people characterized the early fighting as unnatural, as relatives, friends, and former neighbors found themselves on opposite sides of a war after more than a century of common interest in North America. In Machias, people quickly came to understand the war as one between two sovereign powers, Britain and the United States, and they fought vigorously to maintain their newly declared independence. In Liverpool, the conflict remained a civil war. In 1782, as tensions subsided and the peace negotiations progressed, Simeon Perkins noted in his diary that "we hope for a Peace with ourselves, which God of his Infinite Mercy grant, that our Nation may no longer Ly under the awfull Judgement of Devouring one an Other."[1] With the signing of the 1783 Treaty of Paris, however, Nova Scotians found themselves in a dramatically reduced and remade British Empire. They were no longer of one transatlantic British nation, and an international, rather than a provincial, boundary divided them from blood-relatives in New England.

The international boundary made permanent the wartime division between rebel and loyal colonies. It ran along a constitutional fault line that had emerged in British North America in the late seventeenth and early eighteenth centuries. On the rebelling side were the mainland colonies established in the seventeenth century, with the lone exception of Georgia, established in 1732.[2] In their revolutionary protests, the rebelling colonists emphasized the tradition of their direct and individual relationships with the Crown unmediated by Parliament.[3] The North American colonies that remained within the Empire after 1783—Nova Scotia, the Island of St. John (Prince Edward Island after 1799), and Quebec—had been conquered from the French either in the War of the Spanish Succession or the Seven Years' War. East and West Florida, acquired from Spain with the 1763 Treaty of Paris, had also not rebelled, but Britain returned them in 1783, much to the disgust of their loyal British inhabitants. Colonists in those conquered territories, acquired and funded through the expenditure of parliamentary monies and established after the clear emergence of the Crown-in-Parliament, simply could not launch arguments about the loss of their autonomy from Parliament when they had never had it.[4]

Within the broad divide of loyal and rebel colonies were local variations and exceptions, and few have been more compelling and puzzling to historians than Nova Scotia. With approximately half of its population at the time of the Revolution heralding from New England, many scholars have assumed that if any colony were to have been the fourteenth state, Nova Scotia would have been the one. Eighteenth-century American revolutionaries, on the other hand, saw Quebec as a potential threat because the British could launch an attack on the colonies from it, as they did in the fall of 1777. As well, they thought the French Canadians might want to join the resistance to the British. Thus the Continental Congress authorized a two-pronged attack on Quebec for the fall of 1775, one of the only large offensive engagements during a largely defensive war. The revolutionaries did not have similar interests or concerns with Nova Scotia. The standard twentieth-century interpretations for why Nova Scotians stayed out of the revolution emphasize some combination of the following factors: the military might of the British navy with a base in Halifax; the colony's geographic isolation from other colonies; distances between settlements within the colony; and an ideological confusion among settlers from New England caused by their removal from the revolutionary conflict in their homeland.[5]

Machias proves helpful in assessing the merits of these factors.[6] Geographically it had many of the same characteristics as the townships in Nova Scotia. It was as isolated from Boston as Liverpool. Although it was not just down the coast from Halifax, as was Liverpool, it was within the orbit of British naval patrols and staging grounds, which were often in the Bay of Fundy. By water Machias was as close or closer to Halifax than were the Nova Scotian townships on the Fundy shore, and settlements in Maine were as isolated from one another as were those in Nova Scotia. Yet Machias was a hotbed of downeast rebel activity, and it could count on support from settlers in other townships in the region. If people in geographically isolated townships in eastern Maine could sustain revolutionary activity, then we should question whether geographic isolation can explain why Nova Scotians did not rebel.

The Liverpool–Machias comparison prompts us to turn to an assessment of political geography rather than physical geography for an answer to why two similarly remote communities had different responses to the imperial crisis. Both were communities on the margins of political systems and the salient questions relate to their orientation to a political center, the location of the center, the strength of the connection between a center and its peripheries, and the strength of any periphery. Indeed, one of the signal historical problems of the early modern British Empire is to explain how a peripheral area could create a centripetal dynamic of its own, in particular how thirteen North American colonies became strong enough to risk challenging and severing their connection to the imperial center.[7] Machias and Liverpool, and more generally eastern Maine and Nova Scotia, were politically weak and therefore drawn toward the centers of larger systems, but in ways that had less to do with the physical geography than with the political geography of the British Atlantic world as it had evolved over the seventeenth and eighteenth centuries. Quite simply, geographic remoteness is an insufficient explanation for complex political arrangements that had emerged over the previous 200 years. More significant and provocative is why similar communities were oriented toward different political centers in the Atlantic world.

If we ask ourselves how people in Liverpool and Machias responded to changes in imperial governance that were specific to those settlements, then an answer begins to emerge. Most scholars of British America use 1763 as the onset of significant adjustments in the system of imperial governance.[8] At the conclusion of the Seven Years' War the British Ministry and Parliament implemented a series of changes in imperial governance ranging from the Proclamation of 1763, to the levying of new taxes on the colonies, to the Quebec Act, which continued French civil law in a British territory, gave political rights to Catholics, and sanctioned colonial governance without an assembly. But changes in the imperial system did not start in 1763. To be sure, colonists in the older settled areas of the mainland colonies felt the bite of imperial changes and reacted after 1763, and for most analyses of the Revolution that year is a useful starting point. But for eastern Maine and Nova Scotia, the most important changes in British imperial policy were those affecting new areas of settlement, such as land grants and the establishment of town government, policy changes that arose before 1763 and which reflected long-standing British attempts to redefine the Empire, especially on the margins of colonial society.[9] These issues may not have directly touched colonists in the older settled regions, but for people in Nova Scotia and downeast Maine they were central concerns. Thus to understand the response of Liverpool and Machias to the revolution it is necessary to understand their reactions and adjustments to the metropolitan reforms specific to their circumstances. It is their adjustments to these reforms that shed light on their responses to the Revolution.

* * *

In 1760 Yankees arrived in Nova Scotia thinking that they would have the same rights and privileges they had enjoyed in New England and acted accordingly. The Liverpool proprietors petitioned Charles Morris, the provincial surveyor, to issue a warrant for them to call a meeting to choose "a moderator, a clerk, and a committee to manage their affairs."[10] He issued the warrant and they met, but before long they, and settlers throughout Nova Scotia, discovered that the promise of "Government … constituted like those of the neighbouring colonies" did not extend to township affairs and that British officials in Halifax and London would not sanction the endeavors of settlers to replicate civic life as they had known it in New England.[11] Rather, local affairs were to be governed through the Courts of Sessions with magistrates appointed by the governor. Committees of settlers appointed by the executive council were to distribute land in the townships.

Nova Scotia's governor and council closely monitored settlement rates in the new townships, quite unlike colonial governments in New England, which were generally lax in enforcing the terms of grants. In 1761, the summer after the first settlers arrived in Nova Scotia, the council appointed proprietors' committees to admit new grantee-settlers in the places of those grantees who had moved to the province, and instructed the committees on how much land to give each category of people. Farmers with families of seven or more members were to receive one and a half shares, or 750 acres. Farmers with families of six or fewer members were to receive one share. Single farmers under twenty-one years of age were to receive a half-share. The committee for Liverpool had permission to admit fishermen, carpenters, "and other Professions belonging to the Sea." Then in March 1762 Jonathan Belcher, the lieutenant governor, issued a proclamation announcing vacancies in Sackville, Amherst, Granville, Yarmouth, Barrington, Onslow, New Dublin, and Chester townships arising out of the "failure in the Grantees of performance of required Conditions of Settling with their Families within Limited time."[12] The combination of the appointment of proprietors' committees and the gubernatorial invitation for people to join some townships elicited petitions of protest from throughout Nova Scotia. Settlers from the Minas Basin remonstrated that they had been "wholly deprived of those Rights and Priviledges," that they had known in New England and had been led to believe they would enjoy in Nova Scotia, including the right to control membership in the proprietorships.[13] Liverpool's residents protested that "as free men ... born in a Country of Liberty in a Land that belongs to the Crown of England," they had the "right of authority vested in ourselves ... to nominate and appoint men among us to be our Committee and do Other Offices that the Town may Want."[14]

The response from Halifax to the memorials and protests was at best equivocal. In Nova Scotia the divergence from New England practices of local government became entangled with both provincial and imperial politics. In 1759, when Nova Scotia's settlements were still concentrated around Halifax and Lunenburg, the newly-convened assembly attempted to pass a law allowing for the establishment of a municipal government for Halifax. After sparring with the council, which balked at granting municipal privileges, the assembly crafted a bill entitled "Act for Preventing Trespasses," which provided for town officers to be appointed by the grand jury of the Court of Sessions during its annual fall meeting. Such was the extent of local government for Halifax. In 1763, the council, in response to Yankee settlers who protested the absence of the believed-to-have-been-promised New England–style town government, initiated a bill to provide for it. Modifications by the assembly meant that its final form achieved little more than had the March 1759 "An Act for Preventing Trespasses" with the grand juries of the Courts of Sessions remaining in control of appointing town officers. The token concession made to advocates of town government was to allow for annual town meetings to set the poor rate and to elect assessors to collect it. In 1765 the system of local government received its last fine-tuning for many decades when an act established that the grand juries in the Courts of Sessions would nominate town officers and the justices would appoint them from the nominees.[15]

Even had the assembly and council reached a consensus on establishing town government and proprietors' rights, the Crown would probably have disallowed any legislation. In 1761 the assembly passed and the council approved "An Act to enable Proprietors to divide their lands held in common," but the Crown disallowed it. If proprietorships were disallowed, a form of corporation that had even more limited powers and lifespan than town governments, then the Crown probably would have disallowed legislation on local government had the council and assembly been able to agree on the powers to be delegated to localities. As well, such legislation would have conflicted with a four-decade-old metropolitan policy to establish local governments in Nova Scotia on a Virginia model of county government, and not a New England model of town government.[16]

Although the Board of Trade was active in proscribing or disallowing what it knew it did not want in Nova Scotia, it was less directive in determining what it would consider permissible. The disallowance of the proprietors' act left settlers without a good legal mechanism to divide the land until the council appointed committees, which in turn elicited protests about the violation of settler rights. Nevertheless, Liverpool's residents learned that if they did not unduly provoke officials in Halifax they could modify, if not ignore, many of their directives and thereby achieve considerable local autonomy. Liverpool's residents gave a broader definition to the proprietors' committee than Halifax had intended, and used it to distribute land, to add new settlers at their discretion, to elect men for numerous tasks, and to set aside public lands. In 1784 they submitted a disingenuous proprietors' report to Halifax indicating that all the land in the township had been distributed, but over two-thirds of that distribution was on paper only, and for two centuries (until 1978) the proprietors' committee (later called trustees) continued to oversee the allocation of the undivided land.[17] Nothing in Nova Scotia's statutes or executive orders sanctioned most of the committee's actions, but Halifax first turned a blind eye to its activity, and then in the nineteenth century used it for land management issues because it served a useful function.

Liverpool settlers at once drew on their New England heritage for remedies to the institutional weaknesses they experienced in Nova Scotia and yet remained mindful of potential constraints from Halifax. Settlers in Horton assumed similar powers for the distribution of land, albeit without the longevity of Liverpool's committee.[18] It is important to note, however, in each township settlers made adjustments based on local needs, their prior experience, and the degree of oversight from Halifax. The agricultural townships with their valuable land seem to have received more scrutiny from Halifax than did the South Shore fishing villages with their poor rocky ground. In October 1766 the provincial secretary, Richard Bulkeley, informed the justices of the peace in Londonderry that the committee in that township which had taken upon itself the distribution of the undivided lands was illegal. He further stated that "it is a very Extraordinary proceeding to choose persons for the division of the lands after fitt persons had been Appointed by the Government for that purpose, who had they been Negligent in their business would have been removed and others have been appointed."[19] Sitting in Halifax, Bulkeley could think the actions of the Londonderry committee were extraordinary, but the records of Liverpool and Horton show that what it did was quite ordinary in many townships.

Land distribution in Liverpool and Horton reflected the New England practice of proprietorial control, but in Nova Scotia the behavior did not produce the same political and social results as it did in New England. Proprietors in Nova Scotia had no legal corporate rights, so to distribute lands as a group was to act beyond statute law, but proprietors in both townships did it, thereby making possible the sale of township lands. Recent grantees were not to sell land without a license from Halifax, but they nevertheless engaged in a lively, and unlicensed, land trade.[20] Jonathan Belcher, a prolific writer of proclamations, issued one in 1763 prohibiting the sale of land after learning "that many Grantees had alien'd their property and had afterward by Concealment obtained Rights in Other Counties in Manifest abuse of the Special trust Confidence and Liberality of Government in the Respective Grants."[21] Proclamations notwithstanding, neither Belcher nor his successors actively prosecuted these grant violations, partly because they had little interest in doing so. Belcher's warning, however, did make the settlers wary because the possibility remained that the government might step in. Unlike New England proprietors who divided land with the assurance of both custom and statute law behind them, proprietors in Nova Scotia divided their land outside the statute law, using a set of customs that officials in Halifax and London found in principle to be threatening and undesirable.

Settlers in Nova Scotia also found themselves caught between New England practice and Nova Scotia policy on the issue of church support. In New England, most churches were supported through a town assessment for the minister's rate, which all townspeople had to pay unless they were members of an officially recognized dissenting church. In Nova Scotia, the absence of town government made it illegal to tax, whether for religion, roads, or schools, although many settlements raised a minister's rate in their early years. Liverpool's proprietors levied one for four years, then for a brief while the "freeholders" in townshipwide meetings voted, assessed, and collected ministerial taxes. In the late 1770s another form of assessment applied until the time the Reverend Israel Cheever stepped down as the Congregational minister in the town in 1782, which Simeon Perkins referred to in his diary, although neither the proprietors' nor the freeholders' records mention it. Presumably the church and congregation collected a minister's rate, but they had no corporate rights to levy a tax on their members. For twenty years the people of Liverpool had persisted in following a modified version of the New England practice of public support of religion, even when it had no basis in statute law. There is no evidence that the government tried to stop the practice of ministerial assessments, and eventually religious dissent and the lack of town government proved effective prosecutors against them. The important point, however, is that as New Englanders reconstructed their lives in Nova Scotia, they borrowed heavily from their cultural background, all the while recognizing that it might be in conflict with official policy if not the law. And in most instances, the provincial government did little or nothing.[22]

Communication between Halifax and outlying communities over the application of metropolitan and provincial policy fell into some discernible patterns. For the most part Halifax dismissively acknowledged the early protests from townships over the appointment of proprietors' committees or the absence of town government. By the mid-1760s, people in the townships settled by New Englanders largely ceased submitting remonstrances to Halifax, just when colonists in the older colonies began their protests of new metropolitan policy. Not all was quiet, however, in the townships. In Liverpool "Some Publick Marks of discontent were Shewn" upon news of the Stamp Act.[23] When word of its repeal reached the town on June 3, 1766 the people celebrated. Perkins recorded a

> Day of rejoicing over the repeal of the Stamp Act. Cannon at Point Laurence fired, colours flown on shipping. In the evening the Company marched to the home of Major Doggett, and were entertained. People made a bon-fire out of the old house of Capt. Mayhew, a settler here, and continued all night, and part of next, carousing.[24]

This display of discontent, however, was isolated, remained within Liverpool, was not extended to other townships, and was not expressed to officials in Halifax. By the time Parliament repealed the Stamp Act in 1766, communication between townships and Halifax over political rights had been curtailed, thus creating a deceptive silence in the government records that masked continuing local adaptations and developments. By the mid-1760s, Nova Scotia's Yankees had learned that their protests to Halifax elicited little or no response, or if the assembly or council acted in favor of the settlers through legislation or executive orders, the king was likely to veto them. Settlers also learned that if they kept quiet and did not create disturbances they had considerable local control, most of which Halifax tolerated.

Halifax did not indiscriminately tolerate local developments. Colonial governors threatened prosecution if towns called local meetings to discuss colonial or imperial affairs. In 1774 Governor Legge banned meetings to "Disturb the Peace and promote illegal confederacies, combinations, public disorders and the highest contempt to Government." After the Revolution Governor John Wentworth removed justices in Hants and Annapolis counties who organized meetings to protest the dismissal of Naval Officer William Cottnam Tonge.[25] The message was quite clear. In the management of local affairs the government might tolerate, although not guide or sanction, the development of particularistic local institutions, but those local developments were not to be exported or used to agitate against the provincial or imperial governments. Indeed, the governor and council seemed to have issued just enough rebukes to keep the settlers on their guard, but not enough to stop their local adaptations. For the most part, Halifax lacked the coercive power to stop them, although it could make their lives awkward. The assembly and council, for their part, were not in a position to provide the institutional mechanisms to handle local needs. In the gap between prohibitions and absences, localities accommodated themselves as necessity and their customs dictated.

By the time fighting broke out in 1775, Yankees in Liverpool had considerable experience in dealing with undesirable metropolitan policy. Their political education in the colony emphasized reticence toward colonial officials and an inward turning as a way to achieve local autonomy. For over a decade and without clear markers and signals Nova Scotia's Yankees devised local compromises and accommodations that allowed them to reestablish their lives in another colony without inviting government censure. Their behavior served local needs, but would not be auspicious for participating in any organized political action beyond the boundaries of a township and certainly not for organizing a colonywide resistance, which would have been necessary for Nova Scotia to be the fourteenth united state. In suppressing town government without viable alternatives among a people zealous of their local rights, the British had eliminated the institutional mechanisms, and by turn the political behavior, for initiating communications among settlements. One town could not solicit the aid of another town, the assembly could not organize towns, and responding institutions, such as town governments, did not officially exist. The local autonomy that Nova Scotia's Yankees had learned could be theirs would have been jeopardized had people tried to link towns in common action. In the short run, British authorities had created, partly by design and partly by default, a political system that could not organize itself to challenge metropolitan governance.

* * *

Machias, and the other downeast settlements in Maine, contrast sharply with the inward turning localism of Nova Scotian settlements. The Machias grant, the thirteenth between the Penobscot and St. Croix Rivers, finally received the governor's signature in 1770, after three readings in the General Court, but the Crown approved neither it nor the earlier grants of twelve other townships. The lack of royal approbation jeopardized the viability of the thirteen grants and forestalled the establishment of governmental institutions in the region, especially incorporated towns.

The weakness of local government in the Territory of Sagadahoc, like that in Nova Scotia, came from changes in metropolitan policy, but the remedies varied enormously. In Nova Scotia, settlers confronted the implementation of a forty-year-old metropolitan plan to establish the colony without replicating the perceived republican vices of the New England colonies, especially locally vested rights such as town government. In the Territory of Sagadahoc Yankees encountered a variation of the same plan, played out in a decades-old contest between Whitehall and Boston over the control of settlement in the area.[26] To thwart the authority of the Massachusetts government, the Board of Trade blocked the approval of grants and with them the establishment of town governments.

Unlike the situation in Nova Scotia, the settlers in eastern Maine could not even establish clear title to their land. As well, all of eastern Maine was one enormous county, far larger than some colonies. The Massachusetts government could not divide it and create a new county because of the conflict between Whitehall and Boston over jurisdiction in the region. The judicial system in the easterly reaches of Maine was therefore virtually nonexistent, which was not the case in Nova Scotia. Beneath these similarities and differences, it can be said that people in both Liverpool and Machias, and in Nova Scotia and eastern Maine, were dissatisfied with the lack of local, and particularly town, government. But the relationships of the settlements to the larger political world forced people in both areas to respond to these deficits in local government in quite different ways.

The unwillingness of the king to approve the township grants in the Territory of Sagadahoc within the eighteen months allowed by the General Court disrupted the lives of the people who had settled or planned to settle. To bid for more time and to safeguard the security of their investments the grantees applied to the General Court to extend the time limit to receive royal approval. This situation especially affected the first twelve townships granted in 1762. On June 10 and 11, 1765, the proprietors from Townships Four, Five, and Six (now Steuben, Addison, and Harrington) held separate meetings in Falmouth (now Portland), Maine, to vote to request that the General Court extend the time limit for obtaining royal approbation for their grants. Then in a single petition to the General Court, the grantees of all three townships asked the assembly to renew their grants and to give them the right to sell the shares of those proprietors who had not paid their portion of expenses.[27] These people worked together in their negotiations with Boston, and to get three groups meeting within one day of each other meant that prior organization had taken place. In 1767 and 1768, the grantees from the various townships again worked in concert to petition for a time extension.[28] This synchronization of effort among townships, which largely disappeared in Nova Scotia, would prove important to organizing the resistance and revolutionary movement.

Until 1769 Machias was without justices of the peace. In the fall of that year merchant Stephen Parker of Machias wrote to Governor Hutchinson complaining that the absence of any authority had encouraged "licentious" behavior among the inhabitants. As well, the lack of civil authority made merchants wary of supplying Parker, thereby making the provisioning of Machias extremely difficult.[29] Shortly thereafter, Governor Hutchinson appointed Jonathan Longfellow a justice of the peace. In the fall of 1770 four men attacked him and "beat and brused him to such a degree, that he … [was] incapable of going about his business." As the sole magistrate in Machias he could not charge them with an attack on himself. The nearest appointed magistrate able to handle the case was located in Gouldsboro, some twenty leagues (about sixty miles) down the coast, and, according to Longfellow, that magistrate had gone to Boston for the winter. In a memorial in support of Longfellow's report, the people of Machias reasoned that the best way to resolve the problem was to appoint another justice of the peace. Hutchinson responded by appointing a deputy sheriff and a second justice of the peace in Machias.[30]

The lack of justices of the peace also frustrated people in Township Four who reported to the General Court that "neither Law nor Gospel [is] embraced among us every one doing what's right in his own eyes and a great spirit of mobbing and Rioting prevails, Cursing, Swearing, fighting, threatening, Stealing, pulling down Houses and the like as we cant sleep at nights without fear." Without corroborating evidence it is impossible to know if the settlement was as riotous as portrayed, or whether settlers used hyperbolic rhetoric to convince Governor Hutchinson "to interpose in this affair to redress our Grievances" and appoint a justice of the peace, the closest then being either twenty miles to the west in Gouldsboro or over twenty miles to the east in Machias. They recommended Captain Wilmot Wass, a settler from Martha's Vineyard, but added that they would not object should the governor choose a different person.[31]

Hutchinson also commissioned a committee of three from the General Court to travel to eastern Maine and make a report on the status of law and order in the thirteen townships without confirmed grants, in particular Machias, and to assess the damage to the king's woods.[32] The committee recommended that to assure "as much peace and good order at Machias as in the other twelve granted Towns" the existing authority should be strengthened. As an immediate measure they swore in one resident Mr. Sinkler as deputy sheriff, explaining in their report that it "was absolutely necessary, especially as there neither was nor could be a Constable in that place, it not being Incorporated." They also noted that the only jail in the county was over seventy leagues away by water, making it difficult to use for purposes of maintaining law and order, and in winter when the harbors were frozen it was inaccessible. They recommended that the governor use his powers to establish a temporary civil jail at Fort Pownall, about thirty-six leagues from Machias, but he seemingly did not do so.[33]

Under pressure from settlers and the Massachusetts General Court, Hutchinson signed the Machias grant and appointed justices of the peace. His actions were taken against the policy of his superiors on the Board of Trade. But, as he tried to explain to Lord Hillsborough, the General Court would not prosecute the settlers as trespassers and with upwards of 1,500 settlers in the thirteen contested townships some form of governance had to be provided or the people would form their own government much as the regulators had done in the Carolinas. Hutchinson's action in appointing justices of the peace, however, gave sanction to the settlers and reinforced their tie to Boston.[34]

The commissioners sent by Hutchinson to eastern Maine also reported that the people of Machias wanted to be put in a position to hire a minister. In 1772, James Lyon, a Presbyterian minister from New Jersey, who had lived briefly in Nova Scotia, accepted a call to settle in Machias provided that the inhabitants receive permission to tax for his support. They petitioned the General Court for that authority, noting that the area had "not been incorporated, into a Town, District, Precinct or Parish and cannot provide for the support of the Gospel" in the conventional manner. The General Court passed a special act empowering six prominent men to oversee a meeting of the inhabitants to vote up to £120 per year, and to appoint assessors and collectors.[35] The absence of royal approval of the Machias grant blocked the General Court from incorporating the settlement, but it did not stop it from enacting special legislation to provide interim measures until incorporation was possible.

The communication between Machias and Boston, and the twelve other townships and Boston, over how to adjust local affairs continued through the war. Generally, people received what they needed to compensate for the legal tangle created by the Crown's refusal to approve land grants between the Penobscot and St. Croix Rivers. This refusal disrupted the normal growth of civic institutions, and accommodations had to be devised, but unlike the accommodations in Liverpool, which emerged locally in a shroud of official silence, the adjustments in Machias and eastern Maine emerged through a process of requests and negotiations with Boston. Unlike the Nova Scotia townships where the petitions and memorials for redress of grievances virtually ceased after 1765, in Maine they continued throughout the war.

By 1775 the people of Machias and Liverpool had evolved significantly different attitudes about how their respective localities fit into the larger political world. In Machias, the people actively sought the help of the provincial government in Boston, which guided local developments. Through petitions and memorials the people communicated their needs and Boston usually responded favorably. When the Board of Trade blocked confirmation of the grants the General Court and the governor responded with interim measures to allow the people to organize their public lives in familiar ways that could later be merged into the customary institutions of town and county government. In Liverpool the petitions and memorials for the establishment of New England–style local government ceased soon after the settlers arrived in Nova Scotia. The absence of town government and proprietorships and a weak county government created a vacuum at the local level in which developed mutations of New England institutions, and which were efficacious given the peoples' cultural predispositions and local needs, but were at variance with British policy and extralegal, if not illegal. In eastern Maine people avoided local innovation if given centrally guided accommodation. These differences in the way localities communicated with other units of government created very different environments in which people responded to political issues. It is not surprising, therefore, that when armed conflict broke out, people in Nova Scotia townships responded by defending isolated township interests, while those in eastern Maine townships worked in concert with each other, with the provincial government in Boston, and with the Continental Congress to defend the common interests of their polities.

The channels of communication between the Massachusetts government and the towns, and among towns, were critical in developing a resistance movement to the British. The rights of towns to hold meetings at their discretion, to communicate among themselves as legally incorporated entities, and of assembly members to urge action upon the towns were critical to the revolutionaries' efforts. As the resistance movement grew, associations of revolutionaries throughout the colonies utilized existing political institutions, which in New England often meant the town meeting.[36] Indeed the New England town meetings were well suited to forging united opposition to British policy, and other colonies tried to imitate them with large public meetings.[37] Despite being unincorporated, settlements in eastern Maine used customary inter-town patterns of communication to link themselves into the political system. In Nova Scotia comparable channels of communication and networking never developed or were discouraged and suppressed. The weak or passive response of New Englanders in Nova Scotia to the Revolution resulted from their political isolation, not their geographic isolation.

During the Revolution most Nova Scotian Yankees assumed a position of nonengagement that protected their local autonomy. Militarily active loyalism would have conceded too much to the legitimacy of British metropolitan policy. In the townships, accommodation to that policy had involved too much quiet defiance for people to support it suddenly. But their means of accommodation depended on quiescent forms of local adaptation that precluded the development of systems of organization that were needed to sustain rebel activity. Their position was not one of neutrality, nor did it reflect confusion about their choices in Nova Scotia. They had essentially evolved a new political culture of idiosyncratic localism and loyalty to the Empire. They did not openly endorse British policy, but from their local bases neither did they resist it. The metropolitan government had achieved its immediate needs. The prohibition of New England town government in Nova Scotia eliminated competing levels of political authority and allegiance from which people could threaten the Empire. By the outbreak of armed conflict in 1775 there was politically little in Nova Scotia that stood between the town and the empire.

This difference in the political behavior of people in the two areas is nicely illustrated in the issue of neutrality in both Nova Scotia and eastern Maine.

From Yarmouth, Nova Scotia, came an oft-quoted 1775 petition for neutral status, and that scholars have used to argue the case for colonywide neutrality. In eastern Maine there was a movement for neutrality in 1781 during the time that the British were occupying Castine on Penobscot Bay. Beyond the difference in timing there was a more profound difference in the method of requesting neutrality that shows how the political culture of the two areas had diverged in the years after 1760.[38]

The Yarmouth petition for neutral status came shortly after Governor Francis Legge tried to call out the colony's militia units to defend Halifax, which as governor he could do.[39] Throughout the colony militia units refused to muster, those that mustered had no men who would volunteer to go to Halifax, and men refused officers' commissions. The people in Yarmouth also responded to the military confusion with a request for neutral status stating,

> We were almost all of us born in New England, we have Fathers, Brothers & Sisters in that country, divided betwixt natural affection to our nearest relations, and good Faith and Friendship to our King and Country, we want to know, if we may be permitted at this time to live in a peaceable State, as we look on that to be the only situation in which we with our Wives and Children, can be in any tolerable degree safe.

The Governor and Council were unequivocally against the idea. They responded to the Yarmouth memorialists

> that the request & proposition of the Memorialists, cou'd neither be receiv'd or Admitted a Neutrality being utterly Absurd and inconsistent with the duty of Subjects, who are always bound by the Laws to take Arms in defence of Government and oppose and Repel all Hostile Attempts and Invasions, that the duty they owe as Subjects cannot be dispensed with.

Duty or not, most Nova Scotian men refused to do service in Halifax. There is no evidence that people in Yarmouth joined with any other towns to request neutrality, and there were no similar pleas for neutrality from other settlements. The only concerted action taken against the militia call-up was in the Assembly where representatives from the outports fiercely debated the passage of new militia laws.[40]

The movement for neutrality in eastern Maine came after the British had occupied Bagaduce (Castine) at the head of the Penobscot Bay. The General Court in Boston responded to the occupation by asking Brigadier General Peleg Wadsworth to plan a strategy of defense for Lincoln County. He placed all settlements in the county within firing range of an armed vessel under martial law for six months. To residents of islands in the Penobscot Bay he extended neutral status, thereby preempting British compulsion to have them swear oaths of allegiance to the Crown. He indicated that all other settlements in Lincoln County would continue to support the revolutionary cause, which left them subject to British harassment and pressure to take oaths of loyalty. Many also feared that the British Navy would revive its campaign to destroy the seacoast towns in eastern Maine, which British raids on the homes of prominent men only reinforced.[41]

The movement for neutrality began in Gouldsboro under the leadership of Francis Shaw, a magistrate, merchant, and major in the militia. He, according to the reports out of Machias, planned the move in consultation with Nathan Jones, a fellow merchant in Gouldsboro, and Captain William Nickells of Narraguagus. Apparently Shaw worked first through the committees of safety in Gouldsboro, Narraguagus, and Frenchmen's Bay, which agreed to his plan to ask the General Court to declare the region between the Penobscot and the St. Croix Rivers neutral. He then sent a letter to Stephen Jones of Machias asking him to support the proposal there, a draft of which he included in the letter. He also sent letters to the committees of safety at Chandler's River and Pleasant River. Jones showed Shaw's letter and draft petition entitled "Representation of the Inhabitants of all the Tract of Land, lying & being on & between the Rivers Penobscot & St Croix inclusive," to the Machias committee of safety which promptly called a meeting of the inhabitants to discuss it.[42] The people of Machias voted unanimously to oppose any plan for neutrality and to work to defeat it in all other settlements as far west as Frenchmen's Bay. They agreed to write to the governor and General Court disavowing all support of the plan, and passed resolutions censuring the behavior of Shaw "who hath made it evident that he hath his private Interest at heart, more than the good of his Country," an opinion supported by the Pleasant River committee of safety. When it heard of the plan it stated that "not one Person here has coveted to be Neutors at Present Neither do we Desire to be so Sneeking as Leave our Friends at the Westerd to Beat the Bush & we to cathch the Hare."[43]

What the actions of both the Frenchmen's Bay and Machias people show is that they believed that they did not live in isolated communities that could negotiate their own arrangements with the Massachusetts government or with the British in Penobscot Bay. Even if one settlement was the author of a movement, it nonetheless endeavored to persuade other settlements of its position. The process worked two ways. Francis Shaw of Gouldsboro attempted to organize the settlements to support his proposal of neutrality, and the people of Machias worked to defeat it. The networking among towns was an important part of New England political culture, prominently manifested in the Revolution with the committees of correspondence and committees of safety. Even in areas where settlements were not incorporated the practice of seeking widespread support was still employed. In Nova Scotia the British had not been able to suppress the local orientation of New England political life, and local institutions and power structures emerged without central approval. But to maintain that local autonomy the Yankees had to sacrifice the communication among towns that in New England served to temper excessive localism and to knit the towns into a larger political system. The single petition from Yarmouth is a reflection of political, not geographic, isolation.

The meaning of neutrality in Yarmouth and eastern Maine also differed fundamentally. Yarmouth residents wrote their petition on December 8, 1775, in response to the governor's call for men and almost seven months before the signing of the Declaration of Independence. Given this timing, the request only refers to not fighting against the rebels, many of whom were friends, family, and former neighbors, and not to any considered political position with a meaning at odds with the British Empire. Despite the governor's response that the request was "utterly Absurd and inconsistent with the duty of Subjects," precedents existed for British American colonists to refuse to participate in military service, especially in actions against fellow civilians, and yet still claim to be loyal. Colonists had done it during the Seven Years' War and again during the Stamp Act crisis. The request for neutrality from Yarmouth was issue-oriented rather than systemically oriented. They could ask to be treated as neutrals in the decision to bear arms against the rebels without declaring themselves to be disloyal to the Crown or Empire. Issue-oriented neutrality (or nonengagement) and loyalty were not mutually exclusive.

Only with the signing of the Declaration of Independence did a middle ground emerge in English-speaking North America that was beyond the pale of the British Empire. The eastern Maine movement for neutrality carried the implication that militarily and politically a middle ground had emerged, if only temporarily, between the British and Americans. Indeed Shaw used revolutionary ideology to argue that the people of Maine had a right to declare themselves neutral. He claimed that they had "Repeatedly Petition'd the former Government of Massachusetts … for Protection & Support, as that Government did the Kingdom of Great Britain, for Redress of Grievances." Despite the petitions Massachusetts had, Shaw asserted, "Refused or Neglected to give Protection to us the said Inhabitants in Return for our Allegiance." In the absence of that protection and "Compressed between Two Potent contending Powers" the people had a right to ask to be treated as neutrals.[44] This was a very different interpretation of neutrality than that asked by the people in Yarmouth and one that acknowledged a position between Britain and the United States. Indeed some Anglo-Americans fully exploited the position, most notably those in Vermont.[45]

The possibility of a neutral position in Anglo-America came about because of an extreme polarization in positions between colonial Americans and British officialdom. For the people in Machias that polarization made them vilify Francis Shaw and his associates after they attempted to gain neutral status for the area between the Penobscot and the St. Croix Rivers. In their letter to the Massachusetts General Court, they described the plan for neutrality "as the sycophantic production of a few disiging Men, rather than the genuine feelings & sentiments of a faith full & brave People."[46] The Declaration of Independence may have created the possibility of a middle ground in Anglo-America, but in some areas the ideological positions had become so contrary that a neutral one was largely untenable, although Shaw's neutrality movement carried the implication that militarily and politically there was a middle ground between the British and the Americans. Nova Scotians did not entertain this position and throughout the war continued to see themselves within the pale of the empire and the war as a civil rather than an international conflict.

The ideological polarization in some parts of Anglo-America also created new meanings for loyalism and patriotism, definitions that no longer represented ranges on a spectrum of sentiment but rather quite circumscribed points. In Nova Scotia most people continued to use a definition of loyalty that was defined not in the heat of the revolution, but by the range of loyal behavior that had been acceptable in more peaceable times. Thus the "Loyalists," those people in the thirteen revolting colonies who supported the empire and who fled to Nova Scotia, New Brunswick, and Canada after the war, were an American creation. While the remaining parts of the British Empire absorbed those Loyalists and those Loyalists tried to apply their definition of loyalty to all British subjects in North America, it is not a definition that can be widely applied and used to assess the positions and attitudes of all the people who remained loyal at the time of the Revolution.[47] To judge the behavior of Nova Scotians during the war, a British definition of loyalty encompassing more than the time of the Revolution must be used. Thus, if one asks whether Nova Scotians' behavior, despite complaints of governors, fitted within a British definition of loyalty, then the answer is yes. But if one asks, were Nova Scotians Patriots or Loyalists—which is an inherently American question—then the answer is no, but one has asked a question that is inappropriate to Nova Scotia. For most Nova Scotians, one could be both loyal to the Crown and Empire and militarily not engaged. For Patriots and Loyalists in the thirteen rebelling colonies, military action and allegiance were increasingly linked, whereas in Nova Scotian minds they remained distinct. As tensions heightened in the 1770s it would have an impact on how the settlements responded to the bearing of arms.

5

Bearing Arms: The Military Involvement of Liverpool and Machias in the American Revolution

As tensions throughout British America heightened during the 1770s, colonists, regardless of their stance on imperial disputes, recognized that armed force might be used before the issues were resolved: by the British to suppress the protesting colonists; by the colonists to resist British suppression; and by others to protect person and property. Any resort to armed force in the imperial conflict would have touched virtually every adult male in British North America. Most belonged to a local militia unit and when a colony needed to form a provincial army, such as during the Seven Years' War, soldiers were often recruited through local militia units.[1]

Although all militia units in a colony were technically under the command of the governor, customary practice throughout British America accorded local militia units considerable latitude to decide how to respond. During the Stamp Act crisis, for example, militias had refused gubernatorial orders to march against rioters. With such volition, militia units became barometers of local reaction to the political and military conflicts that convulsed the British Empire in the second half of the eighteenth century.[2] This chapter, exploring how New Englanders in Liverpool and Machias responded to the use of armed force during the Revolutionary War, asks three questions. How did each town use its militia? How did each town see its military needs in relation to other units of government including, in particular, the provincial government? How did their military involvement reflect attitudes about the use of armed force and politics?

In both Nova Scotia and Massachusetts the commissioning of militia officers came shortly after the settlement of new townships. Within months of people establishing homes in Liverpool in 1760, three men received commissions for militia officers from the governor: Nathaniel Tory as captain and Joseph Collins and Jonathan Diamond as lieutenants. After two years of rapid population growth the governor commissioned another thirteen officers. With this second round of commissions the Liverpool militia organized three companies, each with a captain and first and second lieutenants; a major oversaw all three companies.[3] The governor and council had organized militias expeditiously for local defensive purposes. New Englanders had intended to move to Nova Scotia in the spring of 1759 but attacks on surveying parties by Mi'kmaq prompted organizers to delay moving for a year while the government negotiated with the Mi'kmaq. A treaty signed in the early spring of 1760 provided some assurance that the Mi'kmaq would not disturb settlers, which proved generally to be the case, despite periodic tensions. But until time had shown that the Mi'kmaq were no longer a threat, domestic security remained a source of concern, and local militias offered the best avenue of defense for settlers.[4]

In Machias, the organization of the militia, like other aspects of establishing the settlement on a firm footing, was delayed by the controversy between Boston and Whitehall over the settlement's legality. In 1769, one year before Governor Hutchinson signed the township grant, the Massachusetts government commissioned three militia officers for Machias, a captain, a lieutenant, and an ensign, yet another adjustment to customary practices in Massachusetts, where militia officers were usually locally elected. The lieutenant, Stephen Parker, either did not accept his commission or resigned it within the year, and in May 1770 Benjamin Foster became lieutenant in his stead.[5] The commissioning of militia officers in 1769 was one of the first official acknowledgments of the settlers in Machias, although it is unclear why Massachusetts acted when it did. The chronic unrest in eastern Maine dating back to the early seventeenth century may have prompted the government to initiate some organization of the militia, perhaps to forestall the organization of regulators, as Hutchinson feared might happen if the government did not grant a township to the settlers of Machias.[6]

Beyond commissioning officers, the militias in Liverpool and Machias were largely inactive until the mid-1770s. In Liverpool, the only settlement in Nova Scotia outside of Halifax to fête the repeal of the Stamp Act in 1766, the militia marched in celebration and partied afterwards at Major John Dogget's. By law Nova Scotia militia companies were to drill once every three months and muster once every six months but there is no evidence that the Liverpool companies did.[7] As imperial tensions increased, Simeon Perkins, lieutenant colonel of Liverpool's militia, called a meeting of the officers in February 1774 to make regulations, nominate men for vacant offices, and ask current officers to examine their company's arms and ammunition. Apparently acting on his own initiative, Perkins called the meeting after receiving news of increasing tensions in New England. With Boston as little as a three-day sail from Liverpool and with regular fishing and trading traffic in the harbor, news of the escalating resistance circulated quickly and kept people in Nova Scotia well apprised of events farther south. Ships' crews relayed news by word of mouth and delivered newspapers and correspondence, thereby guaranteeing that intelligence of all the major turning points in the colonial resistance, and many of the minor twists, reached the town. News of the departure of Governor Francis Bernard from Boston, the Boston Tea Party, British plans to close the Boston harbor (which Perkins perceptively thought would "be productive of disagreeable consequences"), the colonial embargo on British goods, the billeting of soldiers on Boston Commons, and the flight of Governor Thomas Hutchinson to England all reached Liverpool.[8]

Within a month of receiving news of the Boston Tea Party, Perkins consulted with Lieutenant Nathaniel Freeman and decided to call together the militia officers.[9] Temperamentally cautious and prudent, Perkins decided to ready the Liverpool militia for possible conflict six months before Governor Francis Legge's call for militia preparedness, although it is unclear if royalist leanings or protection of the town's trading interests engendered his expression of caution in early 1774. Most likely it was the latter. Legge sent out orders in September 1774 to submit returns of local militia units. When Perkins, in compliance with Legge's instructions, convened local candidates for militia officers, the majority of them refused to accept the governor's commissions. Just six months before, Perkins had asked Liverpool's militia officers to make returns and he encountered no opposition.[10] Two factors may explain the men's opposition, although it is unclear why they had to be recommissioned in the first place. First, during those six months, the conflict in New England intensified, Parliament passed the Coercive Acts, and the colonies called the First Continental Congress, all of which had a polarizing effect throughout British America.[11] Second, the men in Liverpool may have been willing to accept Perkins's direction as an affirmation of local authority, which their refusal of the governor's commissions affirmed.

Over the next twelve months Governor Legge's difficulties with the Nova Scotia outports and their militia companies intensified. The outbreak of fighting in Massachusetts in April 1775, the taking of a royal naval vessel at Machias in June, the commissioning of rebel privateers that preyed on the Nova Scotia coast, and other acts of armed conflict persuaded Legge in September 1775 to recruit 1,000 men from within the colony to form a provincial regiment to defend Halifax. Recruiting competition from the king's regiments forced him to abandon the project. He then decided to use the provincial militia to defend Halifax and tried to call up one-fifth of all the men in the colony and raise taxes to support them, a decision that provoked almost universal resistance in the colony. When the LeHave militia mustered to draft thirty-five men, all refused to be drafted or to enlist. Liverpool men raised a subscription to send Simeon Perkins to Halifax to fill his seat in the assembly that was debating new militia and revenue acts.

By December the tension over the governor's plans for the use of the militia had sufficiently exercised some settlements to provoke them to send petitions of protest to Halifax. Cumberland County inhabitants emphasized that the distant conflict in New England did not justify the governor's measures. They thought it "a piece of Cruelty and Imposition" to be asked to take up "arms against their Friends and Relatives." If necessary they would use the militia locally to "defend ourselves & Property," but to send men to Halifax was unreasonable. The outcry and resistance throughout the outports forced Legge to retreat and return to trying to raise a provincial regiment. Like colonists throughout British America, Nova Scotians would and did pass judgment on what they considered the acceptable use of the militia.[12]

The Nova Scotia outports could refuse to honor the governor's request for men, they could assert that the militia be used only to "defend ourselves & Property," and their representatives to the colonial assembly could fight the governor and council's attempt to raise an internal tax to support the militia, but such behavior also left them largely to their own resources. Despite laws requiring all men to own firearms for their militia responsibilities, few in Liverpool did, and admonitions from the provincial secretary to obey the law had little impact. Colonial militia units expected some public funding, but in Nova Scotia the provincial government balked at sending arms to towns with suspect sympathies. Restrictions on local taxing, save for the poor, further constrained people's ability to raise funds for defensive purposes.[13] For the first year of the war the lack of military preparedness had little consequence for Liverpool. The fighting was off in another part of British America. Rebel privateers took Liverpool vessels on the high seas, but on land life went on relatively undisturbed. The militia did not even muster for practice.

Although Governor Legge failed to command the cooperation of the local militia units, he had marginally more success in prevailing upon local justices of the peace and magistrates to monitor the loyalty of the colony's residents. On June 23, 1775, after the battle of Bunker Hill and the taking of a royal naval vessel in Machias, Legge issued a proclamation stating that anyone moving into Nova Scotia from another British American colony had to give testimony before a magistrate "of their Fidelty and Allegiance to his Majesty's Sacred person & Gov't." In more detailed instructions to Liverpool's magistrates, Richard Bulkeley, provincial secretary, sent a copy of the oath to be administered and orders to report on the character and conduct of all persons coming into the town and the names of any who refused to take the oath. In Liverpool thirteen people swore allegiance to the king on July 19, 1775. In December and January the magistrates administered oaths to all Liverpool residents except Captain Lemuel Drew who refused to swear the oath.[14]

Liverpool's magistrates also defended the town residents against allegations that they were "a lawless & rebellious people." Officials in Halifax prepared a bill to make Liverpool part of Lunenburg County and thereby deprive it of its status as the county seat with courts of law. Simeon Perkins had enough influence in Halifax as a merchant and a member of the assembly to have the bill dismissed. Meanwhile, Richard Bulkeley wrote private letters to William Johnstone, a Liverpool magistrate, a native Scotman, a strident Loyalist, and a government client, asking him to report on "the General conduct & characters of the people." Bulkeley instructed Johnstone that he "need not let it be known that [he had] any direction of this sort."[15]

To bridle or suppress what rebellious behavior Nova Scotians might have exhibited, Governor Legge circulated one proclamation after the next during the summer and fall of 1775. He banned the export of gunpowder, arms, ammunition, or saltpeter for six months to keep it from being shipped through Nova Scotia to the rebels. He prohibited the aiding of any persons involved in the rebellion in New England. Seeing no end to a worsening conflict, he put the province under martial law in December. One proclamation forbade "all persons whatsoever to Utter, publish or print, any such Traterous and Treasonable papers" by which "His Majesty's faithful Subjects here may become corrupted, and they seduced from their duty and Fidelity." The proclamations reflected the governor's perception that most Nova Scotians in the outports were not reliably loyal subjects. Without clear signs of loyalty, Legge balked at issuing government arms to the local militias. Ironically, by forcing people to devise their own local defense, he reinforced the kind of local discretion he found so threatening.[16]

Attacks by New England privateers, rather than proclamations from a suspicious and inept governor, precipitated overt signs of loyalty. After a year of attacking vessels on the high seas, in 1776 New England privateers began entering Nova Scotia's harbors. They harassed people, took small vessels, and occasionally burned or looted homes and shops. This shift in privateers' targets had numerous consequences. John Allan, a former Nova Scotian and United States Indian Commissioner stationed in Machias, deplored the depredations of the small privateers and their "Voricious Dispositions." He reported to Jeremiah Powell, president of the Massachusetts Council, on the return of a Machias-based privateer from a cruise to the Minas Basin where "it is generally supposed they have been burning & Distroying Property." "Such proceeding," he argued, "will Occation more Torys than 100 such Expeditions Woud make good."[17]

Nova Scotians scrambled to devise defensive responses. Liverpool's inhabitants sent a letter to Halifax asking for government protection. The provincial secretary promised that the lieutenant governor "would take immediate measures to prevent such depredations," a promise to be fulfilled, he subsequently wrote, by sending a company of the King's troops to "be posted at Liverpool for the safety, protection and defence of the Inhabitants." It did not happen.[18] British naval patrols off the coast provided little deterrence. On January 10, 1778, Eyre Massey sent a private letter to an unnamed person, probably the Nova Scotia governor, reporting on the navy's response to privateers.

> I think it necessary to inform your Excellency that the Pyrates which have done all the mischief on the Coast of this Province, appear as fishing boats and have concealed arms, and all the Sea Officers have said that Lord Howe has desir'd that they shall not be molested for they take the Merchantmen which the Ships of War speedily retake, in this situation appeared the Pyrate which the Gage lately took.[19]

The navy apparently tolerated rebel privateering as a means to impress sailors from recaptured merchantmen.

In the fall of 1776 privateers entered Liverpool's harbor and stole vessels. With the governor not sending troops or supplies and the navy not taking privateers, Liverpool's leaders began to plan how they could use their limited resources to provide optimum defense and minimize the damage privateers might inflict. Perkins convened the militia officers to discuss keeping a guard because "no protection [was] afforded as yet, from Government." They decided to keep a night guard. Five days later Perkins mustered Liverpool's entire militia, the first time since the fighting had started in 1775. To his surprise he found the men in "much better condition" and "behav[ing] very decently, considering how little experience they have had." For the next two years, local leaders called out the militia at any threat of privateering attacks.[20]

Events entrapped Liverpool's residents in the war. With little leadership from Halifax, except the exhortation to be good loyal subjects, Simeon Perkins deftly used his authority as magistrate and highest-ranking militia officer in Liverpool to manage local affairs. Events did not always make clear the office from which he should act. On March 8, 1777, someone removed two guns from the Point and stashed them on the schooner *Polly* where they were found. A Liverpool constable was assigned to disable the mainsail of the *Polly* to keep it in the harbor until local magistrates could investigate the incident. During the night someone removed the guns from the *Polly*, placed them in a sailboat, and stole the guns and the sailboat, as well as another boat belonging to the Crown. Not knowing whether to treat the incident as an act of war or a civil offense, Perkins made out a warrant to Gamaliel Stuart deputizing him to act as a constable to retake the sailboat if found. He issued a separate warrant to retake the public property of the guns and the Crown's boat. He issued a third warrant to Joseph Freeman, a sergeant in the militia, to muster fifteen men "to assist the Peace Officers in executing their warrants." They found the boats and guns down the coast at Port Mouton, where they seemed to have been taken by privateers, rendering the incident an act of war.[21]

Had it been a civil offense, the use of the militia could have been problematic, hence, Perkins's care in having the militia act at the behest of and under the orders of civil authority. Unable to identify their antagonists as rebels or loyalists, Perkins probably wanted to avoid controversy about whose side the Liverpool militia supported, a goal that the civil definition of the incident helped to serve. Because the incident involved a Crown vessel, it came under the scrutiny of the governor who criticized Perkins's handling of the affair. Perkins recorded in his diary that

> I told him [a naval officer] my situation was more difficult than the Governor immagined, and that I should be happy to be in a private station in these times of difficulty, but as I had been a Magistrate many years in times of tranquillity, it might be out of character to resign in times of difficulty.[22]

By the spring of 1778 fears of a major privateering attack convinced residents of Liverpool that threats to the town exceeded their capacity to respond. Notified of the danger, the lieutenant governor promised "that immediate measures will be taken to protect this shore." When another promise rang hollow, Perkins and the schoolteacher drafted a petition to the lieutenant governor and council requesting protection. But it took an alarming confrontation with a privateer that boldly sailed into the harbor "with Drum and fife going, and whuzzaing," to persuade the government to provide any support. It sent fifty-seven muskets, balls, and powder to be used to arm the militia.[23] Hopes of additional governmental assistance continued through May until dispelled by the return from Halifax of Joseph Freeman, one of the "Heads of the Town," with a paltry "two half barrels of powder, and 250 flints." Freeman reported that the government would spare six soldiers and four six-pounders (cannons) if the people could get them to Liverpool, but the protection of an armed vessel or more soldiers was out of the question, and the town had no safe method of transporting the cannons.[24]

Liverpool's local resources to counter the privateers consisted of a poorly armed militia, no legal way to meet, and no legal way to levy taxes to pay the militiamen should they serve. Almost two decades of living without adequate local institutions had taught Liverpool's residents, if not all Nova Scotians, how to maximize scant local rights and to stretch permissible behavior. Freeman's news of Halifax's weak response reached Liverpool early on the morning of Sunday, May 31, 1778. Utilizing public worship, Perkins asked the "Heads of the town to stop at Mr. West's after the meeting and consult upon measures of safety." They decided to keep a guard of two or three men and dismantle the fort, presumably to remove signs of militancy and signal privateers that the people of Liverpool "might treat with them, and let them know that we would not molest them if they did not attempt landing." After that gathering Perkins consulted "many people of property" who advised him to call out the militia to ask its opinion, whereupon Perkins issued orders for the militia to muster the next day on the parade grounds.[25]

The ensuing meeting illustrates the fine line between legal and extralegal action in Liverpool. The militia mustered and marched to the meetinghouse whereupon Perkins dismissed it for an hour to reconvene at the same place. During that hour's recess Perkins led a discussion of all the adult men in the town, thereby staging a town meeting under the guise of a militia recess. Presumably those not wanting to sit in the meetinghouse for the hour of recess could have left, but Perkins does not indicate that they did. Those remaining agreed on a plan to keep a nightly guard of three men to watch for the approach of privateers. Each guard would receive two shillings per night to be paid with money raised by private subscription. The men also discussed how to respond should a privateer enter the harbor. They decided to sound an alarm to alert townspeople, call out the militia, and initiate negotiations with the privateer's captain. Should a privateer try to land or remove vessels from the harbor, the townspeople would resist them. Otherwise, privateers would be left alone. At the end of the hour's "recess," Perkins "ordered the Militia under Arms" and asked them whether they would accept the duty to which they had just agreed as private men. Only four dissented. Before the day's end money had been committed for nine nights of guard duty.[26]

By adroitly manipulating his legal authority, Perkins staged a town meeting. As the commanding officer of the Liverpool militia, he could order the companies under arms. If he marched them to the meetinghouse and dismissed them to reconvene at the same place an hour later he had not technically exceeded his authority. If the men remained in the meetinghouse for the recess and conversed among themselves, no meeting had been called. Rather, a casual, albeit opportune, gathering had occurred. The line between what was official and unofficial was fuzzy. Was the guard a public act because it had been approved by the entire militia and was paid for only with private money? Or did the private financing make it a private manipulation of public institutions? An entry in Perkins's diary indicates that it was somewhat like a private business deal. He recorded that he had given Mrs. Peleg Dexter, a tavernkeeper, 25s.6d., "my reckoning since our Military affairs commenced," enough for more than four nights of guard duty.[27]

How one interprets these developments depends on the perspective of the observer. Viewed from Liverpool, the exigencies of planning a defensive

Fig. 5.1 Wash drawing of Battery Point blockhouse, Liverpool, 1817, from the J. E. Woolford album, "Sketches of Nova Scotia." (Courtesy of the Nova Scotia Museum, Halifax, Canada; History Collection, 78.45.67.)

strategy with limited matériel, money, and provincial support appear to have legitimized the private extralegal actions made in the interest of the greater public good. The willingness of Liverpool's residents to negotiate with a privateer suggests a kind of protective nonengagement, a recoiling at engaging an armed privateer when local arms were scarce, more than it was a statement about the political underpinnings of the Revolution. Colonial officials in Halifax undoubtedly would have looked on the incident less sympathetically, even though they had failed to provide adequate defense for South Shore communities that were exposed to privateers. Not until the summer of 1782 did the governor agree to fund militia rations, pay for militia duty in Liverpool, and build a battery on Fort Point as protection against privateers.[28]

During the war, the one overriding concern of Liverpool's residents was protection of person and property, a concern largely devoid of ideological articulation, even if it did require a liberal exercise of local authority. The one strategy that stretched the official royalist policy excessively was the 1778 decision of Liverpool's leaders to have "a Treaty opened with the Privateers," a decision both to engage in private negotiations with the "enemy" and to allow private exchanges with privateers in violation of the governor's order of July 1775 "forbidding all intercourse with New England rebels."[29] On Monday, October 19, 1778, two privateers sailed into the Liverpool harbor, anchored, and sent men with a white flag ashore to demand one hogshead of rum and one barrel of sugar, presumably as tribute payment so that the town would not be fired upon or raided. Some militia officers and gentlemen, who were present when the privateers demanded their extortion, responded that they would not deliver the rum and sugar but would sell them. In a short while one of the privateers' captains asked to purchase twenty gallons of rum and twenty pounds of sugar and sent ashore two barrels of bread as payment. This bartering with the enemy "offended" some townspeople, who were "very sangwine in the Cause of Fighting," an indication that some of Liverpool's residents were staunch Loyalists. The bread was left on the beach only to be scavenged later by folk with different scruples or empty bellies.[30]

In November 1778 the governor acceded to Liverpool's requests for assistance in defending the town and notified the magistrates that he would send troops if they could guarantee quarters for them. On December 13 a company of Orange Rangers composed of a captain, first and second lieutenants, an ensign, three sergeants, two or three corporals, forty-eight privates, and some women and children arrived in the town. For the most part "A General Harmony [was] kept up between the Inhabitants & the Officers of the Army." The militia worked with the soldiers to build a battery at Fort Point, and militiamen and troops made joint reconnaissance trips along the coast to check for privateers. The standard problems of desertions, petty thievery, and soldiers selling their military issue to civilians occurred, but for the most part the townspeople and soldiers developed a satisfactory modus operandi.

When the government announced plans in February 1781 to remove the unit, townspeople sent letters and memorials asking that it be allowed to stay, arguing that the threat of destruction by privateers had not yet passed. The government compromised and a detachment of twenty soldiers remained in the town until August 1783 after the cessation of hostilities and the signing of the Treaty of Paris.[31] The government had sent the Orange Rangers to Liverpool to protect person and property and more generally the town. Their presence had no larger strategic meaning. They were not holding territory for the Crown which otherwise might fall to rebels. The threat of an invasion of Nova Scotia ended after an abortive attempt by some men leaving from Machias.[32] The rangers were not recruiting soldiers for action elsewhere. Their purpose was to allow people to go on with the daily routines of their private lives in time of war.

The arrival of the Orange Rangers created a perceptible shift in the expressed loyalty of the people of Liverpool to the king and empire. On June 4, 1779, six months after the arrival of the Orange Rangers, Liverpool began an annual celebration of George III's birthday, which remained a public holiday long after the end of the war.[33] The building of the battery on Fort Point contrasted sharply with the earlier decision to take down the fort on the point, and was a sign that Liverpool would actively resist the depredations of privateers.

Nearly a year after the arrival of the Orange Rangers "Some Gentlemen" decided to purchase a ship on thirty-two shares and outfit it as a privateer, tantamount to a public declaration of being on the king's side, even if only for avaricious reasons.

Having decided to invest in a privateer, the investors asked the government to grant a letter of marque, lend them guns, and give them ammunition, all of which it did. On January 21, 1780, Liverpool's first privateer, the refitted *Lucy*, sailed out of the harbor on its maiden voyage. Over the next three and a half years Liverpool men outfitted six privateers; all met with indifferent success. The history of the *Lucy* illustrates the fluctuating fortunes of a Liverpool privateer and its owners during the American Revolution. It saw two months of duty under the first owners and captured some prizes before being sold. A new combination of owners refitted the vessel and sent it out in the spring of 1780. By June the crew had captured five empty schooners and one laden brig. The owners of the *Lucy* refitted one of the captured schooners and commissioned it as the privateer *Delight*. Readied for its first voyage, the *Delight* was stolen out of Liverpool harbor by Captain Benjamin Cole of Salem, Massachusetts, a notorious New England privateer and a nemesis for Liverpool. Cole had lost a sloop to the *Lucy* earlier that year and to snatch the *Delight* from under the noses of its owners was a sharp retort. George Watson, from neighboring LeHave, indelicately observed that "the privateers will come in & take your Hats off your Heads," a remark that earned him a few hours of detention by Captain John Howard of the Orange Rangers. With the loss of the *Delight*, the owners of the *Lucy* decided to retire that vessel. Perkins, who owned shares in both vessels, calculated he had lost £35 on the two investments.[34]

When Perkins invested in a privateer, he noted that it was to be "Armed for our Defence." His rationale was generous. Owners of privateers seldom kept them close at hand for local defense, but rather sent them out into the shipping lanes to capture enemy vessels and goods or to plunder the enemy's seaport towns. Governments commissioned privateers during wartime as part of larger war strategies; they disrupted the movement of matériel and provisions and undermined wartime economies. Individuals engaged in privateering could "acquire riches and honour," as a 1779 Halifax advertisement for volunteers stated it.[35] Owners fed but did not pay sailors on privateers, compensating them instead with a cut of the prizes taken. Investors had the same incentive. Thus although the rationale for privateering employed the rhetoric of protecting the public, for individual investors it was primarily a private business venture, risky but promising high profits if successful. Not incidentally, if the *Lucy* had been fitted as a privateer primarily to defend the town, the owners probably would not have sold it within two months of its commissioning.

By its very nature, privateering threatened a clash between the avowed public interest of common defense and the practiced private interest of financial gain. On June 28, 1780, a prize of the *Lucy* arrived in Liverpool with ten prisoners on board, four of them deserted British soldiers. Until the magistrates could decide what to do with them, the prisoners had to be incarcerated. They were transferred to another vessel, and a militia guard stood watch. The first night, one militiaman, John Roberts, refused to serve. At his court martial the next day he was fined fifteen shillings, which Perkins reduced to ten. The second night two men refused to stand guard and at their trial they questioned the legality of this militia duty. The court found them guilty of disobeying legitimate orders and fined them twenty shillings; when they refused to pay it they were imprisoned. Meanwhile Captain Howard of the Orange Rangers refused to have his men stand guard arguing that he had none fit for duty.[36]

The conflict revolved around the issue of who had responsibility for prisoners brought back in privateers. Often privateers transferred captured sailors to other ships for transport home or released them on land to find their own way home. Ship captains from Liverpool had returned men to New England; Yarmouth, Nova Scotia, had a reputation as a place from which Yankee sailors could gain passage home.[37] But captains could not release deserted British soldiers. Rather they had to be brought back to British territory and arrangements made for turning them over to military authorities. In the days after the arrival of the prisoners, townspeople debated the issue of whether the town or the investors in a privateer should pay for incarcerating and feeding prisoners. Quite simply, was it a public or private responsibility and expense? The magistrates of Liverpool, many of them investors in privateers, decided, though not without significant dissent, that prisoners taken by privateers were a public responsibility.

The rest of the war had little impact on Liverpool. Privateering offered limited rewards. The Orange Rangers who remained in Liverpool spent much of their time as common laborers working for men such as Simeon Perkins clearing land for new sawmills and roads.[38] The presence of the Orange Rangers helped to assure Liverpool residents that they could go on responding to the war as they had from the beginning, as a complication that they accommodated to their daily lives. Most significantly, they were not going to do the converse and adjust their daily lives to the demands of the war, which is what the people in Machias did.

* * *

In 1775 while militia units in Nova Scotia were refusing to fulfill the governor's request for troops, the militia units in Machias and surrounding settlements had become deeply engaged in the rebellion, largely as a consequence of trying to enforce the trade embargoes enacted first by the Massachusetts Provincial Congress and then the Continental Congress. Up and down the Maine coast, local people had been refusing to ship timber despite the economic sacrifice it entailed. For settlers east of the Penobscot, who obtained most of their food from imports, the timber trade was their lifeline. As timbermen sited mills farther and farther downeast in the 1760s, merchants who supplied wood to Boston and the West Indies had followed in their wake. In 1773 Caleb Davis, a large Boston merchant and later a purchaser of Plantation Number 22 next to Machias, sent Joshua Davis, a ship's master, to "the Eastward to Purchase a Load of Lumber," in exchange for pork, beef, flour, rum, tea, bread, and candles. Within a year Joshua Davis had shipping orders to proceed to Gouldsboro, and not just to an undesignated place to "the Eastward," making the Davises one of the merchant families supplying the settlement of Gouldsboro and buying its lumber.[39] Ichabod Jones, a Boston merchant and the agent for Machias, supplied provisions to settlers in exchange for lumber products.[40]

Fig. 5.2 "Mechios River near the Mills," from *Atlantic Neptune III* by Joseph F. W. Des Barres, 1776. (Courtesy of the Maine State Museum.)

After the passage of the Coercive Acts in 1774, the Provincial Congress put embargoes on trade with the British, especially if goods were destined for the army or navy. In timber-poor Boston, the military needed wood to build barracks and to stoke fires for cooking and heating. In naval shipyards white pine masts from the woods of Maine and New Hampshire were needed to replace broken masts.[41] Merchants who were either politically ambivalent or royalists realized great financial gain in continuing to supply the British army and navy with lumber. Many acquired cargoes of lumber by pressuring destitute settlers in remote towns along the Maine coast to violate the embargo in exchange for provisions. On May 4, 1775, Samuel Thompson led about forty men from the Brunswick, Maine, militia to apprehend Edward Parry, a contractor for the British Navy, to keep him from shipping masts to Halifax. In response to an attempted arrest and being put under bond to appear before the Provincial Congress, Parry acted both revolutionary sympathizer and royalist to suit his needs. In a letter to Henry Mowat, captain of the British naval vessel *Canceaux*, he deplored his detainment by the rebels. In a second letter to the Massachusetts Provincial Congress, he protested his capture and suggested that Samuel Thompson had fabricated the story that the Congress had authorized him to "use all possible and effectual means" to stop shipments of masts to the naval dockyard in Halifax. The Congress dismissed Parry's protestations and sided with Thompson.[42]

In Machias a similar circumstance involving Ichabod Jones resulted in one of the most notorious events of the Revolution in Maine.[43] On June 2, 1775, Jones sailed two provision-laden sloops up the Machias Bay to the settlement at the West Falls with the intention of trading for timber. No stranger to Machias residents, Jones had acted as the agent for the settlers in petitioning for the grant of the township, was himself one of the proprietors, and had earlier supplied the town. He owned a house in Machias and on this voyage he had brought along his wife and daughter to remove them from Boston until the cessation of hostilities. His nephew Stephen Jones was a justice of the peace and had been a captain in the Machias militia. But Ichabod Jones did not believe that his personal collateral and the needed provisions would be sufficient to grease the wheels of commerce among possible rebels, and the British sent along an armed naval cutter, the *Margaretta*.

To use the provisions as leverage Jones drafted a statement for purchasers to sign stipulating that they would guarantee him lumber for shipment to Boston and the protection of his person and property. Aware of the embargo on trade, Machias residents individually refused Jones's conditions. On June 6 they met to discuss their reaction to Jones's terms of trade, and as a group voted not to trade with him. Jones, upon learning of their decision, had Lieutenant James Moore, commanding officer of the *Margaretta*, move the naval cutter to within firing distance of the settlement at the West Falls. Fearing the loss of homes and meager but valuable possessions, the town called another vote and decided by a majority, but not unanimously, to trade with Jones. When Jones unloaded his sloops at the wharf and began to trade he refused to sell to anyone who had voted against him, thereby prompting his opponents to try to stop him from engaging in any trade.

The dynamics of the exchange between Jones and the inhabitants of Machias provide a window into how they saw social and political issues. The first resolution for nonintercourse with the British came from the Provincial Congress, and the people of Machias agreed to uphold it. Jones tried to have them violate that decision by appealing to them as individuals, which they ignored. Rather they met as a group, and collectively rejected his terms. He, in turn, threatened them with force. Coercion persuaded the group to reconsider its position, and a majority voted to allow Jones to proceed about his business.

The vote was not unanimous, but it did not have to be; a simple majority fixed the group's will. Jones, however, decided not to treat it as one decision to which all acceded, but as a multitude of individual decisions and thereby refused to respect what governing powers the people had. If Jones did not have to trade with those that opposed him, then they, in turn, could reject the decision of the group. Jones's action made active resistance a legitimate option. By bullying the town and then negating the collective decision, Jones triggered the action that ultimately led to the taking of his sloops and the *Margaretta*. For some townsfolk, Jones's behavior must have seemed all too much like the kind of tyranny that radicals in places like Boston had said would be the consequence of acceding to the British.

Under the leadership of Benjamin Foster, lieutenant colonel of the militia and a member of the committee of safety, a group of men planned to take Ichabod Jones and his nephew Stephen Jones, whom some suspected of Tory sympathies, at Sunday worship. The town meeting, and presumably Jones's high-handed response, had been on Tuesday, June 6, giving people four full days to plan the capture. They appealed to settlers at Pleasant River and Misapeake (now Addison and Jonesport, respectively) for reinforcements, an action that implied that people in other settlements were sympathetic to the rebel cause and the embargo against trading with the British and would likely come to their aid. At worship on Sunday, the rebels took Stephen Jones, but Ichabod escaped into the woods. Lieutenant Moore and his men, who were also worshipping, fled to their ship and sent back a message that they would burn the town if the people threatened the property of Ichabod Jones. Rather than being a deterrent, the threat provoked the rebels to strip down Jones's two sloops and fire on the British cutter demanding that Moore and his men surrender to America. Moore, too proud to capitulate to a group of rebels in a small insignificant town, took the captain off another trading sloop at anchor in the river and demanded that he pilot the cutter out of the river and harbor.

On Monday morning, June 12, the *Margaretta* weighed anchor and headed downriver on the outgoing tide. The militiamen rallied themselves, and "Armed with guns, swords, axes, and pitchforks," hardly the weapons of a well-armed populace, gave chase in a sloop and schooner. At the mouth of the harbor, they overtook the tender, "a very dull sailor," and captured her.

After tending to the three dead and eleven wounded men, two of whom later died, and confining the prisoners, the Machias committee of safety on June 14 sent an account of the affair to the Provincial Congress, which thanked them for the "good conduct … in preventing the minesterial troops being supplied with lumber." The committee requested and was granted permission to outfit two of the captured vessels as privateers. After considering the implications of operating privateers, the Machias committee of safety realized that it wanted a naval vessel not a privateer. Privateers were private vessels with government commissions to take enemy merchant vessels. The officers and seamen on board operated in a private capacity, and if taken by an armed enemy vessel, they could be, as Benjamin Foster and Jeremiah O'Brien of the Machias committee of safety pointed out, treated as pirates.

To avoid the dilemma of a public committee outfitting private vessels, the committee petitioned the Provincial Congress to issue officers' commissions for the two vessels and put the men under provincial pay. Acceding to the request, Congress passed a resolve commissioning officers and giving them authority to enlist up to thirty men, and stipulating that the officers and seamen would be paid by Massachusetts rather than by Machias or from a portion of any plunder.[44] That resolve made the two Machias "privateers" part of the Massachusetts navy.

The course of action followed by the people in Machias in the *Margaretta* incident carefully balanced local needs with their understanding of the larger issues of the revolutionary effort. Only under duress did they capitulate to Jones's demands and agree to trade for lumber they knew to be destined for British troops in Boston, an exchange prohibited by the Provincial Congress. Their initial rejection of Jones's enticements to trade is even more significant considering the severe food shortages in eastern Maine. Only under the guns of a naval cutter did they weaken to Jones's demands. Just two weeks later committees from ten Maine towns, reaching from Machias in the east to Berwick in the west, met and drafted a petition to the Provincial Congress asking it to revise the embargo relative to grain and provisions so that people in Maine who had no road access to food-producing regions and therefore had to import their food could do so within the law rather than be "reduced to the alternative of Starving, or supplying the ministerial troops with Lumber, either of which they deprecate."[45] Meanwhile, up the Bay of Fundy, merchants and farmers loaded Nova Scotian food, hay, and lumber onto vessels destined for Boston and the British troops.[46]

The Machias people acknowledged the private rather than public character of privateers. To give their armed ships a public definition they petitioned the Provincial Congress for officers' commissions and public pay. Indeed, the difference between the privateers in Liverpool, where they were primarily for private gain, and Machias, where they were for public ends, is striking. In the fall of 1775 Captain Stephen Smith of Machias took one of the armed ships and sailed up to Fort Frederick on the St. John River in Nova Scotia (New Brunswick after 1784) where he and his men captured a brig loaded with provisions and burned the fort. Upon returning to Machias, they divided among the inhabitants the "Cattle, Sheep, Hogs, smoked Salmon & Butter" taken off the brig, except for one-third that the committee of safety reserved for public needs.[47] The division of the booty among all the townspeople and the reservation of one-third complemented the petition to Congress asking to have the embargo on grains and provisions raised so that the people in eastern Maine would not starve.

The willingness of the Machias residents to enforce the trade embargo and their aversion to trading with Ichabod Jones indicate that their response to the imperial conflict would be much different from that of residents in Liverpool. In Machias the people operated in concert with a much larger plan of rebel action, despite the hardships it entailed. Before capturing the *Margaretta* the people were sympathizers of revolutionary Massachusetts but untried rebels. Their success in taking a British naval vessel committed them to an active role in the Revolution, a stand soon reinforced by the taking of another British vessel, the *Diligent*.[48]

Machias was the most eastward revolutionary stronghold in Massachusetts. Many settlers around the Passamaquoddy Bay east of Machias were American sympathizers, but that area was a contested boundary zone between Massachusetts and Nova Scotia. The boundary had not been agreed upon and thus both governments claimed a wide swath of land. The area would be a source of contention until an international arbitration in 1798 established which river was the St. Croix, the official boundary.[49] Thus, Machias was the first significant congregation of settlers who lived in uncontested Massachusetts territory and the largest unincorporated settlement in Lincoln County, both of which contributed to its becoming a focal point for rebel activity in eastern Maine.

After arming and commissioning the captured vessels for naval patrols and manning them with local men, the people of Machias engaged in raids up the Bay of Fundy to disrupt British activity in the area, to gain intelligence of British military movements, and to capture critical supplies of provisions. The British Navy used the Bay of Fundy as a congregating point for British ships, where officers devised strategies for suppressing the rebellion along the New England coast. The taking of the *Margaretta* by the militia of an insignificant and illegal settlement infuriated the British naval command, a group of men already thoroughly provoked by rebels along the New England coast who blocked shipments of lumber and much needed masts to repair the fleet.[50]

For British naval officers, Machias epitomized New England rebelliousness and became a target for its suppression. In the fall of 1775 Admiral Samuel Graves instructed Lieutenant Henry Mowat, commander of the British vessel *Canceaux*, "to burn, destroy and lay waste" vessels, towns, and craft along the New England coast at "Marblehead, Salem, Newberryport, Cape Ann Harbour, Portsmouth, Ipswich, Saco, Falmouth in Casco Bay, and particularly Machias, where the Margueritta was taken." William Gilly of Cranberry Island in Penobscot Bay reported that Mowat visited that island and made "threats against many of the settlements particularly Machias, asking if those Rebels did not think hanging was too good for them." Mowat did not "burn, destroy, and lay waste" to Machias, but he did burn the town of Falmouth (now Portland), Maine, in October 1775, the most thorough destruction of any American town during the Revolution.[51] Fears of a similar raid on Machias kept the people vigilant in watching the movements of naval vessels along the coast, as well as gaining any useful intelligence for the Massachusetts forces or the Continental Army. After a British sloop of war, the *Viper*, took five fishing vessels out of the Machias Harbor in 1776, the committee of safety reported that the vessels had all been taken to Annapolis, Nova Scotia, where two were to be fitted out as tenders to cruise the coast and disrupt shipping. Such dangers enhanced Machias's case for asking the Provincial Congress to "take our Difficult Circumstances into your Consideration and Grant us such Relief as you in your Wisdom shall think proper," a plea employed with varying efficacy throughout the war.[52]

Simply defending the town and maintaining a surveillance of the British navy failed to satisfy all revolutionaries in Machias. Emboldened by their small victories, the Machias committee of safety under the leadership of the Reverend James Lyon, formerly of Londonderry, Nova Scotia, proposed an invasion of Nova Scotia to the Provincial Congress, which was less than supportive. In September 1776, James Lyon, now erstwhile chairman of the committee of safety, wrote a letter to the Massachusetts General Court deploring the government's disinterest in the eastern country and the reports that it thought the territory "a moth, that it has cost more than it is worth." He asked the General Court to support an army "to subdue Nova Scotia" or to allow

some person or persons … leave to raise men, & go against that Province, at their own risque. I believe men enough might be found in this county, who would chearfully undertake it, without any assistance from Government. … Provided that they might call what they took their own in common with the good people of that Province. I confess that I am so avaricious, that I would go with the utmost chearfulness. I hope, however,

I should have some nobler view, for I think it our duty to relieve our distressed brethern.[53]

Just the month before, Lieutenant Colonel Francis Shaw, of the Gouldsboro militia, reported that the Americans' Indian allies had been anxious to attack Fort Cumberland in Nova Scotia; hearsay suggested it could be taken easily. Shaw averred, though, that he would not attempt to take the fort without orders from the General Court, "unless the prospect be so Clear that I should think it a Neglect of Duty not to attempt it."[54]

The ambitions of Lyon and a few other Machias residents fitted neatly with a plan developed in Cumberland, Nova Scotia, for an invasion of the province by the revolutionaries. The plan had its origins in the turmoils of the fall of 1775 when people throughout Nova Scotia were angry at the governor's request to send militiamen to Halifax and to tax the colony's cash-poor residents to support them. On the Isthmus of Chignecto, revolutionary supporters, led by Jonathan Eddy and John Allan, decided to petition George Washington, commander of the Continental Army, and request that an invasion force be sent to take Nova Scotia, not unlike the one sent to Quebec in the fall of 1775. In February 1776, Eddy and two companions, Samuel Rogers and Isaiah Boudreau, left Nova Scotia to take the petition to Boston, where Washington was encamped.

Washington was ambivalent about supporting Nova Scotians, and sent the small embassy, now consisting of just Eddy and Boudreau, on to meet with the Continental Congress in Philadelphia, which declined to support them despite its sympathies. Disappointed, Eddy and Boudreau rendezvoused with Rogers in Providence and returned home. In the summer of 1776, Eddy again journeyed south, and found himself shuttling between the Provincial Council in Boston and the Continental Congress in Philadelphia in search of support for the invasion. All he received was a promise from the Continental Congress that it would support what Massachusetts decided, and Massachusetts gave Eddy permission only to recruit men in the eastern part of the state.[55]

Eddy decided to attempt an invasion, and headed downeast to recruit men. In Machias about 20 men agreed to go with him; at Passamaquoddy a few more joined; 27 men from settlements along the St. John River and 16 Natives boosted the size of Eddy's small army to 72. The committee at Sackville, a community neighboring Cumberland, "Express'd their Uneasiness at seeing so few … and those unprovided with Artillery." Their unease was justified. Eddy laid siege to Fort Cumberland on November 12, 1776, with the 72 men he brought with him and about another 100 from the area. The fort's commander, Joseph Gorham, had a four-month supply of food, and he settled in to wait for the arrival of reinforcements to break the siege. On November 27, 400 reinforcements disembarked their ship. Three days later Eddy's men were in retreat, and the homes of his local supporters were burned to the ground.[56]

In Machias the reactions to Eddy's venture were mixed. William Tupper, the chairman of the Machias committee of safety, wrote the General Court that the people "do not altogether approve of Capt Eddys going there in so loose a manner & with so small a party." Eddy complicated their lives mightily by presenting them with the choice of "Being Either plundred and butchered by their friends, or of incurring the highest displeasure of their own Government the latter alternative [i.e., the first] they preferred and now lie Exposed to the rage of an abandoned administration and their wicked instruments." Given the people's commitment to the rebel cause, Tupper thought it incumbent upon the Massachusetts government to offer them some relief.[57] Even though twenty men from Machias went with Eddy and James Lyon supported the expedition, it had been neither formally endorsed nor organized by the residents of Machias. The town was the last solid revolutionary center before British-held territory and therefore became a staging ground for people interested in challenging the British in Nova Scotia. It remained so throughout the war.

By August 1776, Eddy's former co-conspirator, John Allan, had distanced himself from Eddy. Having fled Nova Scotia as a political refugee, he was in Machias when Eddy was organizing a force, and he labored to convince Eddy of the folly of the plan. Allan, though, was not without his own plans. He convinced the Massachusetts Provincial Congress and the Continental Congress that it was important to the revolutionary cause to ensure the friendship of the Indians in eastern Maine and mainland Nova Scotia with treaties and gifts. Allan was subsequently appointed both the commanding officer of the Massachusetts troops stationed at Machias and the Continental Agent for Indian Affairs, the former appointment being recalled because it was expensive and duplicated Allan's functions as the Indian agent for the Continental Congress.[58]

In the spring of 1777, the intensification of British, Native, and settler activity in Passamaquoddy Bay and the St. John River convinced Allan to petition the General Court to support an expedition to the St. John River to "secure the Inhabitants of the Counties of Cumberland & Sunbury ... but also, for the preservation of all our Settlements lying to the Eastward of Casco-Bay." On June 6, 1777 the Massachusetts assembly approved a plan to raise two regiments to take the St. John River, one regiment of Maine residents and one of Nova Scotia residents. It promptly commissioned officers, who arrived in Machias, where the people committed provisions to them on the understanding that they would have them replaced. In August the Massachusetts Council "laid aside the expedition" until it better knew the movements of the British in other places. The decision to delay, if not cancel, the expedition put the people of Machias in great consternation because they were relying on the enhanced protection that additional soldiers would give them, especially in light of local intelligence suggesting that the British were planning an invasion of the town.[59]

In the two years since the taking of the *Margaretta* in June 1775, the animosity of British naval officers towards Machias had only grown. They planned an attack on the settlement for the summer of 1777, intending to bring the people to submission, if not to burn and destroy the town. Machias residents knew of the danger because scouts had reported that the British were organizing an attack and amassing forces in the Bay of Fundy. Benjamin Foster, colonel of the militia in Machias, reported to the Massachusetts Council on August 8, 1777 that "We have certain Intelligence that a 50 Gun Ship & some Transports have been fitted out at Halifax & were ready to sail for this Place 12 Days ago: These are to be join'd by 500 Men from St John's River; We Expect them every Hour, & God only knows what will become of us! We have no Strength to resist such a Force, & yet Resist we must."[60]

At about three o'clock on the morning of August 13, 1777, scouts returned to Machias with news of "three Large Ships, one Brig, and one Small Schooner at the mouth of the Harbour." Two hours later the *Rainbow*, a brig with eight boats of soldiers in tow, reached the Rim where the East and West Machias Rivers meet. Therewith began the British invasion of Machias. The first day a mere 35 militiamen kept up enough fire on the brig and boats to keep men from landing. Fog on the morning of August 14 allowed some British soldiers to land without being fired on, and the brig moved further up the West Machias River toward the settlement at the falls. Forty to 50 Indians had reinforced the Machias militia, and they positioned themselves on both sides of the river in an attempt to cover as much territory as possible against the superior British numbers. Each adversary waited out the other until the early evening when the Indians began a yell that was reputed to sound like hundreds of warriors, rather than a few dozen. Shortly thereafter the brig lifted anchor and proceeded downriver without firing on the town. Anchoring downriver, the British again tried to land men using open boats, which only drew the fire of the Machias men hidden in the woods. By August 15 militiamen were arriving from other settlements, and by the morning of the 16th the British had abandoned their attempted reduction of Machias, having lost about 100 men, to only 1 man lost and 1 wounded from the downeast forces.[61]

This unanticipated victory bolstered the spirits of the people in Machias, but also made them fear that the British would just regroup and plan another attack. In the fall of 1777 General Eyre Massey in Halifax sent out Major Small to Machias to "destroy that nest of Pirates and Rebels," but Small failed.[62] In January 1778 Massey reported to General Howe that the vanity of Sir George Collier, the commander of the brig *Rainbow*, caused the failure of the August invasion of Machias. British reinforcements sent to join the invasion were stopped by Captain Fotus of the *Vulture*. Collier, who "wanted the whole honour of destroying Machias with his Ships," told Fotus he would not need or want reinforcements. The failure of the invasion gave "fresh spirits to the Rebels." Collier, meanwhile, went down to Boothbay, Maine, and harassed the inhabitants there.[63]

After the British failure to take Machias and the cancellation of the Massachusetts plan to take the St. John River area, the war effort in Machias became one of defending eastern Maine and maintaining a revolutionary presence. In 1779 the British occupied the Penobscot Bay and established a fort at Castine, which cut off Machias and the neighboring settlements from the rest of Massachusetts. With a foothold at Castine, the British pressured downeast inhabitants to take oaths of allegiance to the king or to press for neutrality. As discussed in the last chapter, many people considered neutrality, especially those in the Penobscot region, but the people in Machias and in Townships Four, Five, and Six adamantly refused and managed to suppress the plan. The Machias militia remained active, largely for local defense rather than to plan or engage in any offensive action. And John Allan continued his labors to keep the Indians as American allies. Thus from 1779 to 1783, the primary objective of people in Machias was to maintain an unequivocal revolutionary presence in eastern Maine in order to legitimate the American claim to the region between the Penobscot and the St. Croix Rivers.

* * *

The people in Machias saw themselves as actors within a vast orchestrated enterprise. They believed that their involvement in the revolution had significant consequences and that their actions could produce either harmony or dissonance. In Liverpool, people left scant evidence that they thought their actions would have any impact on the outcome of the conflict or the future of the British Empire. They acted to protect their own local interests without pondering whether they acted in concert with any larger endeavors. In Machias and Liverpool, the people's resort to arms carried profoundly different meanings, and reflected different understandings of the relationship between politics and war and their own responses to it.

In Liverpool, people generally treated incidents associated with the war as an extension of civilian affairs, a reaction consonant with their larger understanding of the conflict. For them, the dispute was among people within the same polity and therefore a civil dispute. When the cannons were stolen from the Point, Perkins gave a warrant as a civilian officer to investigate the affair, even though all suspected that revolutionary privateers had taken them. Only with the decision to commission privateers from Liverpool can we see an acknowledgment by Liverpool's residents that the revolutionaries were to be treated as international enemies rather than as parties to a domestic dispute.

In Machias the opposite quickly became the case as the committee of safety subsumed all local affairs, both civil and military, under its authority.

The return to civil governance was expeditious once the war was over. Upon petition from the Machias settlers, the Massachusetts assembly incorporated the town, and it assumed the governance of the community. But for the years from 1775 to 1783, they conflated civil and military needs, and made local needs subservient to the larger strategic needs of Massachusetts and the United States. At moments, some people resisted this course of action. On August 27, 1777, after the British attempt to take Machias and after the Massachusetts General Court tabled plans for an expedition to the St. John River, Benjamin Foster wrote to the Massachusetts Council and House of Representatives to inform them that the Machias committee of safety had detained supplies belonging to Massachusetts and had decided to pay one hundred militiamen for a month to defend the town and surrounding area even if the cost was not approved by the General Court.[64] This one time people asserted the primacy of their own local needs, but such action could always be justified as protecting American interests in the region between the Penobscot and the St. Croix Rivers.

The difference between the responses of people in Machias and Liverpool to the war was poignantly expressed in political discourse. In records surviving from Liverpool, there is scant mention of the war as a political and ideological issue, except for the annual celebration of George III's birthday beginning in 1779. In Machias, the war permeated many areas of public discussion. Dozens of letters sent from Machias to the General Court after 1775 mentioned the sacrifices experienced by local people in the interest of the greater good. In a memorial from Machias testifying to the revolutionary patriotism of Stephen Jones, the signatories related his stalwart unflinching commitment to the American cause. "[H]e [Jones] allways justified the measures taken by the Colonies … condemn'd in the severest terms those Measures pursued by Administration, and the British Parliament" and was "as sincere a Friend to the American Cause, as any man Whatever." Jones offered a slightly more tempered assessment in the accompanying letter he sent to the Provincial Congress. After representing the memorial as "sufficient evidence of my Attachment to my Native Country," he mentioned his service to the country in both military and civil matters, and ended with a personally noncommittal salutation "Sincerely wishing Success to the American Arms." In the heated rhetoric of the Revolution such a tepid protestation was almost enough to make one's commitment to the "American Cause" suspect.[65]

After the war, petitioners to the Eastern Lands Committee justified their requests for more than one hundred acres of land with testimonials of their revolutionary patriotism. Benjamin Acley was "allways ready to assist in Defending the Country during the whole course of the War." The settlers at Chandler's River noted that they "had many occasions to march to different parts of this Eastern Country, particularly to Machias when attacked by the enemy."[66] The men from Pleasant River deployed all the rhetoric in their verbal arsenal, mixing a recitation of the troubles of settling "a wild uncultivated Desart country" with the trials of war and the virtue of having been Tory-free.

> Your Petitioners Beg Leave to Lay Before your Honours that a Number of us has been Settlers in this Place Seventeen & some eighteen years & upwards, & the gratest Part of us have been here & in this said Plasant River Dureing the time of the unhappy war with Great Britain & some of your Petitioners have Been Soldiers in General Washingtons army three years. And we your Humble Petitioners have suffered & undergone every Difficulty that is Incident to a New Settlement, in Bringing to a wild uncultivated Desart country chiefly Poor Land. And have been exposed Dureing the war to the Ravages & Depredtions of the cruel enemy obliged to Neglect the Improveing our Land to do Duty as Soldiers at Mechias & other Plases on this eastern Shore to help Defend the country. But Happy we that have not nor have had one Tory or Suspected Person Inhabiting this Place. But all have been Loyal to the United States of America During the war. But thro the goodness of God, we have been Protected. And Notwithstanding all those Difficulties, a Great Number of us your Petitioners have thro hard Labours cleared brought to Planted & sowed the wild Land. And here all our Interest Lays.[67]

Such rhetoric continued long after the war in petitions to the General Court for tax relief and other financial compensations.[68]

The resort to military action influenced the way that people saw the relationship between domestic politics and war. For people in Machias, and throughout the United States, war became closely associated with a defense of a political ideology, an act that demanded a personal commitment to the greater whole. In Liverpool the war began and ended at the imperial level and was far enough beyond the means of local people to shape and direct that it lacked any immediate ideological expression. Their first response to war was to defend the physical well-being of the town and its inhabitants. Secondarily, they had a commitment to the king and empire. On the American side of the border, the war became intricately entwined in the defense of domestic politics; in Liverpool, and Nova Scotia more generally, war was an imperial matter and not appropriate for domestic colonial politics.

Liverpool's response to the French Revolutionary and Napoleonic Wars differed little from its response to the American Revolution. When war with Spain threatened in 1792 after the Anglo-Spanish standoff at Nootka Sound, Perkins sent out orders to Liverpool's officers to make returns of the men and arms in their units, appointed a sergeant for Port Mouton, where none had been commissioned, and mustered the militia. "The men Appeared Very well Dressed & accoutered," he noted and calculated that "it is upwards of 8 years ... Since they mustered before." War with France was more prolonged, and then the governor did ask for militias to supply men to protect Halifax.

Unlike during the American Revolution, the local militia units did send men, although few enlisted in provincial regiments. During the American Revolution, the British government promised fishermen that they would not be impressed off their vessels by the British Navy. Fishermen demanded the same in the French Revolutionary and Napoleonic Wars and when the metropolitan government was slow in granting this demand, Nova Scotia's governor feared that fishermen would relocate to the United States. The behavior of Nova Scotians reflected an attitude that as subjects in the empire they would suffer some war hardship, but that it should be minimized and they themselves should not become embroiled in the prosecution of the war. The colonial government in Halifax never planned offensive action comparable to the initiatives Boston took in the wars in the seventeenth and eighteenth centuries. In Nova Scotia, war initiatives had ceased to be a domestic, colony-level political issue.[69]

In Machias, the War of 1812 once again made armed conflict both a national and local issue. The unwillingness of the Massachusetts government to use the militia to defend the coast of Maine, even after the British invaded and occupied the area east of the Penobscot, made the people change their minds about separating from Massachusetts and forming a separate state of Maine. Until then the eastern seacoast towns had remained staunchly Federalist and supporters of continued union with Massachusetts. After the War of 1812 they voted to support a separate state of Maine that could better protect their interests. Again war and domestic politics had become deeply intertwined.[70]

6
The Transformation of New England Congregationalism

At a proprietors' meeting on September 4, 1761, the settlers of Liverpool voted, "That the Town Concur with the Church in Calling the Revd. Mr. Cheever to the Work of the Ministry amongst us." The proprietors had orchestrated the arrangements. They wrote to ministers in Rochester, Massachusetts, asking them to recommend a pastoral candidate. They invited and paid for Cheever to come on trial. They organized the meetings to call him, voted to raise the monies for his salary, and built a meetinghouse. But, as they carefully noted in the call letter, the decision to invite Cheever to be Liverpool's minister was made by the "Brethern of the Church, the sd Proprietors, And Other Inhabitants."[1] The language of both the proprietors' minutes and the call letter indicates how deeply the support of religion was woven into the larger social fabric of the community. Of the groups mentioned—the church, the proprietors, and the other inhabitants—only the church had a singularly religious character.

In Machias preparations for the support of religion proceeded similarly. The proprietors elected a collector of the minister's rate on November 20, 1770. On July 9, 1771, they elected a committee to find a ministerial candidate. On June 6, 1772, they extended James Lyon a call, which he accepted with the proviso that they be empowered by the General Court in Boston to levy and collect a tax to pay his salary. They immediately petitioned for permission to tax all the inhabitants of the township, proprietors and nonproprietors alike, for the support of the minister, which the General Court granted on July 4, 1772.[2]

The religious structures of early Liverpool and Machias reflected the prevailing customs in colonial New England. A "church" was composed of individuals who embraced a religious covenant elaborating a doctrinal position and ecclesiastical structure. The first covenants for Liverpool and Machias are no longer extant, but other evidence indicates that both had Old Light Calvinist Congregationalist covenants. To join, a person had only to give a profession of faith rather than testimony of a conversion experience, as required by New Light churches. Those who were not church members, but who attended worship regularly, were members of the congregation. They had voting rights in some, but not all, church matters. The term "society" was sometimes used in lieu of congregation, generally for followers of a dissenting church rather than for congregants of the "standing" or established church. The membership criteria for a congregation were not as sharply defined as those for a church; congregation often simply meant the "other inhabitants." At the time a township was settled the distinction between congregation and "other inhabitants" was weak, but as a community matured, and as those who attended meetings regularly were distinguished from those who did not, the distinction between the congregation and other inhabitants sharpened. Together the church, congregation, and other inhabitants supported the minister through a townshipwide ministerial assessment.[3]

Eighteenth-century New Englanders generally considered "the support of the gospel" to be a vital part of a community's well-being. Thus the proprietors, or township grantees, used their privileges to call meetings and tax themselves to hire the first minister, to collect money for his support, and to build a meetinghouse.[4] When a settlement became incorporated, the town government assumed the responsibility for taxing the inhabitants for ministerial support, and the proprietors' role in the support of religion ceased. In Machias and Liverpool there were also "proprietors of the meetinghouse." The first meetinghouses in both towns were built by the township proprietors, and seem to have been modest, largely temporary structures. They were replaced with more substantial meetinghouses built with private monies collected through subscription lists. People who subscribed money to a meetinghouse became proprietors of it.

The relative speed with which people in both Liverpool and Machias proceeded to call and hire ministers indicates that the roles and functions of the various groups had compelling cultural definitions that transcended the localities. Within a few decades, however, the fabric of church and society had been strained and permanently rent, more quickly in Nova Scotia than in Massachusetts. The raveling of the multiple connections between church and society, the emergence of the exclusive and largely modern relationship between a minister and church, and the transformation of religious support from an act of public policy to one of private choice paralleled the weakening of Congregationalism in New England culture and the emergence of competing sects such as the Calvinist Baptists, Quakers, Methodists, Freewill Baptists, and Universalists.[5] Historians generally maintain that the roots of this religious modernization dated from the late seventeenth century, if not the Reformation itself. Yet in the specific case of New England Congregationalism, its significantly faster decline in Nova Scotia than in Massachusetts is to be explained not by differences in the factors of dissolution, but by differences in the factors of cohesion, in particular the elimination of town government in the former, a rather remarkable illustration of the relationship between institutional modification and cultural change.

* * *

Like many aspects of local life in eastern Maine, the calling of ministers, the establishment of churches, and the building of meetinghouses became entangled in the uncertainty of township grants that lacked royal approval, the remoteness of the region from long-settled areas, and the upheaval of the Revolution. The commissioners sent by Governor Hutchinson in 1771 to assess conditions in the thirteen townships without royal approbation reported that people in them were eager for a minister's services. The minister traveling with the commissioners preached "twice a day the two Sabbaths" he was in Machias. One gathering had upwards of 150 people, and he baptized thirteen children. At Township Number Four (now Steuben) a calm delayed the commissioners' sailing until a Sunday, and "the people ashore upon their knowing there was an Ordained Minister on board, entreated that we would go ashore and that the minister would perform Divine Service amongst them and Baptise their Children, there not having been a Sermon ever preached there." At that hastily improvised worship service, he baptized nine children and one adult. In a petition to the governor the inhabitants of Township Number Five (now Addison) complained that the lack of "Law" and the "Gospel" in their settlement encouraged "every one doing what's right in his own eyes and a great spirit of mobbing and Rioting prevails." The appointment of a justice of the peace satisfied them, but as their petition suggests, they considered the preaching of the gospel a cornerstone of public order.[6]

Fragmentary evidence suggests that from 1763 to 1771 people in Machias, like those in Township Number Four, had not seen a minister, much less had the steady ministration of an ordained and settled clergyman. When the Machias grant finally received the governor's signature in 1770 the proprietors began making provisions for supporting a minister. Indeed the terms of the grant, like those of most New England grants, stipulated that the proprietors were to build a meetinghouse for public worship, settle a learned Protestant minister, and provide for his support. The grant also reserved one share for the support of the ministry and another for the first settled minister.

By the fall of 1771, the proprietors were negotiating for the pastoral care of the Reverend James Lyon, a Princeton-trained Presbyterian minister.[7]

A man of eclectic gifts, Lyon had a reputation for his musical talents. For his 1759 commencement from the College of New Jersey (now Princeton), he composed the music for "Ode to Peace," a choral piece extolling the greatness of George II and the virtues of the British army in the war against the French. In 1761 Lyon published *Urania*, "A Choice Collection of Psalm-Tunes, Anthems, and Hymns," some "From the most approved Authors," and others "Entirely New," six of which have been attributed to him. During his lifetime, the collection went through at least two editions in 1767 and 1783. After receiving his Master of Arts degree, Lyon went to Nova Scotia in 1764 as an ordained missionary of the Presbyterian Synod of New Brunswick, New Jersey. The arrangement was unsatisfactory. To supplement his meager and uncertain income, Lyon speculated in land, which invited the scrutiny of the New Jersey presbytery. Lyon left Nova Scotia in 1771, and during a stop in Boston he met Stephen Jones of Machias and received an invitation to go there.[8]

Lyon's return to a frontier community after a bad experience in one is ironic, especially considering his strong artistic and intellectual bent more suited to the long-settled regions of the colonies. Besides publishing music, he is the suspected author of a 1763 pamphlet entitled *The Lawfulness, Excellency And Advantage of Instrumental Musick in the Public Worship of God, Urged and Enforced from Scripture and the Example of the far greater Part of Christians in all Ages. Address'd to all (particularly the Presbyterians and Baptists) who have hitherto been taught to look upon the use of Instrumental Musick in the Worship of God as Unlawful*. The pamphlet may have been a response to evangelical criticism about *Urania*, published two years before; it did reflect Lyon's liberalism in religious matters. During the early years of the Revolution he forcefully wielded a pen as the first chair of the Machias committee of safety and then as an individual speaking on behalf of the people of Machias. Late in his life he wrote short homilies for daily meditation, two volumes of which were published posthumously.[9] The return of Lyon, a talented and cultured man, to the periphery of Euroamerican settlement suggests that he did not expect to find himself cut off from the cultured society to which he had earlier contributed.

After a period of trial preaching, "the Proprietors and Inhabitants" voted unanimously to offer Lyon a call to become their "Pastor & Teacher" during his "Natural Life," or so long as his "abilities to perform the duties of a Minister of the Gospel" remained. For his services, he would receive £86 Massachusetts currency, to be paid "in the Common pay of this place, now Merchantable Pine Lumber at the annual market price among us." To speed his settlement in Machias the proprietors added £80 in two £40 installments to build a dwelling house. Lyon accepted the call, "Provided the General Court of this Province shall see fit to empower you and your Successors in Office to collect what you here voted for my Support, If otherways I shall think myself free from the above obligation."

In his letter of acceptance he acknowledged the "destitute circumstances of this Place," and wanted assurances that he would be paid. His experience in Nova Scotia, where communities had no legal mechanism to collect a ministerial rate, surely colored his negotiations. The proprietors and inhabitants petitioned the General Court "to enable or authorize us … to Assess, Levy & Collect … Rates or Taxes" for Lyon's support, noting "the deficiency from authority to Assess or lay any Tax for the support of the Gospel," and, more importantly, to "oblige the Assessed, however reasonable & Just, to pay the same." The General Court passed an act to be in effect for three years enabling Jonathan Longfellow and Stephen Jones, justices of the peace, and Ichabod Jones, Stephen Parker, Benjamin Foster, and James Eliot, gentlemen, together or a majority of them, to levy an annual tax up to £120 on all the inhabitants of Machias, except "professed Churchmen, Baptists or Quakers."[10]

Despite the special legislation, funding for Lyon's salary remained precarious. According to the town minutes of March 16, 1787, the ministerial taxes for 1772 to 1775 were not collected. With the expiration of the special legislation in 1775, Lyon's salary became the sole responsibility of the proprietors, although what monies they collected is unknown. Despite meager pay, Lyon continued his pastoral calling in Machias. Living among the people, he knew their uncertain financial circumstances, especially during the war when the timber trade was virtually stopped. He received a share in the proprietorship as the first settled minister and a house. For the rest, Lyon seemed disposed to wait and have faith that the people would pay him when they could. In the meantime, he supported his family by selling salt he extracted from seawater. During the summer of 1777 he asked the General Court for a twelve-month loan to buy six kettles for his salt works on Salt Island, which it granted him. In 1784, when the Town of Machias was incorporated and it took over support of the minister, nearly £900 of Lyon's salary remained unpaid, a debt the town assumed and paid by the late 1780s.[11]

According to the church records, begun in 1795, Lyon did not establish a covenanted church in Machias until 1782.[12] No solid evidence exists to explain the delay. Possibly both the people and Lyon saw his early years in Machias in the tenor of a frontier missionary rather than as the minister of a covenanted church. As a Presbyterian, Lyon had been trained at Princeton rather than at Harvard or Yale, and was therefore beyond the pale of New England Congregationalism. Eschewing evangelicalism, Lyon apparently weighted his ministry toward preaching the gospel rather than organizing and leading a church of visible saints. Throughout the war he was the only minister east of the Penobscot River, and one of only three as late as 1790.[13] Lyon's years in Machias (1772–1794) occurred during a liberalizing period in the religious establishment in New England. The church he covenanted on September 12, 1782 had open, simple, and liberal "rules and regulations." Persons could be admitted into the Church without making any public relation of their experiences. Acknowledgments for breaching God's commandments were to be related before only church members. Communion was to be administered three times in a year in May, August, and October.[14]

Three rules defined who could be a church member. The first eschewed the evangelical New Light ideal that a person had to have a conversion experience to be considered a candidate for church membership. It implied, though did not state, that the religious conviction necessary for church membership could be acquired through reasoned understanding. The second stated the church's claim to be the arbiter of its members' behavior. Only two of the forty-two church members committed serious enough moral lapses to be suspended from the church: Stephen Parker was suspended "for the notorious crime of Adultery," and James Brown was suspended for not appearing at a church meeting to answer for his behavior on an unspecified charge.[15] The third rule provided for open communion and allowed members of other churches to commune with the Machias members.

Lyon's ministry defined religion as a cornerstone of the social order more than as a stepping-stone to the godly life. He never led a revival; indeed his early music writing indicates that he had few evangelical tendencies. During the American Revolution he advocated the American cause, as did many New England ministers.[16] When he did not receive his salary, he and the people resorted to the public institutions of the General Court and the town, or, before the incorporation of the town, to the quasi-public institution of the proprietorship, to attempt to rectify the deficiency. Lyon's liberal interpretation of the relationship of church and society served Machias, if the absence of serious discontent is any measure. Lyon's successor was less fortunate.

James Lyon served until his death on October 12, 1794. Shortly thereafter a joint town and church committee invited Clark Brown, a young man from Stonington, Connecticut, to preach in Machias for eight weeks. On June 26, 1795 the church and town each voted unanimously to extend him a call. Brown was ordained in Boston on October 7 and on October 12, 1795, a year to the day after Lyon's death, he preached his first sermon in Machias as the called and ordained minister.[17] Within two months his ministry was in trouble. In December the church suspended four members for suggesting that Brown was "destitute of Grace; or not… converted." In light of later events involving Brown's dismissal, this charge was possibly true, but then Lyon had not emphasized the importance of a conversion experience, whether his own or others. New Light minister Edward Manning claimed that Lyon "did not know whether he had been instrumental in a single conversion," an aspiration for ministers of an evangelical turn. Evangelical tensions may have existed in

Machias during Lyon's tenure, but if so, his stature and long service in the town bridled criticism. Or alternatively, Brown's ministry in Machias coincided with more visits by New Light itinerants to eastern Maine, and they may have introduced the ideas that would subsequently help to corrode the town's religious unity. The latter is less plausible because by the 1790s evangelical ferment had been stirring in Northern New England for most of two decades.[18]

Brown's ministry was not as liberal as Lyon's. At a meeting shortly after his arrival, the church suspended four members. At the same time, the church adopted a new and more detailed covenant, one that tightened the rules for membership. Only twenty-one members voted for it. Twelve members were absent and never accepted it; the church suspended them three months later. Under the new rules only covenanted members could have their children baptized; people wishing to have their children baptized must own the covenant and make a public confession of faith. In March the church again revised its rules on membership and baptism. A person only needed to give the church one week of notice, rather than three, to become a member or have a child baptized. The church agreed not to vote on the admission of new members. If a member raised legitimate objections about a prospective member then a meeting would be held to discuss the matter. If no one raised objections then the person was admitted, provided he or she owned the covenant and the confession of faith. Members could not block the admission of new members simply by casting negative votes.

The rule implied that church members had no special capacity to judge the faith of others. Baptized children would be church members until confirmation, whereupon they would be required to own the covenant and make a public profession of faith or give up the benefits of their baptismal covenant. They were not to be halfway adult members by virtue of their infant baptism, a point of contention among New England Congregationalists since the mid seventeenth century.[19]

Those new rules still left some townspeople dissatisfied; under Lyon they had fuller access to the rites of the church, especially baptism for their children. Under Brown the Machias church abandoned the principle of the Half-Way Covenant, the late-seventeenth-century Puritan concession that allowed persons who had been baptized as children to have their children baptized, even if the parents did not own the covenant. The Half-Way Covenant disturbed many who believed that access to the sacraments of baptism and communion should be restricted to church members. By the late eighteenth century some congregations had worked out another compromise to circumvent that problem. Church members could either be covenant members or members in full communion. Covenant members made a public confession of faith and accepted the church covenant but they could not state that they had had a conversion experience, and therefore were not eligible to take communion, but could have their children baptized. Members in full communion made a testimony about their own personal conversion experience.[20]

By April 1797 local pressure over baptism prompted a third consideration of the church rules. In a new preamble, the church explained its desire to adhere strictly "to the Rules of the Gospel, especially as it regards the Administration of Divine ordinance." Every baptized person should "renew their Baptismal covenant after having come to years of understanding," implying thereby that persons who did not renew or confirm the baptismal covenant effectively disavowed it and therefore they had no claim to baptism for offspring. This restriction created "some uneasiness … in the minds of some of the Congregation" and so, "to remove every appearance of restraint as regards the public profession of Religion," the church, "as an indulgence to those persons who think differently from us about the Ordinance of Baptism," voted to administer baptism to the children of baptized persons, even if those persons had themselves not owned the covenant.[21]

Infant baptism implied commitments between God and the baptized child and between the child and the church, which would provide religious instruction "should Parents or Guardians be negligent of their duty." Machias church members balked at assuming that responsibility for the children of nonmembers. They circumvented the problem by rewriting the baptismal covenant to declare that they "consider themselves under More Obligations" to the children of covenanted members than to the children of noncovenanted townspeople. Baptized children of covenanted members could "renew their covenant obligations … after their coming to years of understanding," whereas baptized children of noncovenanted people had to undergo more thorough scrutiny by the church before owning the covenant.[22] The church might be the cornerstone of public order, but a few stalwart members were not going to martyr themselves for the less committed. Their tepid commitment to the religious education of the children of the uncovenanted townspeople indicates another weakening of the larger commitment to the unity of church and community.

While Brown and the church members struggled to craft compromises between their religious convictions and the religious demands of the townspeople, the itinerant New Light ministers Edward Manning and James Murphy from New Brunswick preached in eastern Maine during the summer of 1796 and sowed seeds of evangelical discontent. They challenged Brown's ministerial qualifications and fomented such disruptive divisions that Stephen Jones, one of the town's most prominent men and a member of the church, wrote Manning three letters reproving him and Murphy for intruding "into another man's vineyard." The two itinerants bolstered the opinions of the four suspended church members who thought Brown lacked grace. Manning and Murphy declared publicly that Brown was an "unconverted person," an act

Jones found to be "a breach of Christian charity," and an exhibition of "Great vanity." Alleged signs of Brown's unsaved soul included a liberal education and sermons preached from prepared texts or notes. Manning had charged that Brown memorized prayers; Jones, in contrast, thought the prayers of Manning and Murphy were but "a jumble of words, not half articulated & bellowed out with all the violence of a mad man, & which cannot be understood by the audience."[23]

Clark Brown suffered greatly from Manning and Murphy's charges and the buttressing they gave his Machias critics. At the 1797 annual town meeting, Brown submitted a letter to the inhabitants of Machias asking them to grant "their disappointed and afflicted friend & Pastor" a dismissal. That letter and letters to the church convey a deep disillusionment with his situation, without being explicit about the problems, because, as Brown stated, the "Afflictions & Discouragements which attend me … must be obvious to every person of discernment. … It will not be necessary to recount them." Only two comments hint at specific causes of disaffection. To the church's request that he stay, he responded that "My health will not admit of that intense application to study which is necessary for a Minister in this Country, in which there are no Ministers with whom he can exchange & associate." In another letter he stated that he was "wholly adverse to everything which had the appearance of enthusiasm," an indication of his uneasiness with the evangelical pressures in town. To persuade his supporters to vote with his detractors for dismissal, Brown said that he had "no wish to tarry with them upon any condition whatever."[24]

Brown's friends accepted that he could not stay in the employ of the town, but they were less persuaded that he had no desire to carry on a ministry in Machias "upon any condition whatever." They organized themselves and made plans to petition the General Court to incorporate them as the West Falls Religious Congregational Society in Machias so they could hire Brown independently of the town and be exempted from ministerial taxes. Brown rejected their plan despite the larger salary they promised and sheltering from his critics. The church again asked him to stay, and again he refused. When he did not sail for Boston in May 1797, as he intended, the church once again asked that he stay and preach, if only for a few weeks. Brown agreed to stay for another twelve weeks and then left Machias for good. In November the church gave him an official dismissal in absentia.[25]

Brown's brief tenure marked a new phase in Machias's religious life, one in which people began to explore new institutional accommodations. As tensions strained toward both liberal inclusiveness and evangelical exclusiveness, doctrinal refinements in the church's covenant and rules would not suffice to bind church and people into a whole. Brown's lack of tolerance for evangelical enthusiasm probably weakened his chance to heal the rift between the New Light and the Old Light followers and between the church and the congregation.

But blame for those divisions cannot be laid wholly at Brown's feet, for throughout New England Congregationalist clergy strained to hold together any town's church and congregation under the pressure of religious ferment.[26]

After Clark Brown's departure, the town and church took two years to find a suitable replacement, and another year before Marshfield Steele was ordained and installed as minister. Unlike Brown who was ordained in Boston, Steele was ordained in Machias at the home of Stephen Jones. An ecclesiastical council composed of four ministers and two lay delegates from eastern Maine presided over the ceremony. The local ordination and the presence of eastern Maine clergy, rather than ones from lower New England, indicate a religious maturation of the area. The council also located Steele within a regional circle of ministers, the lack of which Brown had cited as a serious handicap in his ministry in Machias.[27] Besides ordaining Steele, the council also reviewed and revised the covenant and confession of faith of the Machias church, which it found

> essentially defective in point of Doctrine … in that it purposely leaves out the mention of our Savior's Divinity, the entire depravity of the human heart as it is by nature, the agency of the Holy Spirit in changing the heart in a supernatural manner, and the attribute of Divine Sovereignty by which God has a right to do as he will with his own.[28]

Three of the four criticisms were direct attacks on Arminian tendencies, especially among evangelicals, who implied that each individual could personally be instrumental in his or her own conversion, that individuals, not just the Holy Spirit, could change hearts. The criticism, that "God has a right to do as he will with his own," stated the Calvinist position that God, not the individual, determines who will be saved and who damned.

The new sixteen-article confession of faith reflected a return to Calvinist principles. Humanity, as a result of Adam and Eve's disobedience, was depraved, "wholly destitute of moral goodness," and consigned to suffer "the miseries of this life" without hope of eternal life. But God, "of his own good pleasure," before he had created the earth, had "chosen a part of mankind to obtain salvation thro Jesus Christ," and "That God will in time regenerate all the Elect by his Spirit." The church, made up of the elected, was visible in the world and through godly commission provided for the preaching of the gospel to the world. The confession of faith also stated the church's position on baptism, one of the nemeses of Brown's ministry in Machias. Baptism was only for the children of members in full communion or to persons who had reached "years of discretion" and would make a profession of faith before baptism.[29] Once again, children of people who had been baptized but who themselves had not made a profession of faith were excluded from baptism.

The Machias church, backed with the leadership of an ecclesiastical council, retreated from the liberal doctrinal position that some had advocated during Brown's short tenure, after he attempted a modest retreat from the broader liberalism of Lyon's era. This time the tightening of Calvinist doctrine did not spawn the controversy it had generated three years before. Four explanations offer themselves for the quieting of theological controversy. One, when the town invited Marshfield Steele to Machias on trial, it offered a temporary tax exemption to anyone who did not support Steele's candidacy. Sixteen men accepted the exemption, which undercut their ability to challenge him theologically. This tax exemption for religious reasons, the only one before 1812, suggests it was done intentionally to diffuse antagonism to a new minister.[30] Two, Steele was ordained in Machias, a town committee planned it, and the outside delegates were from eastern Maine. Three, an ecclesiastical council from outside the town, but from the region, adjudicated the doctrinal controversies. And last, Steele seemed to provide the strong leadership expected of a standing minister. He was conciliatory without being weak. He acknowledged the "difficulties you were called to encounter by means of a former settlement" and stated that he thought that the town would be "safe only when we distrust ourselves and rely on God."[31] He served a life-tenure in the town (1800–1831) and in 1821 was joined by a second minister, Abraham Jackson, who became the minister for East Machias when the township and church split in 1826.

For over a decade, Steele's ministry checked a growing body of dissenters in Machias. Within his first two months, the church tightened its rules on the admission of new members. Prospective members had to "give evidence of a saving work of God in their hearts" to the pastor. After the pastor's approval, the person was admitted if no member objected. If a member made a "weighty" objection, church members voted on the candidate's suitability. Rules on baptism were revised with a clear design to placate those with Baptist leanings. Adult immersion was allowed if the person had never been baptized, could give testimony of saving grace, and was "conscientious in viewing baptism by immersion as the only Scriptural mode of administering the ordinance."[32] These changes in church rules are virtually the only indications in church records from the first decade of Steele's ministry that religious contentment was not widespread in Machias. Town records are scarcely more forthcoming, although the odd detail hints at religious divisions, which in 1812 resulted in the town's acknowledgment of two religious societies.

In the 1804 notice for the annual town meeting, the sixth agenda item was to see if the town would either "agree to divide the township of Machias into two separate towns" or "set off Elias Foster and others as a Society in said Town for public Religious worship."[33] The town voted to dismiss the item. The religious orientation of Foster and his associates is unclear, but from other evidence we can make some calculated surmises. He probably represented a group of Baptists, many of whom lived in the settlement on the East Machias River. In 1810 twenty-eight men petitioned the Massachusetts General Court to be incorporated as the "First Baptist Society in Machias." Their petition argued that as Baptists in a town where the established church was Congregational they could not enjoy the rights and privileges provided for in the Constitution "of Worshiping the Supreme Being in the way and manner most agreeable to the dictates of their own conscience" and "of applying the monies paid by them for the support of Public Worship to support of a Public Teacher of their own denomination." On June 8, 1810 this petition was sent to the House Committee on Parishes, and on June 8, 1810 the Senate read and concurred with it, but for reasons not explained in the extant legislative papers, the legislature did not enact it.[34]

The lack of legislative sanction did not dissuade the Baptists, and by 1812 they had built a meetinghouse on the East Machias River large enough to be used for town meetings when they were held in that part of town. At the 1812 annual town meeting, the Baptists stated that they had made plans to hire "a religious Instructor of their own persuasion for the year ensuing." The townspeople voted to allow this group "stiling themselves members of a Baptist Church" an exemption from the tax for Steele's salary. The town also recognized a second society known simply as the "Christian Society," probably a separatist group that believed in lay ordinations, whose members "alledged that they have already ordained Mr. Ebenezer Gooch to be their teacher."[35]

The cracks in Machias's religious order widened when Steele interrupted his ministry. The records do not indicate the circumstances surrounding this hiatus, but he left the town in 1812 and did not return until May 1816. During his four-year absence, denominational divisions became an accepted feature of the town's religious landscape.[36] By November 1816, the Congregationalists, with the town's consent, petitioned the Massachusetts General Court to be incorporated as a separate society. In their memorial, signed by approximately one hundred men, they stated that even though they included a majority of the townspeople and wanted to maintain their "Religious priviledges" (i.e., their standing as the established church in the town), they did not want to tax "the feelings or property of others," and therefore thought it best to be incorporated as a religious society. The legislature approved the request and incorporated them as the "First Congregational Society of Machias."

In 1819 the Baptists repetitioned the legislature for incorporated status, justifying their request as deriving from "those inconveniences which naturally flow from the lassitude of unincorporated Bodies." Indeed their need was little more. In the years between their 1810 request for incorporated status, which was not approved, and their 1819 request, which was approved, the town of Machias recognized the Baptists, and they were no longer expected to support financially the Congregationalist church.[37] Neither the town's recognition of three religious societies nor the subsequent incorporation of the Congregationalists and Baptists by the state ended the town's involvement in the "support of the Gospel." For another decade the town tried various combinations of levies, assessments, and distributions of tax monies to support both its religious societies. Not until the 1830s, did support of religion become fully privatized.[38]

The extent to which the Machias town government remained involved in mediating shifts in religious sensibilities is striking. The town collected the arrears of Lyon's salary in the 1780s. It used a tax exemption to acknowledge dissenters when hiring Steele. When it recognized the Baptists as a religious society, it also recognized a short-lived splinter group. The town approved the Congregationalists' petition to the state legislature for incorporation as a society. It used the apparatus of government to help collect monies for both the Baptist and Congregational societies. As religion increasingly became a matter of private conscience in Machias, town government was still an important agent in shaping the course of those changes.

Machias did have proprietors of the meetinghouse, but unlike their Liverpool counterparts, they played no significant role in the resolution of religious differences. The township proprietors built the first meetinghouse, and after the incorporation of Machias in 1784, the town purchased it for £65 and built a second one in East Machias. In 1805 the Western Falls meetinghouse was rebuilt with privately subscribed monies, thus creating the proprietors of the meetinghouse. In 1810 this group petitioned the General Court for incorporation so that they could "finish & complete" the house "and that the charges thereof may be apportioned upon and paid by the several proprietors according to their interest in sd House."[39] In Machias, the proprietors of the meetinghouse were almost solely concerned with their property, but there was no need for them to attempt to resolve religious differences because the town government, buttressed by the state government, continued to serve in that capacity. But in Liverpool the absence of town government created a leadership vacuum that other groups filled. In managing the breakdown of Congregational hegemony in Liverpool, the proprietors of the meetinghouse were the dominant agents.

* * *

When the American Methodist preacher Freeborn Garrettson visited Liverpool in the summer of 1785 he wrote in his diary that "I began to preach at five o'clock in the morning; and the people being mostly raised amongst, and accustomed to the ways of the Presbyterians [Congregationalists] rather thought it to be a work of supererogation."[40] Despite the strong cultural markers that Garrettson recognized, Old Light Congregationalism as an organized denomination in Liverpool would expire by 1790, slower than in many towns in Nova Scotia, but precipitously compared to New England. Three distinct phases define Congregationalism's demise within Liverpool. An Old Light Congregationalist phase, characterized by a unity of church and community, began with the arrival of New Englanders in 1760 and lasted until the dismissal of the settled minister, Israel Cheever, in 1782. From then until 1790, the townspeople struggled and failed to reach a consensus on a new foundation for the unification of church and community. The mechanism for achieving unity was Congregationalism, but by the 1780s a sharp division had emerged between Old Light Congregationalists and a strongly Arminian form of Congregationalism associated with the Nova Scotian evangelist Henry Alline. A third phase began in 1790 when Liverpool's inhabitants abandoned attempts to reforge unity and religious adherence became a matter of private conscience. After that year two denominations predominated: Allinite Congregationalism and Wesleyan Methodism.[41]

The faster breakdown of church and community in Liverpool than in Machias can largely be attributed to the elimination of customary and legitimated institutional forms, in particular, town government. But the redefinition of the township proprietors and the lack of a clerical association in Nova Scotia that could adjudicate problems in conflict-ridden congregations were surely contributing factors. Consequently, the dominant contours of religious life in Liverpool took new forms. Tensions between the laity and the clergy became more extreme, in part because there were no outside adjudicators. A cultural affinity with New England led many in Liverpool to believe that it held a solution to their problems, although realistically it did not because the remaining cultural ties lacked any institutional expression, such as a clerical association. The proprietors of the meetinghouse, through their control of worship space and in the absence of other institutions, became the forum of last resort for adjudicating differences and seeking solutions to the religious conflicts.

The first serious religious tension in Liverpool was financial, not doctrinal. The township proprietors, acting within New England custom, hired Cheever in 1761 and agreed to pay him £85 a year plus a weekly collection, with additions if the sum proved inadequate. What the settlers did not comprehend, however, was that Nova Scotian proprietors would not have the corporate powers that New England proprietors had, nor would Liverpool be incorporated as a town with powers of taxation. Cheever's salary was soon in arrears, and in October 1767 he quit preaching until the community paid his salary or guaranteed more satisfactory means of support.[42] Cheever's financial woes mirrored those of ministers throughout Nova Scotia. James Lyon, Machias's first minister, left Nova Scotia in 1771 because of financial difficulties. In 1769, the church and congregation at Cornwallis, Nova Scotia, wrote to ministers in Boston requesting financial aid. Benjamin Gerrish and Malachy Salter, two Halifax merchants, wrote to the Reverend Andrew Eliot of Boston in 1770 about the financial status of the various dissenting (non-Anglican) churches in Nova Scotia, including Liverpool's, and asked if he could arrange some financial relief from New England.[43] People in New England, however, could not solve the financial problems of Nova Scotia's Congregationalist churches.

Conflict over Cheever's salary arose from regional economic difficulties as much as from the peculiarities of Liverpool, but it exacerbated a more significant tension over lay or clerical control of religious life. As financial support of religion became voluntary, people increasingly justified their withholding of monies on Cheever's deficiencies, rather than on their inability or unwillingness to pay. In 1772, when Cheever called a meeting to request his salary or dismissal, the people adjourned for three days and took the offensive when they reconvened. "There were many debates, enquiries, confessions, and retractions on the side of Mr. Cheever," the substance of which was not recorded. But once both sides aired their grievances, the people voted, by a great majority, to continue with Cheever as their minister. Four years later, "scandelous reports" about Cheever's conduct again circulated. The church and congregation responded by choosing a committee of three to meet with him to discuss the charges, followed by a series of meetings between Cheever and the combined church and congregation.

Both sides jockeyed to control the course of the dispute. The church and congregation called a meeting. Two weeks later Cheever called a meeting. The church and congregation proposed calling a council, although who would sit on such a council in Nova Scotia was unclear, and nothing came of it. Cheever offered to take his dismissal with £100 compensation and "the honors of the Church," which the church and congregation turned down. The dispute subsided temporarily, but three months later a discontented and undeterred group wrote and asked him to take a dismissal from the ministry, but without financial compensation and "the honors of the Church." Cheever refused.[44]

Some prominent members then withdrew from the pastoral care of Cheever and in September 1776 wrote to Mr. Samuel Sheldon Pool of Yarmouth, Nova Scotia, inviting him to come to Liverpool and preach. A 1770 graduate of Harvard, Pool moved to Yarmouth from Massachusetts in 1774 and often served as a lay preacher to the settlers at Cape Forchu. He accepted the invitation and arrived on September 29.[45] Pool's visit created the opportunity for the proprietors of the meetinghouse to become active in the struggle to define the religious character of Liverpool. From then until 1790 the control of worship space was the primary form in which the community's religious struggle found expression.

Liverpool's proprietors built the first meetinghouse in 1761. A modest structure measuring fifty by sixty feet and without pews, it was, for all intents and purposes, a publicly owned building. In 1766 some prominent men upset people when they decided to build pews "for their own comfort." The cause of the disturbance is unknown: people may have been angered at the show of social status by those able to afford pews; or the incident may have exposed a deeply seated religious difference over comfort during worship. It appears, however, that a small group of men, and not the community, made the decision, but by 1766, settlements in Nova Scotia had limited institutional mechanisms for calling meetings to discuss and adjudicate these situations.[46] In the fall of 1774, Liverpool's proprietors' committee voted to build a new meetinghouse. An appointed committee recommended a meetinghouse fifty by forty-two feet, to be financed initially by three or more people who would then sell pews to recover their costs, effectively privatizing the endeavor. Simeon Perkins, William Dean, and Joseph Christopher accepted the task and hired carpenter Josiah Marshall to build it for £805. Before Marshall began building, Perkins, Dean, and Christopher auctioned future pews and townspeople purchased all those for the lower floor and eleven in the gallery, enough to raise £805.[47] The purchasers of the pews became the "proprietors of the meetinghouse."

Construction proceeded slowly. Marshall took two years to build the new meetinghouse during which time the church and congregation met in the old one. When those disaffected with Cheever's ministry invited Sheldon Pool to Liverpool in the fall of 1776, the proprietors of the new meetinghouse opened it, and he preached there, giving the protest a symbolic public meaning that meeting in a home could not give.[48] The new meetinghouse signified Liverpool's religious future, and the laity, not the minister, would control it. Henceforth, when religious disputes arose, determining the use of worship space became the focal point of negotiations. A minister could not unilaterally assert his superior wisdom or the prerogatives of office to force parishioners to use the meetinghouse as he saw fit.

Sheldon Pool preached for a month to a receptive audience, but declined an invitation to stay the winter.[49] After his departure the "agrieved party" continued to worship in the new meetinghouse with the deacons presiding. Finally in April 1777, the discontented enumerated their grievances and asked Cheever to meet with them, not in the old meetinghouse or on neutral ground, but in the new meetinghouse that they controlled. After airing their concerns, they voted to return to one fold and worship in the new meetinghouse. On the following Sunday Cheever preached to the reunited congregation from the first verse of the 122nd Psalm, "I was glad when they said unto me, let us go into the house of the Lord." Perkins recorded that "the people seem greatly pleased that the unhappy disention is made up."[50]

The December 1781 visit of Henry Alline, leader of a colonywide religious revival, finally brought down Cheever's ministry. A New Englander by birth, Alline moved to Nova Scotia from Newport, Rhode Island, as a child and settled with his parents in the Minas Basin in 1760. In 1775, at the age of twenty-seven and after a period of morbid introspection into his spiritual condition, he had a conversion experience and soon after began preaching, first in the Minas Basin and then throughout Nova Scotia.[51] Alline arrived in Liverpool on Wednesday, December 5, 1781, and unlike later itinerant ministers, such as Freeborn Garrettson, he spent his first days unobtrusively.[52] After the Sunday morning service Cheever asked the people whether Alline should preach in the afternoon and "No one Spoke for it." "A Great Number," however, heard him preach at the home of Mr. Stevenson, "and in General Approved of his preaching." That positive reception yielded an invitation for Alline to preach in the meetinghouse the following Friday afternoon, which displeased Cheever because, in his opinion, preaching "in the Pulpit" gave Alline unmerited ministerial credibility. The proprietors of the meetinghouse, however, and not Cheever, determined if Alline could preach from the pulpit during the week; Cheever could, and did, refuse to relinquish the pulpit to Alline for Sunday services.[53]

Alline sojourned in Liverpool for a month and preached at least one other midweek service in the meetinghouse. More often he preached in homes, at times competing with Cheever's Sunday services. On a quarterly communion Sunday "Several of the Communicants Absent[ed] themselves & Attend[ed] Mr. Alline," a sign both of Alline's appeal and of people's deep disaffection with Cheever.[54] After Alline's departure, "some of the Serious people" continued to worship in homes, and attracted many who "have not been remarkable for Religion heretofore [and] are now under great Concern, and making a Grand inquiry what they Shall do to be Saved." Cheever, recognizing open dissension, preached "Very Strenuously against Seperation," and Perkins confided to his diary that "What the event will be God only Knows."[55]

The immediate event was an open confrontation between Cheever and the church and congregation. During February, church members and Cheever met four times. At a fifth meeting, members of the congregation also attended, and the church and congregation voted to dismiss Cheever, the only choice that might have prevented a permanent division. Alline's visit encouraged Cheever's critics to withdraw from worship and communion, explaining that they did not think "Mr. Cheever's Conduct … agreeable to the Character of a Minister." For these people, reconciliation was no longer a viable option. By dismissing Cheever the possibility remained of reforging a unity of church and community.[56]

Religious life in Liverpool did not return to normal. Rather the major antagonists reallocated the space in which the religious struggle took place. The "Heads of the Church" led Sunday morning and afternoon worship in the meetinghouse, but on Sunday evenings the various factions held services in homes. For months after his dismissal, Cheever led services in the homes of sympathizers, and raised the ire of the deacons when he "presumptuously administered [baptism] to some, two or three ignorant and unthinking

People," after having "voluntarily taken his Dismission and thereby has discharged himself from his ordination Vow."[57]

During Alline's second and last visit to Liverpool from November 13, 1782 to February 17, 1783, he served as the only minister and preached in both the meetinghouse and homes. Some people resisted his presence; on Christmas Day, Mr. Millard spoke out against Alline during his sermon only to be reproved by him.[58] Most people, however, accepted him in the absence of another minister, and gradually he encouraged a townshipwide revival. The night before he left, "Mr. Alline made a long Speech, Very Sensible, Advising all Sorts of People to the Religious Life, & gave many directions for their outward walk. This is a wonderful day & Evening." For Simeon Perkins, the event was a new one for Nova Scotia. "Never did I behold Such an Appearance of the Spirit of God moving upon the people Since the time of the Great Religious Stir in New England many years ago." Alline left for Port Medway and Lunenburg and never returned to Liverpool.[59]

Besides sparking a revival, Alline encouraged his followers to adopt a new church covenant. While he was still in Liverpool, the church members met to consult "about Renewing or Coming into a New Covenant." Two deacons were for it, two were against, and after extensive discussion the church came to no agreement. One deacon, Mr. Stephen Smith, and three other members left the meeting to proceed with a new covenant. Most members of the "Standing Church" opposed the "meathod of their withdrawing," as well as "Some Articles in the New Covenant, one in particular Concerning Baptism, Said to be Non-Essensial." The meeting apparently turned not on whether to write a new covenant, but whether the church would accept the new covenant that Alline had written.[60] John Payzant, the first settled New Light minister in Liverpool and Alline's brother-in-law, recorded in his journal that when he arrived "I came to examine the State of the Church [and] I found that Mr. Alline had settled them on a free open communion congregational plane, and Baptised a number of their children." The covenant of the church Alline organized was printed in the mid nineteenth century, but it is unclear whether it was the original 1782 covenant. Article two, under "The Church Visible," states that baptism was not necessary; "We believe that the mode of water baptism, ought not be a bar in the church or term of communion, but each true Christian has a right to enjoy his liberty of conscience in that particular."[61] That statement was consistent with people's complaint in 1782 that Alline believed baptism was nonessential.

A second covenanted church in Liverpool revived the controversy over the use of the meetinghouse for public worship. When no minister was in town, the two churches either met together or separately in the meetinghouse and homes. Itinerant ministers, however, frequently polarized doctrinal differences as each side judged whether an itinerant's qualifications suited him to preach from the pulpit. The return to peacetime shipping in 1783 also increased the numbers of itinerants stopping in Liverpool. The greater range of choice among ministers sharpened people's doctrinal sensitivities and made them more willing to judge someone as unacceptable. In June 1783, the simultaneous presence in Liverpool of William Black, a Methodist minister from the Chignecto region of Nova Scotia, and Donald A. Fraser, a Scots Presbyterian, engendered sufficient disputes over which man should preach in the meetinghouse that people began insisting on "Some Regulations respecting the Public Worship."[62]

The only forum for crafting such regulations was a meeting of the proprietors of the meetinghouse, but people were unclear on what the regulations should cover. Should the proprietors simply determine when the two churches, the Old Light Congregationalists and the New Light Congregationalists, could use the meetinghouse? Or should the proprietors judge ministerial qualifications? A meeting on March 17, 1784 began with New Light complaints about the drinking habits of William Firmage, a Calvinist Methodist minister from England whom the Old Lights let preach in the meetinghouse. Old Lights quickly shifted to doctrinal concerns about Allinite ministers. Simeon Perkins declared that "I would not agree that Mr. Alline or any of his Adherents Should ever Carry on the Publick Worship of the Place in that House, & gave my reasons for it, viz., that Mr. Alline had denied the Fundamental articles of the Christian Religion," probably a reference to baptism being "non-essential." The meeting adjourned for six days, and when the proprietors met again, the discussion became sufficiently contentious that an ad hoc committee of two New Lights and two Old Lights was struck to determine three issues: one, whether and how often Thomas Chipman, an Allinite, would be allowed to preach in the meetinghouse; two, how the property of the meetinghouse might be divided between the two parties; and three, "anything else that may lend to an Amicable Settlement."[63]

On the third point, the committee decided to recruit a new minister out of New England, someone who might be able to restore a unity of church and community. So anxious was the committee for this plan to succeed that they paid Deacon Samuel Hunt to hand-deliver a letter to the Reverend Chandler Robbins of Plymouth, Massachusetts, asking him to recommend a new minister. The problem, however, was not to be quickly remedied. The clerical association to which Robbins belonged had no candidate to send, and the negotiations begun in 1784 dragged on for five years until November 1789 when twenty-one-year-old John Turner arrived from New England. Within two months of Turner's arrival, the five-year conviction that a new minister from New England could heal the divisions had vanished, and in June 1790 Turner returned home.[64]

The old problem of sharing the meetinghouse remained, although with some new parameters. In January 1785, the New Lights began building a new, but smaller, meetinghouse, and by May they were worshipping in it, but a second meetinghouse alleviated only some problems. The old meetinghouse, Zion Congregationalist Church, symbolized the struggle over the definition of Congregationalism in Liverpool. Although prominent New Lights would finance a new meetinghouse, they would not relinquish their property rights in the old one, especially not while negotiations were afoot for a minister from New England. For two years, the New Lights hosted itinerant preachers of their choosing in the new meetinghouse, while in the old meetinghouse Old Lights hosted other itinerants, the greatest number of whom were Methodists. Then in 1787, the contentious Thomas Chipman visited Liverpool again and drew such large and responsive crowds that the New Lights insisted that their property rights in the old and larger meetinghouse be honored and that a minister of their choosing be allowed to preach there if they needed the space. The Old Lights had little choice but to accede to their demands, and negotiations over worship space again became common.[65]

After Turner's brief sojourn demonstrated the futility of believing that a minister from New England could restore religious unity, the controversy over the use of the large meetinghouse intensified. But over the previous decade, the religious contours of the town had changed significantly. During the 1780s, the Methodists became a third religious group in Liverpool, in addition to the Old Light and New Light Congregationalists. Significantly, however, people who became Methodists removed themselves from the disputes over the use of the large meetinghouse (even if they were pew owners) and from the negotiations for a new minister. Those were Congregationalist issues and Methodists were not a part of either side. As long as the numerically dominant Old Lights were party to hiring a minister from New England, they could use their property interests in the meetinghouse to allow itinerant Methodists to preach, who were the greatest clerical presence in Liverpool. When the search for a minister from New England failed, the New Lights asserted dominance in the struggle over the meetinghouse and the meaning of Congregationalism in Liverpool. After Turner's departure, the New Lights blocked the Old Lights from hosting itinerant Methodists in the old meetinghouse, and indicated that they would no longer subject themselves to Old Light judgments on the merits of the preachers they chose.[66]

During the fall of 1790 and the winter of 1791, the Methodists worshipped in the schoolhouse and often drew such large crowds that "Some were obliged to go away, or Stand out of the House." Grumbling soon started. "Many people are talking about ye Meeting House, being uneasy about the New Lights holding meetings there, when they have a House of their own Shut up, & that so Small a Number Should hold the Great House, and Discommode the

Greatest part of the Town." In February, five proprietors of the meetinghouse who were not New Lights requested that a meeting be called to discuss again the use of the building. This time they agreed to auction a year's rental of the building, and the highest bidding party—New Lights or Methodists—would use it. With a bid of £40 the Methodists gained its use.[67]

Unlike previous arrangements, this one was strictly an economic transaction concerning use of property with no provisos about who could preach in the meetinghouse and when. The Methodists rented the large meetinghouse for two years, with the rental monies being used to paint the building and glaze the windows. The New Lights, however, wanted to regain use of the building, and negotiated with Methodist proprietors to sell their interests so the New Lights would have complete ownership. The deal had scarcely been struck when the Methodists began building a meetinghouse of their own. After a decade of conflict, Liverpool's residents accepted their irreconcilable religious differences.[68]

The attempt to coax a phoenix of unification from the dying embers of New England Congregationalism illustrates a complex series of gradual transitions reshaping the religious, social, and political contours of Liverpool. First, the only proposal for unification to receive serious consideration was the plan to hire another Congregationalist minister from New England. Had a new minister come in 1784, the doctrinal differences that Alline's two visits had accentuated might have dulled with time. But settlements throughout northern New England, Nova Scotia, and after 1784 New Brunswick had difficulty hiring ministers. The Congregationalist establishment of lower New England simply could not provide sufficient clerical support, either as missionaries or settled ministers, to all the communities settled by New Englanders after 1760. Consequently, people turned to the services of itinerants, who tended to be New Light evangelicals or Methodists.[69]

In Liverpool, the religious conflict involved both substantive doctrinal issues and the definition of New England Congregationalism. By the early 1780s, both sides erred in thinking that New England held a solution to their differences. Henry Alline clearly began a religious movement distinct from Calvinism, but many people in Liverpool believed it within the bounds of New England Congregationalism. In 'A People Highly Favoured of God': The Nova Scotia Yankees and the American Revolution, Gordon Stewart and George Rawlyk argue that Alline helped New Englanders create a Nova Scotian identity during the American Revolution. The situation in Liverpool, however, was the opposite. Alline's doctrines became a catalyst for a struggle over the definition of New Englandness. Significantly, the New Lights retained the original name of the church, Zion Congregationalist Church, which initially was covenanted in Rochester, Massachusetts, on Buzzard's Bay, thereby indicating a desire to maintain continuity with their New England past rather than break with it. Among the people who became Allinites, at least six families had Rochester roots. This evidence suggests that the Allinite movement in Liverpool was about unresolved New England issues.[70]

The known origins of the Allinites or New Lights reinforces this interpretation. The earliest surviving subscription list for Zion Congregational Church is for 1794, after it was New Light. Of the thirty-four names on the list nineteen were born in, or had parents born in, the Cape Cod region, exclusive of Plymouth. Six were from Chatham; six were from Rochester. Another five had married into families with Cape Cod roots. In total about 70 percent of the Allinites had strong Cape Cod connections. The point of comparison for the Old Lights is the 1791 subscription list for the Methodists, to whom most of them gravitated after the collapse of their church. Of the thirty-five subscribers, only eight had Cape Cod connections, four of them with Eastham, a community not represented by the New Lights. Ten subscribers were from Plymouth, as compared with only three New Lights. After the American Revolution increasing numbers of non–New Englanders, particularly Loyalist refugees and disbanded British soldiers, settled in Liverpool and generally joined the Methodists. Four Loyalists can be identified on the two subscription lists; only one was a New Light who had married into a prominent New Light family. Only three New Lights were not of known New England origins.[71]

The tensions among Liverpool's Congregationalists can be attributed, in part, to tensions within New England Congregationalism that had been transplanted to Nova Scotia. Research on Puritanism in late-sixteenth-century England shows that it contained sectarian tendencies, many of which were transplanted to New England, but were probably localized and contained within township parishes. The geographic pattern of division between Liverpool's Old Lights and New Lights suggests that the migration of people from long-settled townships in New England to new settlements in Nova Scotia unleashed and exposed religious differences that were decades, if not centuries, old.[72]

Two factors explain the tendency of Liverpool's Old Lights to become Methodists. One was the availability of Methodist itinerants after the American Revolution, when Liverpool became a regular stop on New Light and Methodist circuits. Over a period of thirteen years (1781–1793), Simeon Perkins recorded the names of twenty-seven different ministers who stopped in Liverpool; many came more than once and had extended stays. Fifteen were Methodists, eight were New Lights, and four were of other persuasions. The presence of both Methodists and New Lights surely hastened the demise of Old Light Congregationalism, but their presence only gradually redefined religious sensibilities. Too often the religious persuasion of an itinerant minister has been used as a proxy for a town's persuasion, so that scholars have concluded that "a settlement might be described as Methodist or Newlight depending on who happened to be evangelizing." As the struggle over worship space in Liverpool shows, this was not always the case. People's religious beliefs did not change with every passing evangelist. Most of the Old Light Congregationalists in Liverpool embraced Methodism only after the difficulty of finding an acceptable Congregationalist minister became painfully manifest.[73]

The other factor shaping the move to Methodism was a process of Anglicization. The Allinite movement grew out of transplanted New England culture, including a strong tendency toward parish autonomy and laity control. The Methodists, in contrast, represent an Anglicizing trend. Unlike Methodism in the Chesapeake and mid-Atlantic states, where it was an "Americanization" of Anglicanism and an adaptation to the enthusiasms in American religion, the Wesleyan Methodism practiced in Liverpool represented a move away from the clannishness and localism of New England Congregationalism, without requiring an acceptance of Anglicanism. Theologically and culturally, Wesleyan Methodism created a middle ground in Liverpool between Congregationalism and Anglicanism. It emphasized infant baptism, conversion, closed communion, and lay involvement at the local level. Yet its ecclesiastical organization was transatlantic and pan-British, unlike New England Congregationalism, which was regionally specific.[74] That religious shift reflected a broader cultural shift as Liverpool's residents, and Nova Scotians more generally, found new ways to express their place in the British Empire.

* * *

The breakdown of Congregationalism as the established or standing church evolved at very different rates in Liverpool and Machias, despite the strong similarities between the two towns when they were first settled. By 1790 Liverpool residents had accepted their inability to reforge the unity of church and community that had been part of the Congregationalist establishment in New England. Abandoning Calvinist Congregationalism, they split between Wesleyan Methodism and Allinite Congregationalism. In Machias at the same time the Congregationalist establishment was strong enough to see the hiring of four more pastors before the town finally ceased to support the church through taxation. In Machias, East Machias, and Machiasport (separately incorporated in 1826) the Congregational churches remained the dominant denomination, by social status if not by numbers, although East Machias was a Baptist stronghold.

The divergent breakdown of Congregationalism in Liverpool and Machias mirrors its disintegration in Nova Scotia and Maine, including a rapid collapse of Congregationalism in the former and a more gradual movement toward disestablishment in the latter. In Nova Scotia, Calvinist Congregationalism was virtually dead by 1790, with the notable exception of Yarmouth, and when it reemerged in the nineteenth century it was through the agency of English Congregationalism.[75] In Maine the Congregationalists declined much more gradually. In 1780 they accounted for 70.4 percent of all churches in Maine, in 1790, 43.5 percent, in 1800, 32.3 percent, and in 1810, 20.8 percent. In 1810 in the counties of York and Cumberland, which had strong colonial antecedents, the Congregationalists accounted for 39 and 36.9 percent, respectively, of all congregations.[76] Thus the patterns for the decline of Congregationalism diverged not just in Liverpool and Machias, but in Nova Scotia and Maine in general.

Forces for the dissolution of Congregationalism had been evident since before the Puritans left England for North America in the 1620s and 1630s. Many of the theological differences within English Puritanism, some straining toward the heretical, had been masked or bridled when the Puritans came to New England, but they nonetheless persisted.[77] Other forces of dissolution emerged in Massachusetts and Connecticut. The children of the first settlers were not always the "visible saints" their parents had been and were therefore not eligible for full membership in a church, yet they could be neither excluded entirely nor ignored by the church. To overcome this problem the religious leaders formulated the Half-Way Covenant, extending some church privileges, especially baptism, to those people who were baptized but not full covenant members. Other conflicts arose over whether lay or clerical leaders would define the character of local churches.[78] And the frontier with its promise of individual freedom has often been viewed as a disintegrating force.

All of these forces of dissolution were present in both Liverpool and Machias. Cheever angered Liverpool's lay leaders when he baptized and admitted new members without their approval. The Machias church under Clark Brown revised its rules on baptism to accommodate people who wanted their children baptized but would themselves not join the church. Henry Alline's theology deviated far from Calvinism, yet many settlers in Nova Scotia found him within the New England Congregationalist tradition. Brown's geographic isolation from other ministers exacerbated problems in his troubled ministry in Machias.

But divergent patterns in the collapse of Congregationalism in Nova Scotia and Maine were not caused by significant differences in the forces of dissolution but rather by differences in the forces for maintaining cohesion and containing dissent. In New England, churches had the support of clerical councils and town governments backed up by legislative assemblies. In Nova Scotia the proscription on town governments eliminated a crucial source of local power for maintaining religious cohesion and for channeling dissent into appropriate ecclesiastical forms. As well, clerical associations that could help troubled churches were slow to develop in Nova Scotia. Thus differences in the forces for maintaining cohesion rather than the forces of dissolution distinguished the histories of Congregationalism in Nova Scotia from those in New England.

When Governor Charles Lawrence issued his second proclamation in 1759 inviting New Englanders to settle in Nova Scotia he promised religious toleration for all Protestants, even though the Anglican Church was established.

> Protestants dissenting from the Church of England, whether they be Calvinists, Lutherans, Quakers, or under what denomination soever, shall have free liberty of conscience, and may erect and build Meeting Houses for public worship, and may choose and elect Ministers for the carrying on of Divine Service and administration of the Sacrament, according to their several opinions, and all contracts made between their Ministers and Congregations for the support of their Ministry are hereby declared valid, and shall have their full force and effect according to the tenor and conditions thereof, and all such Dissenters shall be excused from any rates or taxes … for the support of the Established Church of England.[79]

The Anglican establishment in Nova Scotia was not the same as the Congregational establishment in Massachusetts or Connecticut. The financial support for it came either from London or from the assembly in Halifax, most of whose revenue came from indirect taxes.[80] A shortage of both Anglican clergy and missionaries sent out by the Society for the Propagation of the Gospel meant that Anglicanism did not penetrate into towns such as Liverpool until the nineteenth century when the issue of a union of church and community had become moribund.[81]

Many Nova Scotia townships settled by New Englanders established a Congregational church and taxed local people for its support, a practice derived from New England custom. But when that local system was challenged and people neglected paying their ministerial taxes, church leaders had no recourse to the law to compel them to finance a religious institution. Whether intended or not, Lawrence's 1759 proclamation, coupled with restrictions on town government, allowed for freedom of individual religious dissent in Nova Scotia decades before it happened in most of New England, Rhode Island excepted. In settlements such as Liverpool a commitment to religious homogeneity and communitywide ministerial support were based on New England custom, and once challenged it disintegrated.

The ramifications of the end of local and direct public support of religion echoed long in Nova Scotia's religious development. Theologically and ecclesiastically, new religious sects in late-eighteenth- and early-nineteenth-century Nova Scotia eschewed the validity of ecclesiastical structure, and many groups only organized in the nineteenth century under pressure from New England Baptists. Among evangelicals, lay exhorting after the sermon became an important mechanism to maintain membership cohesion and reinforced laity control. In the nineteenth century, exhorting was professionalized as part of the role of the clergy, again because of pressure out of New England Baptist circles.[82] The colony experienced religious ferment similar to that found in northern New England, but in New England religious movements very quickly assumed coherent ecclesiastical forms, for example, as Shakers, Universalists, and Freewill Baptists, whereas in Nova Scotia religious movements remained very fluid and their leaders resisted organization.[83]

Part of the explanation for the rapid organization of dissenting sects in New England is that recognition of dissenters and relief from paying taxes to support the established church were generally only extended if one was a member of a dissenting society. Thus it behooved religious dissenters in New England—whether the old Calvinist Baptists, Quakers, and Anglicans or the new Shakers, Universalists, and Freewill Baptists—to organize. In Nova Scotia the lack of an established church that taxed people directly removed much of the need of religious dissenters to organize. Indeed, in Nova Scotia the absence of any organizations to support ministers, such as councils, enhanced and legitimized individual religious dissent, which Massachusetts and Connecticut resisted into the nineteenth century. New England society only acknowledged religious dissent when it assumed an acknowledged corporate form, and therefore dissenters had to organize.

In New England people used the political system to bolster the established church. Machias inhabitants petitioned the General Court for special taxing privileges when they hired James Lyon. When the town was incorporated it assumed responsibility for collecting Lyon's unpaid salary and levying taxes for current support. When disaffection developed with Clark Brown's ministry a group of his supporters organized themselves so they could apply to the General Court for incorporation as a religious society to hire him independently of the town. But when Brown left Machias the town and church decided to work together to hire a new minister. When a group of men rather than the town built a new meetinghouse they petitioned the General Court to be incorporated as proprietors of the meetinghouse. As the number of Baptists in town began to grow, the town recognized them, and they petitioned the General Court to be incorporated as a society. The Congregationalists had incorporated themselves as a society three years previously. The town, however, continued to collect taxes for both societies until the 1830s and apportion monies between the two. Thus even though religious affiliation had become a matter of personal choice and the churches and societies had become independently incorporated they still used the apparatus of town government to collect ministerial salaries.

One of the conclusions of this comparative work on the collapse of Congregationalism in Nova Scotia and Massachusetts and the embracing of new sects is that we need to reexamine the social meaning of religious dissent in eighteenth-century New England. When first trying to unpack the reasons why religious movements among New Englanders in Nova Scotia did not assume coherent and articulated ecclesiastical forms, as they did in New England, I became aware that much of the argument on religious dissent in eighteenth-century New England is deceptive. First, one has to abandon the assumption that evidence of dissent is by itself a sign of growing individualism and democratization. We make that assumption because we know the end of the story. Dissent, whether religious, political, moral, or ethical, is found in any society independent of political orientation. The critical question is how a society responds to dissent. Eighteenth-century New England society chose to recognize religious dissent when it assumed a corporate form. An individual could be excused from paying taxes to the established church if he or she belonged to a recognized dissenting religious society. Only occasionally did towns allow individuals not to support any church or to be independent of any religious society. In general, escaping from the social contract of religious affiliation and support was not an option. Eighteenth-century New Englanders found a way to accommodate religious dissent without accommodating individualism. In the process, it put in place the political mechanisms for creating dissenting corporate bodies and conditioned a society to use them.

The divergence of the governmental systems between Nova Scotia and New England is the greatest single factor in explaining divergent patterns in the decline of Congregationalism, the social response to religious dissent, and the emergence of new sects and denominations. This conclusion contrasts with those of many scholars who put greater emphasis on the influence of the "frontier."[84] The frontier was not an inconsequential variable, but it needs to be carefully qualified. Comparing two "frontier" settlements, this work suggests qualifications on the impact of the frontier on the emergence of new sects and denominations in late-eighteenth- and early-nineteenth-century New England culture.[85]

People from throughout lower New England settled in new communities in Nova Scotia and northern New England. The first Machias settlers came from Scarborough, Maine, but others came from towns in New Hampshire, Massachusetts, and Connecticut. A preponderant number of Liverpool's residents were drawn from two areas, Plymouth and its surrounding area and the Cape Cod and Buzzard's Bay region.[86] In Liverpool those two groups were quite clearly represented in the split between the Plymouth-dominated Old Lights and the Cape Cod–Buzzard's Bay–dominated New Lights. This division suggests that various sectarian sensibilities, which in older settled parts of New England had been isolated and contained within towns, may have come into conflict with other visions of Congregationalism when transplanted to new settlements.[87] The result may well have been religious upheaval when what had been a source of local conformity in an old town became a source of difference and conflict in a new.

Second, one needs to determine whether a town was settled by a group of people or by individuals. Large groups settled both Liverpool and Machias, and each hired a minister. In Liverpool that strong group behavior helped to keep Congregationalism going longer than it might otherwise have done. In Maine Congregationalism was strongest in towns settled by groups before the Revolution and weakest in areas settled after the Revolution, which often had been settled by individuals, especially up the Penobscot and Kennebec River valleys. In 1810 in Lincoln, Somerset, and Kennebec counties Congregationalist adherence was only 17.8, 5.9, and 18.6 percent, respectively, but in the southern counties of York and Cumberland it was 39 and 36.9 percent, respectively.[88] Up the Penobscot and Kennebec River valleys land titles were often uncertain, and settlements were often unincorporated. Machias with its strong group settlement was a Congregationalist stronghold. In contrast, Eastport, on the international border, was settled by unassociated individuals in the late eighteenth century and their land claims were only recognized in the 1790s. There settlers voted against the public maintenance of religion.[89] Thus the determination of whether an area of Maine had a group or individual settlement pattern is an important factor in assessing the viability and vitality of Congregationalism. In areas with group settlement patterns Congregationalism was stronger than in areas with individual settlement patterns.

Third, those areas of New England where settlements were only slowly incorporated as towns, such as in the Kennebec River valley, exhibited a greater tendency toward religious fragmentation and the emergence of new sects. Similarly, in Nova Scotia the absence of town government left local leaders without the political apparatus that had helped to enforce religious adherence in New England. Machias's strong town government, in contrast, was used to support the Congregationalist establishment, albeit not without some occasional dissent.

What the frontier provided was a way to reproduce society, whether as a close replication of the old, a significantly reformed and refashioned new, or a radical revision. The practice for colonial New England was a conservative replication of the old social order, reflected in grants with their stipulations for hiring a minister, building a meetinghouse, reserving shares for the first settled minister, and supporting religion and education.[90] The British knew that the frontier in Nova Scotia presented an opportunity to reform and refashion New England practices and to eliminate the excesses they thought New England represented. In the late eighteenth century the rapid geographic expansion of New England often exceeded the region's institutional growth, and there the fluidity found room for considerable social innovation that at times tended toward the radical, as happened in central Maine, as well as New Hampshire and Vermont.[91]

Social and political conditions rather than the physical condition of the frontier influenced religious developments in Nova Scotia and New England. The settlers in Liverpool and Machias initially followed the colonial New England pattern of conservative replication, as the proprietors and inhabitants made provisions for hiring a minister. Machias, with the sanction of the Massachusetts government, long maintained an established Congregational church. Congregationalism's influence was gradually eroded by internal religious dissent, but that erosion was kept well checked and channeled through the use of town government and the state incorporation of religious societies. Liverpool settlers tried hard to maintain the old New England pattern of conservative replication, but the political alterations wrought by metropolitan policy left Liverpool's leaders without the apparatus of town government to help maintain the Congregational church as the standing church. Left without one of the critical factors for maintaining religious cohesion, Old Light Congregationalism collapsed within three decades, followed by another three decades of religious fragmentation and the emergence of the Allinites, Methodists, Baptists, and Anglicans.

We return to where we began with the distinction between factors of dissolution and factors of cohesion. Conditions in areas with new settlements were not inherently different from those in more settled regions, except that they presented the possibility that the factors for maintaining social cohesion would not be successfully transplanted to a new area and that the factors corroding customary social institutions would therefore be left unchecked. It is important to note that the frontier itself was not a factor of dissolution but a condition in which the factors of dissolution might, but not always, gain ascendancy over factors of cohesion. The religious histories of Liverpool and Machias both demonstrate how well New Englanders could transplant their customary institutions. Even without political sanction Liverpool replicated New England Congregationalism and maintained it for a generation. When the people found themselves without the forum of town meetings to discuss and bridle religious differences, the importance of the proprietors of the meetinghouse and the church and congregation for framing religious discussion and resolving differences was enhanced. But these social groupings lacked the right to deploy law against dissent that town governments enjoyed. Machias, which remained within the fold of New England political institutions, was a conservative replication of Congregationalism and New England social and cultural life more generally.

7
The Structure and Functions of Local Government

In the seventeenth century, Puritans established colonies in North America, in part to escape the centralizing tendencies of the Stuart monarchy, and town government came to be both the symbol and the substance of local control.[1] After a century and a half, New Englanders had become confident of its existence and convinced of its critical importance as a unit of civil government. Secure in its validity, they could at once utilize their localism to incubate a revolution and to forge bonds of cooperation with other jurisdictions to fight it. The British, in contrast, had long seen New England town government as problematic. After the formal cession of Acadia/Nova Scotia by the French to the British in 1713, the Board of Trade indicated that this new colony would have a county system of local government similar to that of Virginia rather than town governments, like those of neighboring Massachusetts, a colony that was seen as "affect[ing] too great an Independence."[2] County governments with royally appointed officials, unlike town governments with locally elected officials, better reflected the principle that the Crown was the source of civil governance. The county governments of Nova Scotia with their Courts of Sessions, Inferior Courts of Common Pleas, and appointed magistrates were an explicit extension of the colonial government in Halifax, which in turn was an extension of the metropolitan government. Through county courts and appointed justices the British tried to retain control of local affairs and provide for administrative needs.[3] Thus New Englanders moving to Nova Scotia took their commitment to town government with them only to confront the centralizing tendencies of the state that their ancestors had left Stuart England to escape.

The shift from town to county government in Nova Scotia became an effective mechanism for the British to steer New Englanders' political habits in new directions. In this regard, I argued in Chapter 4 that the absence of town governments in Nova Scotia helped to curtail communications among settlements and isolated them politically. In New England, intertown organizations, particularly the committees of correspondence, were critical in sustaining revolutionary action.[4] The political isolation of settlements in Nova Scotia and the political networking among towns in New England were major factors in conditioning divergent responses to the imperial crisis and the ensuing war. But not just during a political upheaval and crisis did the two systems of local government produce divergent reactions from the people. After the return to peace in 1783, the continued differentiation in governmental institutions in New England and Nova Scotia makes clear that the changes in the prerevolutionary decades had become part of the permanent political landscape.

Through an analysis of the structures and functions of the local governments of Machias and Liverpool, this chapter demonstrates how institutional modifications affected the routine administration of public business and in turn peoples' attitudes about it. It argues that changes in local government in Nova Scotia, and subsequently throughout post-1783 British North America, helped to solidify the statist turn that imperial governance had taken at the

Fig. 7.1 Wash drawing of part of the bridge and town of Liverpool, from the J. E. Woolford album, "Sketches of Nova Scotia." (Courtesy of the Nova Scotia Museum, Halifax, Canada; History Collection, 78.45.68.)

end of the seventeenth century,[5] and reinforced vertical administrative linkages that reached from Whitehall and Westminster to individual settlements in the colonies. In New England, in contrast, provincial governments served as an insulating buffer between the metropolitan government and local governments, thereby limiting the effect of vertical linkages and reinforcing lateral linkages among towns, as well as making town governments the primary purveyors of government services.[6]

At first glance, New Englanders' commitment to town government and the metropolitan government's dislike of it had little to do with its routine functions.[7] Scholars who have looked at the frequency of town meetings have found that after a town was settled and well established few meetings would be held aside from the annual meetings to elect town officers. If extraordinary business arose, such as the need to find a new minister, then a meeting would be held. If no uncommon business arose during a year then a single annual meeting would serve a town's needs.[8] In this sense, town governments, as administrative units, were quite innocuous, yet, as both New Englanders and officials in Britain knew, the issue centered not on the number of meetings held in a year, but rather on whether towns could call meetings at their discretion. The latter left open the possibility that meetings might be held to discuss colonial or imperial affairs or other issues that were not explicitly of a local nature.

The power to call meetings independently of the control of a provincial government made town government a live, although generally dormant, threat to higher authorities. In 1774 Parliament addressed that threat by putting an article in the Massachusetts Government Act to restrict town meetings to a single annual meeting, an act that only produced active defiance from many Massachusetts towns. Parliament's intent was to restrict the powers of towns to the routine administration of local needs and to check the use of town meetings to agitate against metropolitan policy. Although many towns had a history of doing little more in their meetings than the Massachusetts Government Act allowed, their actions had been determined by the needs of the town and not by the demands of laws made in Westminster and New Englanders wanted it left that way.[9]

Most business of local government was concerned with providing the basic public services needed to carry on daily life and to minimize conflict: hog reeves caught stray livestock; constables apprehended the unruly and rowdy; and overseers of the poor dispensed welfare to the disadvantaged and dispossessed. In most instances, it made little difference whether magistrates in a Court of Sessions appointed local officers, the practice in Nova Scotia, or townspeople elected them at an annual meeting, the practice in Massachusetts. Indeed the willingness of the Board of Trade to allow towns in Nova Scotia to elect overseers of the poor and levy a poor rate acknowledged the point that for the provision of some services, the difference between town and county government was negligible.

Both Machias and Liverpool had a similar range of local officials, elected in the former and appointed in the latter. Table 7.1 lists the town officers for Machias in 1784, the year the town was incorporated, and ten years later in 1794. The next four columns list the town officers for East Machias and

TABLE 7.1 Local Officials in Machias, East Machias, and Liverpool*

Nature of Office	Machias		East Machias		Liverpool	
	1784	1794	1826	1834	1826	1834
Moderator	1	1	1	1	—	—
Town clerk	1	1	1	1	1	1
Selectmen/overseers of the poor	5	3	—	—	—	—
Selectmen	—	—	3	3	—	—
Overseers of the poor	—	—	1	3	—	—
Overseers of the poor and surveyors of lines and bounds	—	—	—	—	10	13
Assessors	4	3	3	3	8	14
Collector(s)	2	2	1	1	8	—
Treasurer	1	1	1	1	1	1
Clerk of licenses	—	—	—	—	1	1
Constables	2	2	3	6	28	34
Surveyors of highways	7	8	9	13	36	52
Surveyors of lumber	7	16	18	22	17	31
Surveyors of dried fish	—	—	—	—	10	3
Gaugers of casks	—	—	—	—	3	1
Gaugers and inspectors of oil	—	—	—	—	3	2
Surveyors of hoops and staves	—	—	—	—	4	3
Inspectors of bricks and lime	—	—	—	—	2	2
Clerks of the market	—	—	—	—	2	3
Surveyors and weighers of hay	—	—	—	—	—	2
Inspectors of grain, salt, and coal	—	—	—	—	—	5
Fence viewers	4	6	3	3	21	17
Hog reeves	4	8	—	—	—	58
Hayward/field drivers	2	3	5	7	—	—
Sealers of leather	3	2	—	—	—	3
Surveyors of weights and measures	2	—	—	—	—	—
Inspectors of thistle cutting					—	7
Wardens	2	—	—	—	—	—
Harbor master(s)	—	1	—	4	—	—
Tythingmen	—	2	1	5	—	—
Fish committee	—	3	3	5	—	—
School committee	—	5	3	3	—	—
School agents	—	—	6	6	—	—
Fire wardens	—	—	—	5	5	—
Engine men	—	—	—	—	6	—
Measurers of wood and bark	—	—	—	3	—	—
Surveyor of cord wood	—	—	—	—	1	—

*Officers listed in italic were specific to Liverpool.

Liverpool/Queens County in 1826 and 1834. Those two years were used because they are the first two years for which we have records of local officials from the Queens County Court of Sessions. The record of town officers for Machias for those years are not extant, and so the records from East Machias, formerly part of Machias and separately incorporated in 1826, are used.[10] All the towns over all the years had a similar core of officers: a town clerk, overseers of the poor, a town treasurer, tax assessors and collectors, constables, surveyors of highways, surveyors of lumber, and fence viewers. The purpose of many local officials in Machias, East Machias, and Liverpool was simply to regulate or monitor potential or actual conflicts of private interest. Fence viewers made sure that fences were in repair so that livestock did not roam onto other people's property. Surveyors of lumber inspected the quality of the wood products that local timbermen produced so that a town's commercial reputation would not be jeopardized by sloppy work. These and other local officials, from surveyors of weights and measures to surveyors and weighers of hay, were elected or appointed to ensure that the enterprises of private individuals conformed to public standards.

As the towns matured, the kinds and numbers of officers changed.[11] The large and growing numbers of surveyors of lumber in Machias, East Machias, and Liverpool reflect the increasing importance of the timber trade in eastern Maine and Nova Scotia.[12] In Liverpool, the decline in the number of surveyors of dry fish, gaugers of casks, gaugers and inspectors of oil, and surveyors of hoops and staves indicate the lessening importance of the fishery and the ancillary trade of coopering. As population density increased, new problems emerged that required new local officials, such as fire wardens. The major difference in the patterns of town officers among Liverpool and Machias and East Machias was that Liverpool had a larger number of specialized officers related to economic regulation, and Machias and East Machias had more officers who facilitated the provision of public education and religious services.

Local officers, whether elected in Machias and East Machias or appointed in Liverpool, generally provided unpaid services, which most townspeople did as part of their civic responsibility, and thus raising taxes to pay for them was not an issue. Indeed, local officeholding can be seen as a kind of tax on men of wealth and status, who tended to hold the most important positions.[13] Whether one was nominated to office by a grand jury and then appointed by the magistrates or elected by one's fellow citizens probably had little influence on the types of local offices people held. Seventeenth- and eighteenth-century New Englanders generally elected local leaders who might well have been chosen by court magistrates or by provincial officials. The most important town officers—the moderator, selectmen, and treasurer—were men who tended to be prosperous and often older than other men, and towns frequently elected the same individuals year after year, giving them long tenure in office.[14] The fragmentary evidence from Liverpool and Machias indicates leadership patterns that scholars have identified in other places.

In Liverpool, Nathan Tupper, a deacon of the Liverpool church, was elected moderator of the first proprietors' meeting and in 1761 his fellow settlers chose him to be one of Liverpool's first two representatives to the Nova Scotia assembly. In 1772, the governor commissioned him a justice of the peace for Queens County.[15] Simeon Perkins, another Liverpool representative to the assembly, was also chosen by townspeople to be both the proprietors' and town clerk. The governor commissioned him to be a justice of the peace, magistrate in the Inferior Court of Common Pleas, and lieutenant colonel of the Queens County militia. Elisha Freeman was a member of the first proprietors' committee, a justice of the peace, and surrogate of wills and probate. Two other members of the first proprietors' committee, Jonathan Diman and Peleg Dexter, were appointed officers in the militia. Merchant Benajah Collins, among the wealthiest men in town and a prominent New Light, was also a justice of the peace and a magistrate in the Inferior Court of Common Pleas. One of the few men in Liverpool who was a government appointee, but not a community-selected leader, was William Johnstone, the Loyalist Scotsman. He served in the provincially appointed positions of justice of the peace, magistrate, and the customs collector for the district of Liverpool.[16]

Among the Machias town officers chosen in 1794, the moderator, Stephen Jones, was also a justice of the peace, clerk of the proprietors, and owned the largest house in town, valued at $1,100. The town clerk, Ralph Bowles, was also the U.S. postmaster, an office he held by government commission. John Cooper, the county sheriff by gubernatorial commission, was a selectman and overseer of the poor, an assessor, and a member of the fish committee. The treasurer of the town and a local merchant, George Stillman, had held a military commission from Massachusetts during the war. James Avery, a surveyor of the highways, was also a justice of the peace, and had served as both the town's agent and representative to the state legislature.[17]

The above similarities in leadership patterns in Liverpool and Machias show that men who received government commissions were also likely to have been chosen by their fellow townspeople for local leadership. The exceptions to this pattern in Liverpool were the outspoken supporters of metropolitan policy, such as William Johnstone. Loyalist John McAlpine, who settled in Liverpool after the American Revolution, used his government connections to garner the commission of deputy naval officer for Queens County. After offending townspeople with his strict enforcement of instructions for issuing passes for fishing vessels and for collecting customs, they drove him out of town, but not without community confrontations with naval and civil officials.[18] Metropolitan desires aside, local leaders, whether in Massachusetts or Nova Scotia, whether under systems of county or town government, had to be publicly acceptable bridges between their localities and provincial or state governments. Effective local government in the early modern era depended on a close fit between local leaders and their constituencies. Part of the British government's logic in allowing Catholics in Quebec to hold public office, as the Quebec Act stipulated, was so French Canadians could be appointed to lead in their communities.

The relationship among the provincial government, local leadership, and attitudes about local discretion shaped quite different political geographies in New England and Nova Scotia. New England had a long-standing practice of dividing one town into two or more towns, often precipitated by competing loci of leadership.[19] Early in Machias's settlement two distinct villages developed near the mill sites on the West and East Rivers. After the town's incorporation in 1784, the location of the annual meeting alternated between the two villages.[20] With time, an intratown rivalry seems to have developed, but only in 1826, after local negotiations, did the townspeople agree to petition the Maine legislature to have the town divided into three towns: West Machias, East Machias, and Machiasport, the last of which encompassed the area's deep water harbor where a third nucleation of settlement had grown up.[21]

Few clues exist to explain the circumstances that led Machias residents to divide themselves into three separate towns, but a battle over the use of the name Machias suggests contentious underlying issues. A year after the division, West Machias appointed a committee to petition the legislature to drop the "West" in its name. In the petition, the committee argued that the western part of old Machias had always been known as simply Machias, that the federal post office and customs house located there were still considered to be in Machias and not West Machias, and that therefore the name should be changed back to its former usage. Both houses of the Maine legislature approved the request, but the petition and legislative approval were withdrawn when the people of East Machias remonstrated against the change. They contended that the names agreed to at the time of separation were "the *only* condition upon which a separation could have been agreed upon, as each division was tenacious of the old name [emphasis in the original]." If the name "Machias" were to be applied to any part, the remonstrance recorded, it should be the eastern part because the real Machias, meaning in the local Indian language "bad little falls," was on the East Machias River. The Indian name for the falls on the West River was *Rawapskitchwock* according to Morse's *Gazetteer* and the petitioners.

In 1830, eight men from West Machias again petitioned the legislature to drop the "West," reiterating that because the federal post office still used the name Machias for West Machias, it would be appropriate to have the names conform to each other. The legislature approved the petition, and West Machias became Machias.[22] But the struggle was not over. In the fall of 1839,

East Machias petitioned the legislature to change the name of the town to Mechisses, a spelling of Machias occasionally seen on seventeenth- and eighteenth-century documents. The name change became effective on February 12, 1840, but a year later the legislature reversed its decision, perhaps after grasping the absurdity of having two towns with the same name, albeit with two spellings, side by side.[23] The use of the name Machias had finally become a dead issue, although as the battle illustrates, the division of the old township did not fully alleviate the old rivalry between the western and eastern parts.

The important point here is that the town system of local government in New England allowed for political divisions if there were conflicting loci of power. Two more towns were subsequently carved out of Machias: Whitneyville in 1845, where a large sawmill had been built by a group of businessmen from Boston, and Marshfield in 1846, a small unpretentious rural village. Divisions also occurred in neighboring townships. In Jonesboro, the fishing village hived off from the lumbering and farming area in 1832 and became the town of Jonesport. In 1891, Rogue Bluffs was set off from Jonesboro, and in 1925 the long-standing autonomy of Beal's Island from Jonesport was recognized with separate incorporation.[24]

Nova Scotia did not experience the fragmenting of local government that Maine experienced, but its county system was not immune to demographic pressure and the emergence of new centers of local power. An analysis of the formation of new counties in Nova Scotia shows that as new well-defined loci of leadership emerged in the colony, they created pressure to divide counties. Until 1759, Nova Scotia had no counties. In that year five were created largely in anticipation of the settlement of New Englanders.

At the time of its founding, Liverpool was in Lunenburg County, but in 1762 the County of Queens was created, which separated the South Shore townships settled by New Englanders from the German and French settlements in Lunenburg County. With Liverpool as the new county seat, Queens County included the South Shore from Liverpool on the east to Yarmouth on the west. In 1774, the people of Yarmouth petitioned Halifax to be set off as a separate county, to stretch from Barrington on the east and up to the Annapolis Sound with Yarmouth as the county seat. Their primary justification for a new county, as well as an abatement on the county levy to pay for a jail, was the great distance from Liverpool. Their request was not honored, but it reflected the tendency to try to make the county system responsive to population growth and local preference.

In 1784, the arrival of Loyalist refugees prompted the creation of the county of Shelburne on the South Shore, to acknowledge the large influx of settlers and a new locus of leadership there, leaving the County of Queens with only Liverpool and Guysborough (Port Mouton) townships in it. The process of creating new counties in Nova Scotia continued until there were eighteen, six with two sessional districts. When the provincial government in Halifax forced municipal incorporations on the province in 1879, twelve of the counties were incorporated as rural municipalities, and the six counties with two sessional districts were split into two municipalities, for a total of twenty-four municipalities.[25]

Counties in Nova Scotia averaged fewer inhabitants than did counties in Maine, and principal towns in them accounted for a greater proportion of a county's population that did principal towns in Maine. In 1827, the people in the township of Liverpool accounted for 77.2 percent of Queens County's 4,225 inhabitants. The combined population of Machias, East Machias, and Machiasport in 1830 was only 13.1 percent of Washington County's population. In Queens County, Liverpool was the only significant center of population; in Washington County, Calais, Eastport, Lubec, and Harrington all had populations over a thousand people. Eastport, alone, had 2,450 inhabitants. A comparison of county populations in Nova Scotia and Maine in 1827 and 1830, respectively, shows that the Queens County–Washington County comparison was not anomalous. (See Table 7.2.) The average population of Maine counties at 39,944 was nearly three times the Nova Scotia average at 13,761. In 1830, Maine's most populous county, Cumberland County, was three times larger than any county in Nova Scotia, except Halifax County, which was divided into four sessional districts. Colchester and Pictou districts became separate counties in 1835. The division of Halifax County with its 46,519 souls (still fewer people than three counties in Maine) into three sessional districts substantiates the point that counties in Nova Scotia were more subject to demographic pressure than were counties in Maine.[26]

TABLE 7.2 Population of Counties in Nova Scotia and Maine, 1827 and 1830

Nova Scotia, 1827		Maine, 1830	
County/District	Population	County	Population
Halifax County	46,528	York	51,722
Halifax Peninsula	(14,439)	Cumberland	60,102
Halifax District	(10,437)	Lincoln	57,183
Colchester District	(7,703)	Kennebeck	52,484
Pictou District	(13,949)	Oxford	35,211
Hants	8,627	Waldo	29,788
Kings	10,208	Somerset	35,787
Annapolis	14,661	Penobscot	31,530
Shelburne	12,018	Hancock	24,336
Queens	4,225	Washington	21,294
Lunenburg	9,405	Total	399,437
Cumberland	5,416		
Sydney	12,760	Average Population	39,944
Total	123,848		
Average Population	13,761		

That demographic pattern also applied to counties in other states in the United States and other colonies in British North America. (See Table 7.3.)[27] In 1830, five states (Massachusetts, Maine, New Hampshire, Connecticut, and New York) had counties with populations that averaged over 30,000 people, all states where towns or ridings handled most of the day-to-day business of local government. Another five states, which also had strong systems of local government below the county level, had counties that averaged over 20,000 inhabitants, and a sixth, Rhode Island, was only a few hundred residents shy of an average of 20,000.[28] The states in which counties were the primary unit of local government tended to have smaller counties than in British North America, particularly states in the South; the average white population of counties in North Carolina, Virginia, South Carolina, and Georgia, all of which had been

TABLE 7.3 Comparison of County Sizes in British North America and the United States

British North America	No. Counties		Avg. Population		Total Population
Lower Canada	40	—	12,797	—	511,877
Upper Canada	27	—	11,633	—	322,203
New Brunswick	11	—	10,860	—	119,457
Nova Scotia	9	—	13,761	—	123,848

United States	No. Counties	Avg. Free Population	Avg. Total Population	Free Population	Total Population
Illinois	51		3,087		157,445
Missouri	32	3,605	4,389	115,364	140,455
Mississippi	26	2,729	5,255	70,962	136,621
Indiana	63		5,445		343,031
Louisiana	36	2,949	5,993	106,151	215,739
Georgia	76	3,938	6,800	299,292	516,823
Kentucky	83	6,298	8,288	522,704	687,917
Alabama	37	5,189	8,366	191,978	309,527
Virginia	111	6,682	10,914	741,648	1,211,405
Tennessee	62	8,715	10,998	540,300	681,903
North Carolina	64	7,694	11,531	492,386	737,987
Ohio	73		12,820		935,884
South Carolina	42	6,328	13,838	265,784	581,185
Rhode Island	5		19,440		97,199
Vermont	13		21,589		280,657
New Jersey	14		22,916		320,823
Maryland	19	22,792	23,528	433,046	447,040
Delaware	3	24,485	25,583	73,456	76,748
Pennsylvania	51		26,436		1,348,223
New Hampshire	8		33,666		269,328
New York	56		34,163		1,913,131
Connecticut	8		37,209		297,675
Maine	10		39,944		399,437
Massachusetts	14		43,601		610,408

former colonies, ranged between a high of 7,694 and a low of 3,938. (Those population figures nearly double when the African American population of slaves is included in the average, but the higher figures are not representative of the distribution of political power.)

In contrast, the British North American colonies (excluding Newfoundland and Prince Edward Island) had counties with average populations over 10,000 people: New Brunswick (10,860), Upper Canada (11,933), Lower Canada (12,797), and Nova Scotia (13,761). In short, the demographic evidence suggests that throughout most of the United States, local elites had significantly greater control over their local governments than did their counterparts in British North America. The British government had successfully diminished local power, enhanced the power of the provincial government, particularly the executive, and firmly linked it to the metropolitan government in the colonies that remained within the empire after 1783.

In Nova Scotia the Courts of Sessions handled most of the routine business of local government from the appointing of hog reeves to the licensing of tavern keepers, much of which would have been handled by town governments in New England. Courts of Sessions in Maine dealt with more singular aspects of local government, such as building county jails, acting on petitions for county roads, and apportioning the county revenue requests to all the towns and unincorporated townships. In Washington County, the Court of Sessions licensed retailers of liquor and inn holders, but the applications had been collected and vetted by town selectmen who submitted the license applications to the court.[29] It did not, however, become involved in the more pedestrian details of local life, such as the abatement of an individual's taxes or appointing town officers, both of which were central tasks of the Queens County Court of Sessions and occupied much of its time.[30]

The population density necessary to sustain the institutions of local government that provided routine public services through its own constituents, such as towns in New England, was smaller than the population density for institutions that provided more incidental services. Thus the unit of government electing fence viewers and overseers of the poor could be much smaller than the unit of government monitoring roads traversing more than one jurisdiction. In Nova Scotia, where administration of both the ordinary and extraordinary aspects of local government were combined in one institution, the county Court of Sessions, the size of the population served was larger than that served by most towns and smaller than that served by counties in Maine.

County size was not entirely insignificant in Maine. Initially Machias had been in Lincoln County, which stretched nearly two hundred miles as the crow flies up the long and indented Maine coast. On April 27, 1786, the town of Machias initiated a move to have the area from the Union River to the St. Croix River erected into a separate county. Massachusetts had already created a separate district for the registering of deeds with the registrar's office located in Machias. With Maine's population growing rapidly and Lincoln County covering a large and unwieldy territory, it was only a matter of time before a division occurred. To speed the proposal through the Massachusetts legislature, the town of Machias hired Boston merchant Caleb Davis to be its agent. They stated their wish and supplied him a "List of Suitable persons for Office in the proposed New County," most of whom were prominent men in Machias.[31] By 1789, the legislature authorized the division of Lincoln County into Lincoln, Hancock, and Washington counties, all three of which subsequently lost part of their northern tiers of townships to new counties. In the early nineteenth century, Washington County had its advocates for dividing the county into judicial districts. In 1819 and 1821, the towns of Eastport and Lubec petitioned the state to establish a Court of Common Pleas in their area, and both times the town of Machias fought and defeated it.[32]

The New England practice of dividing towns until they were quite small allowed powerful local factions to use the system to create towns that they controlled, a way for private interest to posture as public utility. Whitneyville, separately incorporated in 1845, was the village that grew up around the sawmill established by a group of Boston businessmen who had bought the undivided land from the proprietors in 1835.[33] Within ten years of purchase they petitioned for separate incorporation, a request for public autonomy from the town of Machias that matched their private interests. From the early years of colonization in the seventeenth century, New England towns existed in a gray zone between public inclusiveness and private exclusiveness. Kenneth Lockridge labeled seventeenth-century towns "closed corporate communities" because their membership was exclusive. Although some of the exclusivity of towns, manifested poignantly in their right to warn-out people, ended in the late eighteenth and early nineteenth centuries, the hiving off of new towns from old ones maintained the tension in town government between what was an extension of private desire and what was an expression of public need.[34]

The blurring of the public and private in towns derived, in part, from their corporate status. Corporations in the seventeenth and eighteenth centuries were bodies politic existing by royal or parliamentary grant to provide government, either "special or general." As the population of colonial Massachusetts diversified, it became necessary to define membership in towns more inclusively, as well as to remove town functions that had become incompatible with a town's inclusiveness. Often the services that were removed from a town's control or responsibility became the preserve of new corporate groups whose memberships were defined exclusively.[35] These new corporations were often given many of the privileges of towns, especially the right to tax their own members, sue and be sued, elect officers, and pass bylaws.

In colonial New England, land proprietorships were the most widespread manifestation of this tendency to create private corporations, but religious societies, proprietors of meetinghouses, turnpike corporations, banks, and an array of organizations with primarily economic purposes assumed some of the rights of bodies politic and mimicked the structure of incorporated towns.[36] In 1822, the proprietors of the east meetinghouse in Machias requested that the Maine legislature incorporate them, appealing in their petition to an 1818 Massachusetts law "Authorizing the Proprietors of Churches, Meeting Houses, and other Houses of Public Worship to regulate and manage their property and interests therein." The legislature incorporated them, but two years later the proprietors petitioned for a new incorporation arguing that the old one had been deficient and requesting that they be given "such priviledges & powers as are usually granted to similar associations." The legislature honored the request and in the second incorporation explicitly gave them powers similar to those of a town, in particular the right to levy taxes on their own members to pay for expenses.[37] Some corporations were given considerable power over individual members. Article three of the act to incorporate the Machias Congregational Society stated that a member had to join another religious society in order to be discharged, a restriction that three men unsuccessfully petitioned the legislature to strike in 1820.[38] The restriction on leaving religious societies was a reflection of the belief that all people had to belong to and financially support religious institutions. That power of religious societies blurred the boundaries between public and private, as did the powers of many corporations that flourished in postrevolutionary New England.[39] Significantly, Nova Scotia and the other post-1783 British North American colonies did not have a similar growth of corporations because of restrictions on incorporations that derived from both imperial policy and the Bubble Act, which Parliament passed in 1720 after the South Sea Bubble and extended to the colonies in 1741.[40]

The absence of town government in Nova Scotia engendered a sharp divergence with New England practices in the financing of local services. If we return to the lists of town officers in Table 7.1, the presence of school committees and school agents in Machias and East Machias and their absence on the Liverpool–Queens County list is a striking illustration of this shift. In Maine, towns were responsible for providing public education, and they elected committees and agents to hire teachers, maintain buildings, and generally manage school affairs. In Nova Scotia, the first serious attempt to provide for public education came with two pieces of legislation in 1811, but it was not until 1864 that legislation provided for a free school system. One of the 1811 acts provided for school trustees, who were selected for Queens County.

In 1818, at a Liverpool town meeting, the townspeople nominated trustees for the schools from whom the Court of Sessions made appointments. In 1820 the Queens County district of Herring Cove nominated trustees, as did the inhabitants of Guysborough township and Port Medway in 1821. In 1826, the Court of Sessions, in response to new legislation, defined the bounds of six school districts and required districts without trustees to submit names of nominees to the court the following year. The debates leading up to the 1826 legislation had included provisions to make general assessments to support education mandatory throughout Nova Scotia, but the proposal failed in the face of vehement opposition.

School trustees in Queens County did not serve one-year terms, but life terms or until they stepped down. As they had fewer financial resources at their disposal than did their counterparts in Machias, their primary function in the first half of the nineteenth century was to monitor the quality of the existing private or quasi-public schools in a district rather than oversee the provision of public education, which, as stated above, would not become available in Nova Scotia until 1864. Not surprisingly, the pattern in New Brunswick was similar with legislation passed in 1871 to provide for a free school system.[41]

The difference between Machias and Liverpool in the provision of education can be traced back to the role of town government in New England and its absence in Nova Scotia and then throughout post-1783 British North America. New England towns traditionally collected most taxes; the county, provincial, and then state governments were heavily dependent on towns to send in tax revenues. In colonial and early national Massachusetts neither the county nor the state were involved in the direct collection of taxes from the citizenry. The colony of Massachusetts derived some revenues from import and export duties, but relinquished control over those revenues with independence. At the conclusion of the Revolution when Massachusetts was struggling with an enormous war debt, it attempted to sell its unsettled lands, especially those in Maine, and to apportion larger assessments on the towns, which resisted paying them. For the most part, public revenues in New England were both collected and dispersed at the town level, and most of the taxes were used for local services, in particular for the support of the poor, a minister, education, and the building of roads.

The responsibility of towns for the provision of these services was reflected in the grants of both Machias and Liverpool. One share of land was reserved for the support of the schools, one for the support of the ministry, and one for the first settled minister. These provisions of land carried the expectation that the towns would assume responsibility for both the secular and spiritual education of the community. Land divisions also allowed for road easements, and New England practice provided for statutory labor for their construction and upkeep. The reservation of shares of land for the support of religion and education in the Nova Scotia townships granted to New Englanders, such as

Liverpool, indicates that provincial and metropolitan officials did not fully comprehend the impact that the proscription on town government would have on the ability or willingness of local jurisdictions to provide these services.

New Englanders moving to Nova Scotia took with them the idea that towns were both the source and dispenser of public revenues, only to discover that there would be no towns with taxing privileges, except to raise monies to support the poor. Rather than raise substantial sums at the county level, communities in Nova Scotia did without many services or paid for them privately. Support of ministers very quickly became privatized and remained so. Education became a private matter. Liverpool had schools and teachers, but they were supported through private subscription or tuition. Public roads were built using labor assessments, county revenues derived from license fees or provincial funds. Most highway repairs in Liverpool were financed with money from liquor license fees collected by the Court of Sessions. Tax revenues for support of the poor continued to be voted for at the township level, but were apportioned on the county's inhabitants through court-appointed assessors, and were a major expense of the county.[42]

Few financial records for Liverpool have survived, but those that do exist for 1829, 1830, 1832, and 1835 reveal a number of important details of taxation in early Liverpool.[43] (See Table 7.4.) First, most taxes were used for support of the poor, an average of 59 percent for the four years. Less than 20 percent of the tax revenues on average were used for general purposes, shown in the "County Rate" column. Second, the county rate and jail rate were assessed directly on the individual in Queens County, whereas in Washington County they would have been assessed by the county on the towns. Third, no county taxes were assessed specifically for schools, and most monies for roads came from license fees or provincial revenues, many of which were collected from duties on foreign trade collected at the colony's various ports of entry. In the United States, in contrast, duties on foreign trade were federal revenue and did not tend to find their way back into localities in the way the duties did in Nova Scotia.[44]

TABLE 7.4 Taxes for Liverpool, 1829–1835

Purpose	1829	1830	1832	1835[a]	4-Yr Avg
Poor rate (£)	150:0:0	175:0:0	190:0:0	175:0:0	—
% of total taxes	77.8	74.5	51.3	48.2	59
County Rate (£)	43	60	38:19:2	58:15:4	—
Jail Rate (£)	—	—	141:13:4	89:11:8	—
Total (£)	193:0:0	235:0:0	370:12:6	362:16:8	—
Avg. Tax/Person[b]	1s.2d	1s.5d	2s.3d	2s.3d	1s.9d

[a]Total includes £25 for a bear bounty and £14:6:8 for roads.
[b]Based on a population of 3,261.

Comparable figures for East Machias for the period 1826 to 1831 are given in Table 7.5.[45] The tax burden for East Machias was considerably higher than for Liverpool. The average per capita tax in East Machias for the six years was 6.9 times higher than the average per capita tax in Liverpool. The highway tax in East Machias, which accounted for approximately half of the tax burden, could be paid in labor, but factoring it out still left the cash tax value more than three times higher than Liverpool's. Schools and roads were the primary public goods people in Maine paid for at the local level and that people in Nova Scotia did not provide through local assessments. At the beginning of the nineteenth century, Governor John Wentworth began building roads in Nova Scotia that were financed from provincial revenues. Rural assemblymen discovered that they could manipulate the dispersal of funds and very quickly gained "almost complete control over the expenditures which concerned them most," in particular the road monies, a local dispersal of provincial patronage that had no seventeenth- or eighteenth-century British American precedent, but which persisted well into the nineteenth century in Nova Scotia.[46]

As the New England colonies, and then states, developed needs that involved more than one town, such as the establishment of a college or the building of turnpikes, they tended to create new corporations, or corporate-like entities, rather than provide them through the provincial government itself. The creation of corporations was particularly marked after the Revolution, when the states were no longer subject to the restrictions on incorporations deriving from the Bubble Act. That act was specifically intended to curb the creation of commercial corporations, but also reflected the attempt by the British government to check the centrifugal tendencies that rapid economic and colonial expansion had unleashed in the seventeenth and eighteenth centuries, much of it undertaken by incorporated ventures. In the new United

TABLE 7.5 Local Taxes for East Machias, 1826–1831

Purpose	1826	1827	1828	1829	1830	1831
Schools	300	300	300	300	300	426
Ministry	400	500[a]				
Town Officers	100	100	100	95	100	100
Contingencies	150	100	150	100	100	100
Poor Rate	200	200	300	50	200	200
Militia	50	50	25	25	25	25
Highways	1,000	1,000	1,200	700	1,000	1,000
County Roads			350	100	200	50
Poor House				100	112	
Burying Ground Fine						100
Total ($)	2,200	1,750	2,425	1,470	2,037	1,901
Estimate in £ (3$/£)[b]	733	583	808	490	679	634
Avg. Tax/Person	13s.9d	10s.11d	15s.2d	9s.2d	12s.9d	11s.10d

[a]Vote rescinded.

[b]The conversion rate is the one used in the town records.

States some leaders worried about the growth of corporations, which they recognized as reinforcing a tendency towards institutional localization and privatization rather than centralization. James Sullivan, while attorney general of Massachusetts, argued that the "creation of a great variety of corporate interests, in themselves powerful and important … weakens government."[47] In the nineteenth century, states learned how difficult it was to reverse that process, illustrated graphically in the Supreme Court case, Trustees of Dartmouth College v. Woodward, in which the court sided with the trustees that the legislature of New Hampshire could not change the college's charter. It effectively privatized that college and most other colleges that had been established in the colonial era.[48]

The concern of James Sullivan about the concentration of power in private corporations at the expense of state governments was similar to the concerns that the British government had long had about chartered or incorporated entities, including the colonies that rebelled. The British solution in new colonies was to limit incorporations of most kinds, but particularly municipal governments, which as we have seen in the case of Liverpool (and throughout Nova Scotia) resulted in a short-term decline in social services. But in the nineteenth century, when the pressure for services increased throughout British North America, the colonial governments introduced them as provincial-level initiatives with provincial-level oversight, funding, and regulation. What the case of Liverpool, and Nova Scotia more generally, suggests is that the centralization of the British imperial state at the provincial and local levels involved a dismantling of the social infrastructure before it could be reconstructed into a more centralized system.[49] What the case of Machias, and Massachusetts and Maine more generally, suggests is that state sanctioning of the divisions of townships into ever smaller units blurred the line between public and private power, and reinforced an ideology that state-level governments (and formerly colonial provincial-level governments) were to facilitate and protect, more than check, those local expressions and concentrations of power.

Conclusion
Divergent Structures of Power in the Anglo-Atlantic World

The six comparative cases in this study have shown that divergences in the kinds of political choices that people in Liverpool and Machias made were heavily conditioned by institutional changes made at higher levels of government and which local residents had little or no say in formulating. These changes were particularly marked in Nova Scotia: ownership of township land as tenants-in-common was prohibited; municipal governments were proscribed for decades; and localities had limited fiscal powers to provide services such as schools and roads. In eastern Maine, part of the older colony of Massachusetts, the British metropolitan government attempted similar changes, but there the provincial government could block the implementation of many changes or mitigate their impact. The refusal of the Crown to approve land grants in eastern Maine is one such case; in response the Massachusetts General Court enacted a number of compensatory measures, such as extending the time to get royal approbation of the grant.

Despite externally imposed changes, people in both Liverpool and Machias crafted their own local responses to them. In Machias, the settlers' acceptance of the trade boycotts after 1774, despite the hardships they engendered, contributed to the tensions that led to the capture of the *Margaretta* in June 1775. The unwillingness of Machias residents to support the petition for neutral status in 1781 was probably critical in making the area between the Penobscot and St. Croix Rivers part of the United States. In Liverpool, the proprietors' committee submitted disingenuous reports about the distribution of township lands to the provincial government. The need for the proprietors' committee to steward the undivided land perpetuated the committee's existence for two centuries despite the original intent of the provincial executive council that it should be short-lived. In both Machias and Liverpool people drew heavily on their New England heritage to craft adjustments, although in Machias they tended to be in concert with the provincial government, whereas in Liverpool they were locally devised adjustments. The proprietors of the meetinghouse were a New England institution, but their adjudication of the religious tensions in Liverpool was particular to the township and had no external legitimation. Similarly, the proprietors' committee in Liverpool incorporated New England practices, but its eventual powers were both an embellishment of New England practice and of Nova Scotian intentions and circumstances.

The discretion that people in Liverpool and Machias exercised in implementing various policies tended to fit within, rather than challenge, parameters of permissible action set by the provincial level of government. That tendency was normative rather than exceptional, in both New England and Nova Scotia. The most marked local exception was the rebellion in Cumberland, Nova Scotia, but even that rebellion was imported as much as it was indigenous. If the divergences between Liverpool and Machias that this study has documented were both normative within their own jurisdictional contexts, rather than one being normative and the other being anomalous or one being the norm from which the other diverged, then we can say that they illustrate two primary ways of structuring governmental power in the Anglo-Atlantic world: one associated with the colonies that rebelled and another associated with the colonies that remained within the Empire. Thus what remains to be done is to describe the macro-level differences in these two distinct ways of structuring governmental power that had developed in British America in the early modern era.

From the founding of the Massachusetts Bay Colony in 1629 and 1630 to the passage of the Massachusetts Government Act in 1774, metropolitan officials had been anxious about the ways in which New Englanders devolved power onto towns. Officials believed that changes in local government, particularly in Massachusetts, would alleviate many of the problems associated with governing colonies, and at various times they challenged the rights and privileges of New England towns. In the seventeenth century, royal officials questioned the legality of towns owning undivided lands, which precipitated the creation of land proprietorships. When Nova Scotia received a British government after the conquest of Acadia in 1710, instructions to governors emphasized that the colony was to have a county system of local government like that of Virginia, rather than town governments like the neighboring New England colonies. When thousands of New Englanders moved to Nova Scotia in the 1760s, they learned how earnest the Board of Trade was about the proscription on town governments.[1] After the Boston Tea Party in December 1773, Parliament passed four pieces of legislation to punish and restrain Massachusetts. One of the Coercive Acts was the Massachusetts Government Act, which included a provision limiting towns to one meeting a year, an attempt to make them little more than administrative units of the provincial government rather than semiautonomous bodies politic.[2]

According to this metropolitan logic, people in Nova Scotia and Virginia, both with county systems of local government, would have had more in common than had people in Nova Scotia and Massachusetts or Massachusetts and Virginia. That logic contributed to the serious misjudgment of Parliament when it passed the Coercive Acts in 1774. Rather than punishing and isolating Massachusetts from the other colonies, as Parliament intended, it brought most of them into common cause. Delegates from New England to the Carolinas gathered for the first Continental Congress in September 1774 to formulate a concerted response to this newest, and intentionally punitive, round of parliamentary legislation. Significantly, Nova Scotia did not send delegates, and generally it has been argued that the colony's residents were intimidated by the British officials governing the colony. Although there may be some truth to this position, the single event of Nova Scotia not participating in the Continental Congress is yet another discrete instance of Nova Scotia's divergence from what is often perceived to be normative British American behavior. But rather than judging each discrete divergence separately, they need to be examined as a group that can explain another pattern of British American behavior on its own terms rather than as a deviation or an anomaly.

The Anglo-Atlantic controversy that led to the independence of thirteen colonies turned on the question of the role of Parliament in the Empire. Two elements of the debate are significant for our purposes. The first concerns the jurisdictional definition of colonies and the second the jurisdictional reach of Parliament. The most narrow definition of colonies was that they were little more than municipal corporations, a position espoused by some metropolitan observers. Most British Americans, in contrast, contended that the colonies were autonomous dominions of the Crown with their own assemblies modeled on Parliament. According to this colonial line of reasoning, which had a considerable body of precedent to substantiate it, the internal governance of any colony was the preserve of a colony's provincial government, and the most important provincial-level institution was the assembly.[3] While Parliament could legislate for the mutual concerns of British subjects in the extra-European world, such as transatlantic navigation, colonial assemblies legislated on matters internal to the colonies. Various permutations of this debate can be traced back to the early seventeenth century, though until the 1760s the negotiations between colonies and the metropole had largely revolved around the balance between prerogative powers of royal officials in the colonies and the rights and privileges of colonists.[4] Parliamentary legislation, beginning with the Sugar Act in 1764, was perceived by many colonists as a new and dangerous twist in a long-standing struggle over the distribution of power between colonial governments and the metropolitan government.

In this ongoing controversy, the provincial governments of the colonies, and particularly the assemblies, served both as buffers against metropolitan intrusions and as enablers of local authorities, whether at the county or town level. In this structure of power, most provincial governments were not so much one level in a hierarchy of power reaching from Whitehall and Westminster to the colonies, but rather horizontal barriers against strong vertical linkages of power. Over time, the practice of provincial governments serving as barriers against metropolitan intrusions assumed both institutional and ideological expression. We can see this formulation of power operating in the case of Machias. When the Crown refused to approve the thirteen grants in the Territory of Sagadahoc, the General Assembly treated that refusal as a temporary and unwarranted exercise of prerogative power. It could not override the Crown's decision, but it could and did enact a wide range of interim measures that allowed settlers a modicum of security for their land claims and the rudiments of self-government through their proprietorships.

By the 1760s, one of the important commonalities, or convergences, among most of the mainland colonies was the sensibility that provincial governments should serve as a barrier against prerogative, and later parliamentary, intrusions and should enable and then protect local rights of self-government. Colonists from New England to the Carolinas, as well as some in the island colonies, had no difficulty in mustering both constitutional and ideological arguments to defend this formulation about the function of provincial-level governments in British America.[5] Although there were fairly substantial institutional variations among provincial governments, there had nonetheless emerged a fairly substantial constitutional and ideological convergence about the idea of provincial autonomy.[6] Hence in the years after the Seven Years' War, when the Ministry and Parliament passed legislation that challenged those beliefs, colonists from New England to the Carolinas could agree to concert their protests and resistance. The rhetoric Machias residents used when explaining their support of the American Revolution indicates how deeply into society those attitudes resonated in most of the British North American colonies.[7]

Nova Scotia lay outside that constitutional and ideological formulation of provincial governments. Its government was largely the result of metropolitan initiatives, both by the Ministry and by Parliament, in quite stark contrast to the origins of most other provincial governments in companies or proprietorships, notwithstanding the subsequent royalization of most of them. Between the conquest of Acadia/Nova Scotia in 1710 and the 1748 British decision to build Halifax as the colony's capital and the northern American port for the Royal Navy, the colony had a feeble provincial government. The vast majority of its residents were either French Catholic Acadians or Mi'kmaq. People from neither group could legally hold public office, if they had wished, because they were not Protestants, nor were they clearly recognized as British subjects. The colony had little money, because it lacked residents who could be taxed and a mechanism to raise adequate taxes, even after the Acadians swore an oath of allegiance.[8]

In 1748 Parliament allocated monies to build Halifax and to fund a more robust provincial government. Some money was used to recruit Protestant settlers from Germany, Switzerland, and France; other funds subsidized the settlement of New Englanders in the 1760s. When merchants in Halifax failed to persuade Governor Charles Lawrence to convene an assembly, they appealed to the Board of Trade, which insisted to Lawrence that the colony would have an assembly, which first met in October 1758. In Nova Scotia, a functioning provincial government was the intentional construction of the metropolitan government. Consequently, rather than serving as a barrier against metropolitan intrusions, it became part of an interconnected system of power reaching from Whitehall and Westminster to settlements such as Liverpool. While residents of Nova Scotia recognized the difference, they were not simply obsequious subjects. They agitated for an assembly. They documented the glaring inadequacies of Governor Francis Legge and petitioned for his removal. Assembly members drafted a petition to Parliament in 1775 recommending a plan for the colonies to contribute financially to the running of the Empire.[9]

In the case of Nova Scotia, the configuration of power among the metropolitan, provincial, and local governments was vertically linked and made the colony a province within an empire. In contrast, the provincial governments of the colonies that rebelled had weaker and more contested vertical linkages with the metropolitan government, and colonists in them insisted they were not so much provinces within an empire, but discrete overseas provinces of the Crown. As well, they had a deep ideological suspicion of the metropolitan government's interest in creating those linkages, whether to Massachusetts, Nova Scotia, or any other British American colony.

Again, we can go back to the cases of Machias and Liverpool and see how those differences in the constructions of power manifested themselves at the local level. By 1850, the original township of Machias had been divided into five separately incorporated towns. In contrast, the original township of Liverpool had never been divided, although it had a number of distinct communities, including Milton, Port Medway, Brooklyn, and Berlin. As was shown in Chapter 7, the fragmenting of local governments, whether town or county, was common throughout the United States. The pressure to make local governments conform to the power base of local elites blurred the boundaries between public and private power and tended to keep the vertical integration between local and state governments weak. Most public services were provided through local governments, thus creating a great range of quality. That practice also conditioned an ideology of localism.

In contrast, until the 1830s, the basic unit of local government in Nova Scotia, and throughout post-1783 British North America, was counties that averaged larger populations than comparable units of government in the United States, whether towns or county. The sharp curtailment of local taxing privileges meant that over time residents in Nova Scotia lost what ideological commitment to the local provision of services they might have had. By the end of the eighteenth century the restrictions on local taxation appear to have reduced the number of services available in Nova Scotia in comparison to New England, most notably in the area of education. In the long run, those changes seem to have made Nova Scotians, and British North Americans more generally, more receptive to provincial-level discretion in how services would be provided. The commitment in the United States to local, if not private, control was also observable in the years after the American Revolution in the rapid and widespread alienation of public lands, whereas the British North American colonies retained a much higher percentage of Crown lands.

Beginning in the 1750s, many observers of the North American colonies, such as Archibald Kennedy, William Smith, and Thomas Pownall, began to advocate greater coordination among the colonies and between Britain and the colonies.[10] At the Albany Congress in 1754, Benjamin Franklin proposed a plan for union that the colonies rejected because they would give up too much power and the metropolitan government rejected because greater unity among the colonies would give them more power.[11] As the imperial crisis deepened in the 1760s and 1770s, many elite Loyalists fruitlessly tried to convince their fellow colonists to consider a more federal imperial system, although it is not clear that metropolitan authorities would have accepted such a plan. Many of these Loyalists, like the assembly in Nova Scotia when it drafted its 1775 petition on imperial reform, were far from obsequious sycophants to metropolitan dictates. Indeed, many expressed frustration at the seeming inability of the Ministry and Parliament to think creatively, rather than condescendingly, if not punitively, about colonial needs. Rather what often distinguished them from revolutionaries was that they had a different vision of how the linkages of power within the British Atlantic world might be configured and they were ideologically committed to working within a system with greater vertical linkages.[12] The revolutionaries, however, were more ideologically opposed to such a structure of power, and more committed to preserving and protecting local expressions of power.

In this sense, the American Revolution was a war against the extension of a modern bureaucratic state into the oldest colonies of British North America, while the newer colonies were willing to accept the idea of a more integrated imperial state, in part because they were products of it.[13] Ironically, in the

1780s, the newly independent Americans discovered that the states were too weakly coordinated under the Articles of Confederation and that the United States needed a stronger federal system. The Constitution of 1787 remedied the greatest institutional weaknesses of the earlier constitution, but it could not eliminate the deeply entrenched ideological mindset that suggested that provincial-/state-level governments were to function as barriers against a higher level of government, as well as enable and protect local governments. Consequently, in the United States political debates continued to revolve around the question of whether a strong federal government is necessary. In contrast, in British North America, and later Canada, political debates tended to begin from a premise of a strong state and thus to turn on questions of how power should be distributed within it and what its basic responsibilities should be. The origins of those significant ideological differences can be traced back to institutional reforms that the British government attempted to implement overseas in the seventeenth and eighteenth centuries. Resistance to those reforms in the colonies established in the seventeenth century and their implementation in colonies acquired in the eighteenth century created imperial fault lines that influenced the daily lives of people in places like Liverpool, Nova Scotia, and Machias, Maine, as well as shaped the long-term political geography of North America, if not the English-speaking world more generally.

Notes

Introduction

1. On social convergence see Jack P. Greene, *Pursuits of Happiness: The Social Development of Early Modern British Colonies and the Formation of American Culture* (Chapel Hill: University of North Carolina Press, 1988). On cultural convergence see T.H. Breen, "The Baubles of Britain: The American and Consumer Revolutions of the Eighteenth Century," *Past and Present* 119 (May 1988): 73–104. On ideological convergence see Bernard Bailyn, *The Ideological Origins of the American Revolution* (Cambridge, MA: Harvard University Press, 1967). On constitutional convergence see Jack P. Greene, *Peripheries and Center: Constitutional Development in the Extended Polities of the British Empire and the United States, 1607 –1788* (Athens: University of Georgia Press, 1986); and idem, "Metropolis and Colonies: Changing Patterns of Constitutional Conflict in the Early Modern British Empire, 1607–1763," in *Negotiated Authorities: Essays in Colonial Political and Constitutional History* (Charlottesville: University Press of Virginia, 1994), 43–77.
2. For analyses of divergences within the British Empire, see Elizabeth Mancke, "Another British America: A Canadian Model for the Early Modern British Empire," *Journal of Imperial and Commonwealth History* 25 (1997), 1–36; and idem "Negotiating an Empire: British and Its Overseas Peripheries, c.1550–1780," in *Negotiated Empires: Centers and Peripheries in the New World, 1500–1820*, eds. Christine Daniels and Michael V. Kennedy (New York: Routledge, 2002), 235–265.
3. Louis Hartz, *The Liberal Tradition in America: An Interpretation of American Political Thought Since the Revolution* (New York: Harcourt, Brace and World, 1955); and idem, ed., *The Founding of New Societies: Studies in the History of the United States, Latin America, South Africa, and Canada* (New York: Harcourt, Brace and World, 1964), and Kenneth D. McRae, "The Structure of Canadian History," in ibid., 219–274.
4. Kenneth D. McRae, "The Structure of Canadian History," in L. Hartz, ed., *The Founding of New Societies*, 219–274; Gad Horowitz, "Conservatism, Liberalism, and Socialism in Canada: An Interpretation," *Canadian Journal of Economics and Political Science* 32 (1966), 143–171; Gordon T. Stewart, *The Origins of Canadian Politics: A Comparative Approach* (Vancouver: University of British Columbia Press, 1986); and the essays in Janet Ajzenstat and Peter J. Smith, eds., *Canada's Origins: Liberal, Tory, or Republican?* (Ottawa: Carleton University Press, 1985).
5. One of the most persistent examiners of the differences between the United States and Canada, and who works in the Hartzian tradition, is the sociologist Seymour Martin Lipset; see *Continental Divide: The Values and Institutions of the United States and Canada* (Washington, DC: Canadian American Committee, 1989); and *American Exceptionalism: A Double-Edged Sword* (New York: Norton, 1996), 77–109.

6. See, for example, John Herd Thompson and Stephen J. Randall, *Canada and the United States: Ambivalent Allies*, 3d ed. (Athens: University of Georgia Press, 2002), 3, 9–14; Reginald C. Stuart, *United States Expansionism and British North America, 1775–1871* (Chapel Hill: University of North Carolina Press, 1988), 3–27; and Gordon T. Stewart, *The American Response to Canada Since 1776* (East Lansing: Michigan State University Press, 1992).

7. For example, see Theda Skocpol, *States and Social Revolutions: A Comparative Analysis of France, Russia, and China* (Cambridge: Cambridge University Press, 1979); and Thomas Ertman, *Birth of the Leviathan : Building States and Regimes in Medieval and Early Modern Europe* (Cambridge: Cambridge University Press, 1997).

8. For two excellent studies of transnational local comparisons see John W. Cole and Eric R. Wolf, *The Hidden Frontier: Ecology and Ethnicity in an Alpine Valley* (New York: Academic, 1974); and Peter Sahlins, *Boundaries: The Making of France and Spain in the Pyrenees* (Berkeley: University of California Press, 1989).

9. For an institutional examination of political differences that challenges the Hartzian approach see Elizabeth Mancke, "Early Modern Imperial Governance and the Origins of Canadian Political Culture," *Canadian Journal of Political Science/Revue canadienne de science politique* 32, 1 (1999): 3–20.

10. Mancke, "Another British America," 1–36; and idem, "Negotiating an Empire," 235–265.

11. Michael J. Braddick, "The English Government, War, Trade, and Settlement, 1625–1688," in Nicholas Canny, ed., *The Oxford History of the British Empire, Vol. 1, The Origins of Empire: British Overseas Enterprise to the Close of the Seventeenth Century* (Oxford: Oxford University Press, 1998), 286–308; and Elizabeth Mancke and John G. Reid, "Elites, States, and the Imperial Contest for Acadia," in Reid et al., *The 'Conquest' of Acadia, 1710: Imperial, Colonial, and Aboriginal Constructions* (Toronto: University of Toronto Press, 2003), 25–47.

12. Elizabeth Mancke, "Chartered Enterprises and the Evolution of the British Atlantic World," in Elizabeth Mancke and Carole Shammas, eds., *The Creation of the British Atlantic World* (Baltimore: Johns Hopkins University Press, 2005).

13. Greene, "Metropolis and Colonies," 43–77; idem, "Political Mimesis: A Consideration of the Historical and Cultural Roots of Legislative Behavior in the British Colonies in the Eighteenth Century," *American Historical Review* 75 (1969): 337–367; and idem, "The Role of the Lower Houses of Assembly in Eighteenth-Century Politics," *Journal of Southern History* 27 (1961): 451–474.

14. Mancke, "Early Modern Imperial Governance," 14–16.

15. Mancke, "Another British America," 1–5; and Mancke, "Early Modern Imperial Governance, 8–13.

16. John Brewer, *The Sinews of Power: War, Money, and the English State, 1688–1783* (London and Boston: Unwin, 1989).

Chapter 1

1. Geoffrey Plank, *An Unsettled Conquest: The British Campaign Against the Peoples of Acadia* (Philadelphia: University of Pennsylvania Press, 2001), 140–157; Stephen E. Patterson, "1744–1763: Colonial Wars and Aboriginal Peoples," in Phillip A. Buckner and John G. Reid, eds., *The Atlantic Region to Confederation: A History* (Toronto: University of Toronto Press, 1994), 125–155; and Fred Anderson, *Crucible of War: The Seven Years' War and the Fate of Empire in British North America, 1754–1766* (New York: Knopf, 2000), 112–114.

2. William C. Wicken, *Mi'kmaq Treaties on Trial: History, Land, and Donald Marshall Junior* (Toronto: University of Toronto Press, 2002), 191–209; Daniel N. Paul, *We Were Not the Savages: A Micmac Perspective on the Collision of European and Aboriginal Civilizations* (Halifax: Nimbus, 1993), 120–147; L.F.S. Upton, *Micmacs and Colonists: Indian–White Relations in the Maritimes, 1713–1867* (Vancouver: University of British Columbia Press, 1979), 57–60; and Emerson W. Baker and John G. Reid, "Amerindian Power in the Early Modern Northeast: A Reappraisal," *William and Mary Quarterly*, 3d ser., 61 (2004): 77–106; and John G. Reid, "*Pax Britannica* or *Pax Indigena*? Planter Nova Scotia and Competing Strategies of Pacification," *Canadian Historical Review* 85 (December 2004).

3. Petition of Thomas Westgatt and others, 3 October 1763, *Documentary History of the State of Maine* (hereafter *DHMe*), James P. Baxter, ed., 24 vols. (Portland: Maine Historical Society, 1889–1916), 13:315–316; Petition to the General Court of Massachusetts, November term 1759, *DHMe*, 13:180–581. For similar expressions see the petition of Ebenezer Thorndike and others, 2 January 1762, *DHMe*, 13:242–243; and Petition of a Number of Soldiers, 1 April 1761, *DHMe*, 13:232–233. Speech by T. Pownall to the General Court, 2 January 1760, *DHMe*, 13:199; Jeremy Belknap, *The History of New Hampshire*, 2 vols. (Boston, 1784–1792), 2:283–284, 302–314; Proclamation by Governor Lawrence, 12 October 1758, Nova Scotia Archives and Records Management (hereafter NSARM), RG 1, Vol. 188, No. 30–32.

4. Graeme Wynn, "A Province Too Much Dependent on New England," *Canadian Geographer/ Le Geographe Canadien* 31, 2 (1987): 100; Bernard Bailyn, *Voyagers to the West: A Passage in the Peopling of America on the Eve of the Revolution* (New York: Knopf, 1988), 10. The estimate is based on the figures in Robert V. Wells, *The Population of the British Colonies in America Before 1776: A Survey of Census Data* (Princeton, NJ: Princeton University Press, 1975), 69–89. In 1767 NH's population was 52,700, in 1764 MA's was 245,698, in 1762 CT's was 145,590, and in 1774 RI's was 59,670 or approximately 500,000 for New England ca. 1765. Using Wells's sex and age ratios, half were male, and half the males were between the ages of sixteen and sixty, or approximately 125,000 adult men.

5. Machias Grant, Act of the House of Representatives, 4 April 1770, Commonwealth of Massachusetts Archives (hereafter CMaA), Vol. 118:446; Liverpool Grant, 1 September 1759, NSARM, MG 100, Vol. 176, No. 26Q.

6. Nova Scotia Census 1767, NSARM, RG 1, Vol. 443, No. 1; Wynn, "A Province Too Much Dependent on New England," 100; J. Potter, "The Growth of Population in America, 1700–1860," in *Population in History: Essays in Historical Demography*, D.V. Glass and D.E.C. Eversley, eds. (Chicago: Aldine, 1965), 638–639; J.M. Bumsted, "1763–1783: Resettlement and Rebellion," in *The Atlantic Region to Confederation*, 162–165; and Charles E. Clark, *The Eastern Frontier: The Settlement of Northern New England, 1610–1763* (New York: Knopf, 1970), 354.

7. Kenneth Lockridge, "Land, Population and the Evolution of New England Society 1630–1790," *Past and Present* 39 (1968): 62–80; Darrett B. Rutman, "People in Process: The New Hampshire Towns of the Eighteenth Century," *Journal of Urban History* 1, 3 (1975): 268–292; William D. Williamson, *The History of the State of Maine*, 2 vols. (1832; rpt., Freeport, ME: The Cumberland Press, n.d.), 2:364–365; Catherine Fox, "The Great Fire in the Woods: A Case Study in Ecological History" (M.A. thesis, University of Maine, 1984), 30 and passim; Jamie H. Eves, "The Acquisition of Wealth, or of a Comfortable Subsistence: The Census of 1800 and the Yankee Migration to Maine, 1760–1825," *Maine History* 35 (1995): 6–25.

8. Jean Daigle and Robert LeBlanc, "Acadian Deportation and Return," in R. Cole Harris, ed., *The Historical Atlas of Canada, Vol. 1, From the Beginning to 1800* (hereafter *HAC*) (Toronto: University of Toronto Press, 1987), Plate 30; N.E.S. Griffiths, *The Acadian Deportation: Deliberate Perfidy or Cruel Necessity?* (Toronto: Copp Clark, 1969); idem, "The Acadians of the British Seaports," *Acadiensis* 4, 1 (1976): 67–84; Jean Daigle, "Acadia, 1604–1763: An Historical Synthesis," in *The Acadians of the Maritimes: Thematic Studies*, Jean Daigle, ed. (Moncton, NB: Centre d'étude acadiennes, 1982), 43–46; and Plank, *An Unsettled Conquest*, 140–157.

9. J. Hector St. John de Crèvecoeur, *Letters from an American Farmer* (New York: Dutton, [1912]), 42–43.

10. How New England influenced Nova Scotia has been variously interpreted. For the older arguments, see John Bartlet Brebner, *New England's Outpost: Acadia Before the Conquest of Canada* (1927, rpt. New York: Burt Franklin, 1973); and George A. Rawlyk, *Nova Scotia's Massachusetts: A Study of Massachusetts–Nova Scotia Relations, 1630–1784* (Montreal: McGill–Queen's University Press, 1973). For more recent interpretations see Plank, *An Unsettled Conquest*, 10–39; and Mark Power Robinson, "Maritime Frontiers: The Evolution of Empire in Nova Scotia, 1713–1758" (Ph.D. diss, University of Colorado, 2000).

11. Elizabeth Mancke, "Imperial Transitions," in Reid et al., *The 'Conquest' of Acadia, 1710*, 178–202.

12. Winthrop P. Bell, *The Foreign Protestants and the Settlement of Nova Scotia: The History of a Piece of Arrested British Colonial Policy in the Eighteenth Century* (Toronto: University of Toronto Press, 1961); and Kenneth S. Paulsen, "Settlement and Ethnicity in Lunenburg, Nova Scotia, 1753–1800: A History of the Foreign-Protestant Community" (Ph.D. diss., University of Maine, 1996).

13. D.C. Harvey, ed., "Governor Lawrence's Case Against an Assembly in Nova Scotia," *Canadian Historical Review* 13, 2 (1932): 184–194; and Brebner, *New England's Outpost*, 133–143.

14. Proclamation, 11 January 1759, NSARM, RG 1, Vol. 188, No. 39–44.

15. Brebner, *New England's Outpost*, 73, 136–137, 239; and Report of Charles Morris and Richard Bulkeley, October 1763, NSARM, RG 1, Vol. 222.

16. The interpretation of the 1759 proclamation has been a source of discussion for over 200 years. New Englanders in the 1760s misunderstood it. Thomas Haliburton, an early-nineteenth-century Nova Scotian historian, erroneously called it the "Charter of Nova Scotia," although no charter obligations were made in it; see Gordon Stewart and George Rawlyk, '*A People Highly Favoured of God': The Nova Scotia Yankees and the American Revolution* (Toronto: Macmillan of Canada, 1972), 15–16, 21.

17. Report of H.M.'s Attorney and Solicitor General, 29 April 1755; Letter from Governor Lawrence to the Lords of Trade, 8 December 1755; and Extract from a Letter of the Lords of Trade to Governor Lawrence, 25 March 1755, in "Establishment of the House of Assembly of Nova Scotia, 1758," Appendix C, *Report*, 1956, Public Archives of Nova Scotia (Halifax, 1957), 22, 24, 26.

18. Leonard Woods Labaree, ed., *Royal Instructions to British Colonial Governors, 1670–1776*, 2 vols. (1935; rpt., New York: Octagon, 1967), 2:540, 537–541.

19. Liverpool Grant, 1 September 1759, NSARM, MG 100, Vol. 176, No. 26Q. For examples of Massachusetts grants see *DHMe*, 13:322–330 and 14:80–82.

20. John Frederick Martin, *Profits in the Wilderness: Entrepreneurship and the Founding of New England Towns in the Seventeenth Century* (Chapel Hill: University of North Carolina Press, 1991), 9–45; and Lillian F. Gates, *Land Policies of Upper Canada* (Toronto: University of Toronto Press, 1968), 6–7, 30–32.

21. Board of Trade to Belcher, 12 December 1760, CO 2/8/6, 2–4, NSARM, MF 13953.

22. Martin, *Profits in the Wilderness*, 257–280. See also Roy Hidemichi Akagi, *The Town Proprietors of the New England Colonies: A Study of Their Development, Organization, Activities and Controversies, 1620–1770* (1924; rpt., Gloucester, MA: Peter Smith, 1963). For evidence on the prevalence of copying, see Labaree, ed., *Royal Instructions*, passim.

23. Order in Council, 15 August 1761, NSARM, RG 1, Vol. 211, No. 210; Memorial from Peleg Coffin, et al., 8 July 1762, NSARM, RG 1, Vol. 211, Nos. 250–251. D.C. Harvey cites this petition as evidence of concerns about town government, although the incident that provoked the memorial was the appointment of a proprietors' appointment and not town officers. Cf. Stewart and Rawlyk, '*A People Highly Favoured of God*', 17–20. For a useful discussion of towns and New Englanders' ideas of corporate rights see Martin, *Profits in the Wilderness*, 267–293; and Oscar Handlin and Mary Flug Handlin, *Commonwealth, A Study of the Role of Government in the American Economy: Massachusetts, 1774–1861*, rev. ed. (Cambridge, MA: Harvard University Press, 1969), 92.

24. Report of Charles Morris and Richard Bulkeley, October 1763, NSARM, RG 1, Vol. 222; and Dominick Graham, "Charles Lawrence," in *Dictionary of Canadian Biography* (hereafter *DCB*), Vol. 3, *1741–1770* (Toronto: University of Toronto Press, 1974), 361–366.

25. D.C. Harvey, "The Struggle for New England Township Government in Nova Scotia," *Canadian Historical Association Report* (1933), 18; Council Minutes, 28 October 1766, NSARM, RG 1, Vol. 212, No. 21.

26. A List of the Proprietors of the Township of Liverpool [1761], NSARM, RG 20, Series C, Box 43, doc. 1; Nova Scotia Population, 29 October 1763, NSARM, C. B. Ferguson Collection, Box 1897, F 2/3; Grant of Liverpool, 20 November 1764, NSARM, MG 4, Vol. 77.

27. Margaret Ells, "Clearing the Decks for the Loyalists," *Canadian Historical Association Report* (1933), 47.

28. Grant to John Godfrey et al., 5 January 1771, NSARM, MG 4, Vol. 77; Return of the Township of Liverpool, 19 March 1784, NSARM, MG 4, Vol. 77.

29. Instructions for an unspecified person from Richard Bulkeley [1759], NSARM, RG 1, Vol. 163, doc. 173; Council Minutes, Questions asked by the men from Connecticut and Rhode Island, 18 April and 17–18 May 1759, NSARM, RG 1, Vol. 188, 53–64; Council Minutes, 30 November 1759, NSARM. RG 1, Vol. 188, 112; and J.B. Brebner, *The Neutral Yankees of Nova Scotia: A Marginal Colony During the Revolutionary Years* (1937, rpt. New York: Russell & Russell, 1970), 31–32.

30. Sailing Orders for S. Cobb, Halifax, 19 April 1760, NSARM, RG 1, Vol. 165, docs. 52–53. See also NSARM, RG 1, Vol. 165, docs. 3, 19, 26, 36, 64, 70–71, 80–82, 90–91, 127, 184; and NSARM, RG 1, Vol. 163, docs. 161, 169, 164; and Phyllis R. Blakeley, "Silvanus Cobb," in *DCB*, Vol. 3, *1741–1770*, 128–130.

31. Letter from Richard Bulkeley to John Dogget, 29 October 1760, NSARM, RG 1, Vol. 136, 2; Council Minutes, 4 March and 14 April 1761, NSARM, RG 1, Vol. 204, docs. 163, 173; Council Minutes, 22 May 1761 and 31 December 1762, NSARM, RG 1, Vol. 211, docs. 192, 288; Report on the Counties of Nova Scotia, October 1763, NSARM, RG 1, Vol. 22.

32. Mancke, "Another British America," 1–36.

33. Richard Maxwell Brown, *The South Carolina Regulators* (Cambridge, MA: Harvard University Press, 1963); Jack P. Greene, *The Quest for Power: The Lower Houses of Assembly in the Southern Royal Colonies, 1689–1776* (Chapel Hill: University of North Carolina Press, 1963), 380–387, 399–437; and Michael Bellesiles, *Revolutionary Outlaws: Ethan Allen and the Struggle for Independence on the Early American Frontier* (Charlottesville: University Press of Virginia, 1993), 25–51; "Charter of Massachusetts, 7 October 1691," In *The Glorious Revolution in Massachusetts: Selected Doucments, 1689–1692*, Robert Earle Moody and Richard Clive Simmons, eds. (Boston: The Colonial Society of Massachusetts, 1988), 617.

34. Fox, "The Great Fire in the Woods," 30–49. The first mill at Machias was sketched by J.F.W. Des Barres in his *Atlantic Neptune* (London, 1776). See Paul E. Rivard, *Maine Sawmills* (Augusta, ME: Maine State Museum, 1990), 39.

35. The Proprietors' Book of Records of Machias, copy of the original in the Washington County Court House, Machias, Maine, 3; Petition of Machias Inhabitants for a Township Grant, 4 June 1767, CMaA, Vol. 118: 290–291; Petition of the Inhabitants of Machias for a Grant, 7 January 1768, CMaA, Vol. 118: 314–316; Act of the House of Representatives, 4 April 1770, CMaA, Vol. 118:446.

36. Williamson, *The History of the State of Maine*, 2:509.

37. For the 1762 defense by Massachusetts of its claim to the land between the Penobscot and St. Croix Rivers, see *DHMe*, 13:296–302.

38. Mancke, "Chartered Enterprises and the Evolution of the British Atlantic World."

39. Grant to S. Waldo and others, 6 March 1762, *DHMe*, 13:264–266. Notably, land claims west of the Penobscot River were only gradually resolved in the late eighteenth and early nineteenth centuries. For an analysis of these land conflicts see Alan Taylor, *Liberty Men and Great Proprietors: The Revolutionary Settlement on the Maine Frontier, 1760–1820* (Chapel Hill: University of North Carolina Press, 1990); and Gordon E. Kershaw, *The Kennebeck Proprietors, 1749–1775* (Portland: Maine Historical Society, 1975).

40. In *DHMe*, 13:308–311.

41. Gov. Bernard to the Lords Commissioners, 25 April 1763, *DHMe*, 13:311–315.

42. There are numerous letters by Hutchinson to the Board of Trade concerning affairs downeast and his actions in signing the grant for the township of Machias. Some of the more important are found in CMaA, Vol. 26: 493–494 and Vol. 27: 26, 57–61, 79.

43. The Proprietors' Records of Machias, 1–4.

44. Grant to Paul Thorndike & others, 27 January 1764, *DHMe*, 13:322–330; Petition for Extension of Grant, 6 June 1766, *DHMe*, 13:445–446; Petition of the Proprietors of Townships Number Four, Five, & Six, 12 June 1765, *DHMe*, 13:412–414; The courses and Boundaries of the High Marsh Lots in the Township of Machias, The Proprietors' Records of Machias, n.p., back of book.

45. James S. Leamon, *Revolution Downeast: The War for American Independence in Maine* (Amherst: University of Massachusetts Press, 1993), 104–134, 174–181.

46. Memorial and Petition of a number of the Inhabitants of Machias, 27 January 1779, *DHMe*, 16:168–170; Original Grantees of the Township of Machias, [1779], *DHMe*, 16:148; Settlers in Machias and not in the Original Grant, [1779], *DHMe*, 16:149; Proprietors' Book of Machias, 24–31; see Chapter 3 for a further discussion of nonproprietors in Machias.

47. The 1784 petitions for land in Lincoln County are found in the CMaA, Eastern Land Papers, Box 14.
48. Bucks Harbor Petition, CMaA, Eastern Land Papers, Box 14; a Deed for Plantation No. 22, Registry of Deeds, Washington County Court House, Machias, Maine, Vol. 1: 129–131.
49. Chandler's River Petition, CMaA, Eastern Lands Papers, Box 14; and Letter from Joseph Pierpont to Caleb Davis, 10 November 1791, Caleb Davis Papers, MHS, Vol. 17.
50. Report of the Commissioners on Machias, 12 September 1771, *DHMe*, 14:137; for these sentiments see the petitions from Plantation Nos. 4, 6, and the back section of 6, CMaA, Eastern Lands Papers, Box 14.
51. On Halifax's increasing dominance in Nova Scotia's trade, see Lewis R. Fischer, "Revolution without Independence: The Canadian Colonies, 1749–1775," in *The Economy of Early America: the Revolutionary Period, 1763–1790,* Ronald Hoffman, et al., eds. (Charlottesville: University Press of Virginia, 1988), 88–125. On the relationship between Halifax merchants and outport politics, see Brian Cuthbertson, *Johnny Bluenose at the Polls: Epic Nova Scotian Election Battles, 1758–1848* (Halifax: Formac, 1994).
52. Adam Shortt, "Municipal History, 1791–1867," in Adam Shortt and Arthur G. Doughty, eds., *Canada and Its Provinces: A History of the Canadian People and Their Institutions by One Hundred Associates, Vol. 18, Province of Ontario* (Edinburgh: Edinburgh University Press, 1914), 405–452.
53. Peter S. Onuf, "Settlers, Settlements, and New States," in *The American Revolution: Its Character and Limits,* Jack P. Greene, ed. (New York: New York University Press, 1987), 172–173.

Chapter 2

1. For overviews of the area see Harris, ed., *HAC*, 47–51 and Plates 19–32; Buckner and Reid, eds., *The Atlantic Region to Confederation*, 3–155; and Richard W. Judd, Edwin A. Churchill, and Joel W. Eastman, eds., *Maine: The Pine Tree State from Prehistory to the Present* (Orono: University of Maine Press, 1995), 31–142.
2. Harris, ed., *HAC*, 1:47–48; John Mannion and Selma Barkham, "The 16th Century Fishery," in ibid, 1:Plate 22; John Mannion and Gordon Handcock, "The 17th Century Fishery," in ibid, 1:Plate 23; Harold A. Innis, *The Cod Fisheries: The History of An International Economy*, rev. ed. (Toronto: University of Toronto Press, 1954), 11–51; and Clark, *The Eastern Frontier*, 11–38.
3. Gillian T. Cell, *English Enterprise in Newfoundland, 1577–1660* (Toronto: University of Toronto Press, 1969), 53 –96; John G. Reid, *Acadia, Maine, and New Scotland: Marginal Colonies in the Seventeenth Century* (Toronto: University of Toronto Press, 1981), 3–33; and Neal Salisbury, *Manitou and Providence: Indians, Europeans, and the Making of New England, 1500–1643* (New York: Oxford University Press, 1982), 50–96.
4. Bruce J. Bourque, *Twelve Thousand Years: American Indians in Maine* (Lincoln: University of Nebraska Presss, 2001), 86–87, 108; and Andrew Hill Clark, *Acadia: The Geography of Early Nova Scotia to 1760* (Madison: University of Wisconsin Press, 1968), 71–108.
5. Charles M. Andrews, *The Colonial Period of American History,* 4 vols. (New Haven, CT: Yale University Press, 1934–1938), 1:249–299, 1:344–374, 2:1–196; C. Grant Head, *Eighteenth Century Newfoundland* (Toronto: McClelland and Stewart, 1976), 100–102, 111–132.
6. Clark, *The Eastern Frontier*, 63–77.
7. Reid et al., *The 'Conquest' of Acadia,* passim.
8. Mancke and Reid, "Elites, States, and the Imperial Contest for Acadia," in ibid.; *The Importance of Settling and Fortifying Nova Scotia; With a Particular Account of the Climate, Soil, and Native Inhabitants of the Country. By a Gentleman lately arrived from the colony* (London, 1751), 29–30; "Remarks on some parts of Nova Scotia and New England respecting Navigation, &c." NSARM, RG 1, Vol. 222, No. 40 (n.d. ca. 1770).
9. William Wicken, "Mi'kmaq Decisions: Antoine Tecouenemac, the Conquest, and the Treaty of Utrecht," in *The 'Conquest' of Acadia,* 86–100; idem, *Mi'kmaq Treaties on Trial,* 25–159.
10. Clark, *The Eastern Frontier*, 111–114; John G. Reid, "1686–1720: Imperial Intrusions," in *The Atlantic Region to Confederation,* 78–103; George Rawlyk, "1720–1744: Cod, Louisbourg, and the Acadians," in ibid., 107–124; and J.S. McLennan, *Louisbourg: From Its Foundation to Its Fall, 1713–1758,* 4th ed. (Halifax: The Book Room, 1979).

11. Patterson, "1744–1763: Colonial Wars and Aboriginal Peoples," in *The Atlantic Region to Confederation*, 125–155.

12. Reid et al., *The 'Conquest' of Acadia, 1710*, passim. Useful assessments of the Acadians include Clark, *Acadia*, 186–261, 330–369; Naomi E.S. Griffiths, *The Contexts of Acadian History, 1686–1784* (Montreal and Kingston: McGill–Queen's University Press, 1992), 33–94; and Daigle, "Acadia, 1604–1763: An Historical Synthesis," 17–46.

13. Anderson, *Crucible of War*, 503–506.

14. Nova Scotia Census, 1767, NSARM, RG 1, Vol. 443, No. 1. The Acadian population was probably underreported in this census. For more in-depth discussions of this census, see J.M. Bumsted, "1763–1783 Resettlement and Rebellion," in *The Atlantic Region to Confederation*, 165; and Wynn, "A Province Too Much Dependent on New England," 98–99. For an assessment of the impact of the Acadian deportation on Nova Scotia's economy, see Julian Gwyn, *Excessive Expectations: Maritime Commerce and the Economic Development of Nova Scotia, 1740–1870* (McGill–Queen's University Press, 1998), 15–42.

15. Neil MacKinnon, *This Unfriendly Soil: The Loyalist Experience in Nova Scotia, 1783–1791* (Kingston and Montreal: McGill–Queen's University Press, 1986), 29–32; D.G. Bell, *Early Loyalist Saint John: The Origin of New Brunswick Politics, 1783–1786* (Fredericton, NB: New Ireland Press, 1983), 17; W.S. MacNutt, *The Atlantic Provinces: The Emergence of Colonial Society, 1712–1857* (Toronto: McClelland and Stewart, 1965), 64–65, 181–182; and Ann Gorman Condon, "1783–1800: Loyalist Arrival, Acadian Return, Imperial Reform," in *The Atlantic Region to Confederation*, 84–209.

16. [1767] NSARM, RG 1, Vol. 443, No. 1; [1817] T. C. Haliburton, *An Historical and Statistical Account of Nova Scotia*, 2 vols. (Halifax: Joseph Howe, 1829), 2:276; [1827] ibid., 2:277; [1851] "Statistics of Each County of the Province of Nova Scotia," *Journals and Proceedings of the House of Assembly* (Halifax, 1851), Appendix 16.

17. Clark, *The Eastern Frontier*, 336, 354; Report of Commissioners on Machias, 12 September 1771, *DHMe*, 14:139; Report on the Number of Inhabitants in Lincoln County, 11 December 1781, CMaA, Vol. 162: 527–528; and Philip J. Greven Jr., "The average size of families and households in the Province of Massachusetts in 1764 and in the United States in 1790: An overview," in Peter Laslett and Richard Wall, eds., *Household and Family in Past Time* (Cambridge: Cambridge University Press, 1972), 550–556.

18. Michael J. Troughton, "From Nodes to Nodes: the Rise and Fall of Agricultural Activity in the Maritime Provinces," in Douglas Day, ed., *Geographical Perspectives on the Maritime Provinces* (Halifax: St. Mary's University, 1988), 25–46.

19. Graeme Wynn, "'Deplorably Dark and Demoralized Lumberers'? Rhetoric and Reality in Early Nineteenth Century New Brunswick," *Journal of Forest History* 24, 4 (1980): 168–187; and Daniel Vickers, "Work and Life on the Fishing Periphery of Essex County, Massachusetts, 1630–1675," in David G. Allen and David Hall, eds., *Seventeenth Century New England* (Boston: Colonial Society of Massachusetts, 1985), 83–117.

20. Charles Morris, "Description and State of the New Settlements in Nova Scotia in 1761," *Canadian Archives Report* (1904): 289–300; *The Diary of Simeon Perkins*, 5 vols. (Toronto: The Champlain Society, 1948–1978), 1:8 February 1773; 1:20 March 1773; and 3:19 June 1780. (Hereafter *Perkins's Diary*. All citations are by volume and date except when the reference is to a volume introduction or a footnote.)

21. Report of Commissioners on Machias, Sept 12, 1771, *DHMe*, 14:137, 139; "Petition from Chandler's River," May 7, 1784, CMaA, Eastern Lands Papers, Box 14, No. 22.

22. Frederick S. Allis Jr., *William Bingham's Maine Lands, 1790–1820*, 2 vols., (Boston: Colonial Society of Massachusetts, 1954) 1:54, 2:775–776.

23. Coolidge's trials are found in a series of his letters to Caleb Davis, 15 October 1788; 2 November 1788; 13 November 1788; 11 May 1789; 13 July 1789; 14 September 1789; 28 February 1791; 24 May 1791; 28 May 1791; 18 June 1791; 13 August 1791; 29 September 1791; 10 November 1791; 12 December 1791; 13 April 1792; 24 June 1792; 8 October 1792; 3 October 1792; 28 November 1792; 31 December 1792; 28 July 1793; 18 November 1793; December 1793; 28 February 1794; 6 March 1794; 24 May 1794; 28 July 1794; and 20 August 1794; Caleb Davis Papers, Massachusetts Historical Society, Vols. 15–18, 18A, 18B, in date order.

24. John Cooper, "A Topographical Description of Machias in the County of Washington," *Collections of the Massachusetts Historical Society*, 1st ser., 3 (1794):144–148; and Stephen Jones, "Historical Account of Machias," *Maine Historical Society Quarterly* 15, 2 (1975): 47–56.

25. Valuation of Machias, 1786, CMaA, Vol. 163:302.

26. Moses Greenleaf, *A Survey of the State of Maine in Reference to its Geographical Features, Statistics, and Political Economy* (1829, rpt., Augusta: Maine State Museum, 1970), 193, 201, 451.

27. From "A General Return of the Several Townships in the Province of Nova Scotia—the first day of January 1767," NSARM, RG 1, Vol. 443, No. 1; and Haliburton, *A Historical and Statistical Account of Nova Scotia*, 2:372.

28. Mancke, "Another British America," 1–36.

Chapter 3

1. Grant of Liverpool, NSARM, MG 100, Vol. 176, No. 26Q; and Machias Grant, 4 April 1770, CMaA, Vol. 118:446. At 80 square miles, the township would have 51,200 acres. (One square mile equals 640 acres.) I estimated that approximately 20 percent of the area was water, leaving approximately 40,000 acres to be divided among 80 grantees. The exact location of the St. Croix River remained a source of international dispute until 1798; see David Demeritt, "Representing the 'True' St. Croix: Knowledge and Power in the Partition of the Northeast," *William and Mary Quarterly* 3d ser., 54 (1997): 515–548.

2. Akagi, *The Proprietors of the New England Colonies*, passim; Martin, *Profits in the Wilderness*, 149–161, 257–280.

3. Daniel Vickers, "Competency and Competition: Economic Culture in Early America," *William and Mary Quarterly* 3d ser. 47 (1990): 3–29.

4. "An Act to enable Proprietors to divide their Lands held in common and undivided," 33 George II, Chapter 3. The King-in-Council repealed this act in 1761; see *Nova Scotia Acts*, 50.

5. Labaree, ed., *Royal Instructions*, 2:540, 537–541; McKinnon, *This Unfriendly Soil*, 38; Gates, *Land Policies of Upper Canada*, 27–44; and G.F. McGuigan, "Administration of Land Policy and the Growth of Corporate Economic Organization in Lower Canada, 1791–1809," Canadian Historical Association *Report* (1963), 65–73; Peter S. Onuf, *Statehood and Union: A History of the Northwest Ordinance* (Bloomington: University of Indiana Press, 1987), 21–24, 30, 38–39, 44. In general, the amount of land distributed to settlers after the American Revolution, in both the United States and British North America, was less than before the war.

6. Grant of Liverpool, 1 September 1759, NSARM, MG 100, Vol. 176, No. 26Q; Grant of Liverpool, 20 November 1764, NSARM, MG 4, Vol. 77; and Morris, "Description and State of the New Settlements in Nova Scotia in 1761," 289–300.

7. Proprietors' Records of Liverpool, Nova Scotia, NSARM, MG 4, Vol. 77: 4, 5. A few absentee proprietors remained, but they were men who received a share of land as a political favor and not through the township grant; see Return of the Township of Liverpool, Nova Scotia, 19 March 1784, NSARM, MG 4, Vol. 77.

8. Morris, "Description and State of the New Settlements in Nova Scotia in 1761," 292–293; Nova Scotia Census, 1767, NSARM, RG 1, Vol. 443, No. 1; and Proprietors' Records of Liverpool, 4. On the problems of fishermen holding land in Massachusetts, see Daniel Vickers, *Farmers and Fishermen: Two Centuries of Work in Essex County, Massachusetts, 1630–1850* (Chapel Hill: University of North Carolina Press, 1994), 197–203.

9. The following quantitative analysis of the settlers in Liverpool is based on these documents: Grant of Liverpool, 1 Sept 1759; 1761 Census, NSARM, RG 20, Series C., Vol. 43; Grant of Liverpool, 1764; Grant to John Godfrey and Others [supplemental grant], 5 January 1771, NSARM, MG 4, Vol. 77; Return of the Township of Liverpool Nova Scotia, 19 March 1784, NSARM, MG 4, Vol. 77; Proprietors' Allotments, Liverpool, Nova Scotia, NSARM, MG 4, Vol. 77. The original allotment book is in the possession of the Municipality of Queens County, Liverpool, Nova Scotia, and covers a longer period of time than does the copy at NSARM.

10. Return of the Township of Liverpool, 18 March 1784.

11. Order in Council, 15 April 1761, NSARM, RG 1, Vol. 211, No. 210; Memorial from Peleg Coffin, et al., 8 July 1762, NSARM, RG 1, Vol. 211, Nos. 250–251; Liverpool Proprietors' Records, 11 July 1791, 23 February 1796, and 23 March 1802.

12. Records of the Town of Machias, Town Hall, Machias, Maine, passim; Original Grantees of the Township of Machias, [1769], *DHMe*, 16:148; Revolutionary War Militia Records, CMaA, Vol. 36: 89, 90, 92, 123, 195, and Vol. 37: 12–20; and The Proprietors' Book of Records of Machias, Washington County Court House, Machias, Maine, 14, 16, 17. This last is a copy of the records done sometime before the dissolution of the proprietorship in 1835; the signatures for the distribution of the dividends are original.

13. The Proprietors' Book of Records of Machias, 14, 16, 17.

14. The Proprietors' Book of Records of Machias, 29–31.

15. The Proprietors' Book of Records of Machias, 32–36.

16. Ernest A. Clarke and Jim Phillips, "Rebellion and Repression in Nova Scotia in the Era of the American Revolution," in F. Murray Greenwood and Barry Wright, eds., *Canadian State Trials: Law, Politics, and Security Measures, 1608–1837* (Toronto: University of Toronto Press, 1996), 180–184, 210n.

17. The Proprietors' Book of Records of Machias, 44–46, 55–56, 71.

18. Registry of Deeds, Washington County Court House, Machias, Maine, Vol. 1: 21, 28–29; and The Proprietors' Book of Records of Machias, passim.

19. Graeme Wynn and Debra McNabb, "Pre-Loyalist Nova Scotia," in *HAC*, Plate 31; Debra McNabb, "Land and Families in Horton Township, N.S., 1760–1830" (M.A. thesis, University of British Columbia, 1986); and idem, "The Role of the Land in Settling Horton Township, Nova Scotia, 1766–1830," in Margaret Conrad, ed., *They Planted Well: New England Planters in Maritime Canada* (Fredericton, NB: Acadiensis, 1988), 151–160.

20. Proprietors' Records of Liverpool, 4, 5; Phyllis R. Blakely, "Silvanus Cobb," *DCB*, 128–129.

21. George W. Drisko, *Narrative of the Town of Machias* (1904; rpt. Somersworth, NH: New Hampshire Publishing, 1979), 14–19, 23; Registry of Deeds, Washington County, Vol. 1: 56, 66–67, 141, 234; and Proprietors' Book of Records of Machias, 3.

22. Proprietors' Records of Liverpool, 22 May 1760; 1 July 1760; 29 June 1761; 11 January 1762; 12 February 1761; 9 March 1762; and 27 April 1764. On the changing role of mills in towns see Gary Kulik, "Dams, Fish, and Farmers: The Defense of Public Rights in Eighteenth-Century Rhode Island," in Hebert G. Gutman and Donald H. Bell, eds., *The New England Working Class and the New Labor History* (Urbana: University of Illinois Press, 1987), 187–213.

23. Proprietors' Records of Liverpool, 10 May and 14 June 1768.

24. Proprietors' Records of Liverpool, 1 December 1777, and 1 April 1785.

25. Proprietors' Book of Records of Machias, 9–12; "The Courses and Boundaries of the High Marsh Lots," in ibid., n.p., back of the book; Proprietors' Allotments, Queens County Registry of Deeds, Liverpool, Nova Scotia. Local lore claims that the men who settled Machias in 1763 had "found" it in 1762 on a voyage downeast in search of marsh where they could cut hay. It is entirely possible. Lower New England suffered from severe drought in the summer of 1761 and 1762, which might well have caused a shortage of hay. See Drisko, *Narrative of the Town of Machias*, 10–11. The total acreage of marsh in Machias is calculated from the distribution list in the Proprietors' Records; cf. the much lower figures in Table 2.4.

26. Proprietors' Book of Records of Machias, 19 April 1777, 7–8, and "The Courses and Boundaries of the High Marsh Lots."

27. Proprietors' Records of Liverpool, 8 July 1760; and "A memorial rec'd from Nathan Tupper and 28 others," Council Minutes, 23 April 1762, NSARM, RG 1, Vol. 204.

28. Quoted in Harvey, ed., *The Diary of Simeon Perkins*, 2:xix.

29. Proprietors' Records of Liverpool, 8 and 15 July 1760.

30. Anthony Lockwood, *A brief description of Nova Scotia, with plates of the principal harbors; including a particular account of the island of Grand Manan* (London, 1818), 69; and "Miscellaneous Remarks and Observations on Nova Scotia, New Brunswick, and Cape Breton. Supposed to be Written by the Surveyor General of Nova Scotia," *Collections of the Massachusetts Historical Society* 3 (1794):98.

31. Proprietors' Records of Liverpool, 1 and 8 July 1760, and 10 and 29 June 1761.

32. Absentee Grantees, NSARM, MG 4, Vol. 77.

33. Plan of 200 Acres of Land at Little Port Jolly, NSARM, RG 20, Series C., Vol. 43; and Indenture, 11 July 1978, signed by Archibald Burke, Q.C., and R. Eric Millard, Edward B. Ritchie, and Roger F. Melanson, Trustees of the Liverpool Township, in Proprietors' Allotment Book. I am indebted to Andrew Faulkner for this information. For the nineteenth-century distribution of land, see the Proprietors' Allotment Book.
34. Boston and Eastern Mill and Land Company Papers, Maine Historical Society, MS 248; Proprietors' Book of Records of Machias, 73–77, 87–69, 99, 111–114. The record of the distribution of the dividends is in the back of book, n.p.
35. Proprietors' Book of Records of Machias, 20 November 1770, 9 and 11 July 1781, December 1781, 12 May 1784, 16 August 1784; and Proprietors' Records of Liverpool, 8 July 1760, 29 June 1761, 28 August 1761, 4 September 1761, 23 January 1763, 15 September 1774.
36. Proprietors' Records of Machias, 8 March 1796.
37. Proprietors' Records of Liverpool, 14 June 1768, 8 May 1769, 9 July 1772, 8 and 28 March 1785, 23 February 1796, 30 April 1805, 20 September 1866.
38. McGuigan, "Administration of Land Policy," 66–73; Gates, *Land Policies of Upper Canada*, 27–44.
39. Handlin and Handlin, *Commonwealth*, passim; and Pauline Maier, "The Revolutionary Origins of the American Corporation," *William and Mary Quarterly*, 3d ser., 50 (1993): 51–84.

Chapter 4

1. *Perkins's Diary*, 2:21 June 1782.
2. Mancke, "Another British America, 1–36; and idem, "Early Modern Imperial Governance and the Origins of Canadian Political Culture," 3–20.
3. Greene, *Peripheries and Center*, 79–150; idem, "Metropolis and Colonies: Changing Patterns of Constitutional Conflict in the Early Modern British Empire, 1607–1763," 43–77.
4. Elizabeth Mancke, "The American Revolution in Canada," in Jack P. Greene and J.R. Pole, eds., *A Companion to the American Revolution* (Malden, MA and Oxford: Blackwell, 2000), 503–510.
5. Brebner, *The Neutral Yankees of Nova Scotia*, passim; and Stewart and Rawlyk, '*A People Highly Favoured of God*', passim. Brebner's thesis remains dominant despite its serious flaws. See, for example, Thompson and Randall, *Canada and the United States*, 13. For a dated but still useful overview of interpretations see George A. Rawlyk, *Revolution Rejected 1775–1776* (Scarborough, ON: Prentice-Hall, 1968). For interpretations of Nova Scotia as a predominantly Loyalist colony, see Wilfred Brenton Kerr, *The Maritime Provinces of British North America and the American Revolution* (1941; rpt. New York: Russell and Russell, 1970); and especially Ernest Clarke, *The Siege of Fort Cumberland, 1776: An Episode in the American Revolution* (Montreal and Kingston: McGill–Queen's University Press, 1995). For an economic interpretation of Nova Scotia's response to the American Revolution, see Fisher, "Revolution without Independence: The Canadian Colonies, 1749–1775," 88–125.
6. For the history of the American Revolution in Maine see Leamon, *Revolution Downeast*. For an account of the Revolution in Machias see John Ahlin, *Maine Rubicon: Downeast Settlers During the American Revolution* (Calais, ME: Calais Advertiser Press, 1966). The basic narrative of this account is sound, but its interpretation is deeply flawed.
7. For essays exploring this problem for all the European empires in the Americas, see Daniels and Kennedy, eds., *Negotiated Empires*. For revolution in the British Atlantic see Eliga H. Gould, "Revolution and Counter-Revolution," in *The British Atlantic World, 1500–1800*, eds., David Armitage and Michael J. Braddick (Basingstoke, UK and New York: Palgrave, 2002), 196–213.
8. For one challenge to that chronology, see Jack P. Greene, "A Posture of Hostility: A Reconsideration of Some Aspects of the Origins of the American Revolution," *Proceedings of the American Antiquarian Society* 87 (1977), 27–68.
9. Mancke, "Another British America;" idem, "Negotiating an Empire: Britain and Its Overseas Peripheries, c.1550–1780," 235–265. James Leamon suggests that the imperial controversy did not affect Maine until 1774, although he does consider unsettled conditions in much of eastern Maine. He attributes the unsettled conditions to rapid population growth, but many of the underlying causes had to do with contests over provincial and imperial control of the region. See Leamon, *Revolution Downeast*, xv, 6.

10. Liverpool Proprietors' Records, NSARM, MG 4, Vol. 77: 2–4.
11. Proclamation, 11 January 1759, NSARM, RG 1, Vol. 188, No. 39–44.
12. Proclamation, NSARM, RG 1, Vol. 165, p. 213; J.S. Martell, "Pre-Loyalist Settlements around the Minas Basin," (M.A. thesis, Dalhousie University, 1933), 122.
13. Proclamation, 25 March 1762, NSARM, RG 1, Vol. 165: 213; Memorial from Peleg Coffin, et al., 8 July 1762, NSARM, RG 1, Vol. 211: 250–251; Stewart and Rawlyk, 'A People Highly Favoured of God', 19–20.
14. Council Minutes, 15 August 1761, NSARM, RG 1, Vol. 188: 263–264; Memorial from Peleg Coffin, et al., 8 July 1762, NSARM, RG 1, Vol. 211: 250–251.
15. Brebner, The Neutral Yankees, 211–217; J. Murray Beck, The Government of Nova Scotia (Toronto: University of Toronto Press, 1957), 134–135; Harvey, "The Struggle for the New England Form of Township Government," 15–23.
16. Mancke, "Imperial Transitions," 183–185.
17. See Chapter 3 for an analysis of land distribution in Liverpool and Machias.
18. McNabb, "Land and Families in Horton Township, N.S., 1760–1830," 22–41.
19. Richard Bulkeley to Richard Upham, David Archibald, & John McKean, Esqrs., Londonderry, 29 October 1766, NSARM, RG 1, Vol. 136, No. 96.
20. McNabb, "Land and Families in Horton Township, N.S., 1760–1830," 47–56.
21. Proclamation, 25 March 1763, NSARM, RG 1, Vol. 165, No. 260.
22. Liverpool Proprietors' Records, 28 August 1761; 8 October 1762; 1 December 1763; 29 May 1764; NSARM, MG 4, Vol. 77; Perkins's Diary, 1:4 June 1777; 1:26 February 1778; 1:3 March 1778; 2:12 March 1781; 2:5 February 1782.
23. Brebner, Neutral Yankees, 157.
24. Perkins's Diary, 1:3 June 1766; Governor to the Board of Trade, 19 September 1765, NSARM, RG 1, Vol. 37.
25. Quoted in Beck, The Government of Nova Scotia, 136. See also Margaret Ells, "Governor Wentworth's Patronage," Collections of the Nova Scotia Historical Society 25 (1942): 49–73.
26. Williamson, The History of the State of Maine, 2:359–360.
27. Minutes of Meetings, DHMe, 13:412–413; Petition, DHMe, 13:413–414.
28. Petition of Samuel Doane and Mathew Thorton, 28 January 1767, DHMe, 13:20–21; Petition of Nathan Jones and Others, 28 January 1767, DHMe, 13:21–22; Resolve of the House of Representatives, 5 February 1767, DHMe, 13:23; Petition of David Bean and Others, May 1768, DHMe, 13:83; Resolve of the House of Representatives, 28 June 1768, 13:83–84.
29. Letter, Stephen Parker to Thomas Hutchinson, 11 November 1769, CMaA, Vol. 25:339–340.
30. "Jonathan Longfellow's Memorial to Governor Hutchinson," 8 November 1770 and "Memorial of the Inhabitants of Machias," 9 November 1770, DHMe, 14:112–115; Jones, "Historical Account of Machias," 49; Letter, Hutchinson to Lord Hillsborough, 30 November 1770, CMaA, 27:59–60; Letter, Hutchinson to Lord Hillsborough, July 1771, CMaA, 27:196; Letter, Hutchinson to Jonathan Longfellow, 17 December 1770, CMaA, 27:79; Letter from Hutchinson to Col. Goldthwaite, 9 May 1771, CMaA, 27:162–163.
31. "Petition to Govr. Hutchinson by Inhabitants of the Fifth Township," n.d., DHMe, 14:92–93.
32. Order by Thomas Hutchinson to William Brattle, James Bowdoin, and Thomas Hubbard, 26 July 1771, CMaA, Vol. 279:23.
33. Report of Commissioners, 12 September 1771, DHMe, 14:137–139; Letter from Thomas Goldthwait to Hutchinson, 12 October 1772, CMaA, Vol. 25:540–541.
34. Hutchinson's Message to the House of Representatives, 19 June 1771, DHMe, 14:132–34; Hutchinson to Hillsborough, 15 July 1772, CMaA, Vol. 27:363. See also Hutchinson's Speech, 1770, DHMe, 13:103–106.
35. "An Act to Encourage the Preaching of the Gospel," CMaA, Vol. 14:258–259.
36. Richard D. Brown, Revolutionary Politics in Massachusetts: The Boston Committee of Correspondence and the Towns, 1772–1774 (Cambridge, MA: Harvard University Press, 1970).
37. Pauline Maier, From Resistance to Revolution: Colonial Radicals and the Development of American Opposition to Britain, 1765–1776 (New York:. Knopf, 1973) 117–118.

38. Cf. the following discussion of issues of neutrality in Nova Scotia and Maine with Brebner, *The Neutral Yankees*; Stewart and Rawlyk, *'A People Highly Favoured of God'*; Leamon, *Revolution Downeast*, 131–134; Clarke, *The Siege of Fort Cumberland*, xi, 16; and Donald Desserud, "Nova Scotia and the American Revolution: A Study of Neutrality and Moderation in the Eighteenth Century," in Margaret Conrad, ed., *Making Adjustments: Change and Continuity in Planter Nova Scotia, 1759–1800* (Fredericton, NB: Acadiensis University Press, 1991), 89–112.

39. Labaree, ed. *Royal Instructions*, 1:7–8, 392.

40. Brebner, *Neutral Yankees*, 308–310; Letter from Richard Bulkeley, Provincial Secretary to Justices of the Peace in Yarmouth, 16 December 1775, NSARM, RG 1, Vol. 136:231; James D. Snowdon, "Footprints in the Marsh Mud: Politics and Land Settlement in the Township of Sackville, 1760–1800" (M.A. thesis, University of New Brunswick, 1974), 94.

41. Proclamation of Martial Law, 18 April 1780, *DHMe*, 18:222–224; Martial Law Proclaimed in Lincoln County by John Allan, 26 June 1780, ibid., 18:333–335. See also James S. Leamon, "The Search for Security: Maine after Penobscot," *Maine Historical Society Quarterly* 21, 3 (1982): 119–153.

42. The documents to piece this story together can be found in the *Documentary History of Maine*. They are: Letter of the Chairman of the Committee of Correspondence, Pleasant River, 9 April 1781, 19:191; Machias Committee of Correspondence to the Governor Hancock, 11 April 1781, 19:193; Memorial of the Inhabitants of Machias to the Governor Hancock, 1781, 19:225–228; Letter of Francis Shaw to Stephen Jones, 17 March 1781, 19:235–236; Minutes of the Meeting of the Inhabitants of Machias, 29 March 1781, 19: 236–238; Letter of the Machias Committee of Correspondence to Governor Hancock, April 1781, 19:238–241; Deposition of Jonas Farnsworth, 11 April 1781, 19:241–243; Copy of the Representation written by Francis Shaw, 17 March 1781, 19:243–246; Letter of Francis Shaw to the Governor and Council, 3 May 1781, 19:246–249.

43. Letter of the Pleasant River Committee of Correspondence, 9 April 1781, *DHMe*, 19:191.

44. Copy of Representation of the Inhabitants of all the Tract of Land, lying & being on & between the Rivers Penobscott & St. Croix inclusive, by Francis Shaw, *DHMe*, 19:243–246.

45. Bellesiles, *Revolutionary Outlaws*, passim.

46. Memorial of the Inhabitants of Machias, 29 April 1781, *DHMe*, 19:228.

47. MacKinnon, *This Unfriendly Soil*, 67–88; J.M. Bumsted, *Understanding the Loyalists* (Sackville, NB: Centre for Canadian Studies, Mount Allison University, 1986), 39–49.

Chapter 5

1. Labaree, ed. *Royal Instructions*, 1:7–8, 392; John Shy, *A People Numerous and Armed: Reflections on the Military Struggle for Independence*, rev. ed (Ann Arbor: University of Michigan Press, 1990), 29–41; Bruce C. Daniels, *The Connecticut Town: Growth and Development, 1635–1790* (Middletown, CT: Wesleyan University Press, 1979), 132–139; and Anderson, *A People's Army*, 26–27, 41–42.

2. Maier, *From Resistance to Revolution*, 16–26, 63, 92, 140, 179; and Michael A. McDonnell, "Popular Mobilization and Political Culture in Revolutionary Virginia: The Failure of the Minutemen and the Revolution from Below," *Journal of American History* 85 (1998): 946–981.

3. Commissions, NSARM, RG 1, Vol. 164: 104, 178, 179; see also NSARM, RG 1, Vol. 171: 83–84.

4. Council Minutes, 18 April 1759, 17 and 18 May 1759, NSARM, RG 1, Vol. 188: 53–64; Report from Capt. Cobb, 16 July 1759, ibid., 88–90; Proclamation of Treaty with the Indians Report from 11 March 1760, ibid., 142; Wicken, *Mi'kmaq Treaties on Trial*, 191–209; Reid, "*Pax Britannica* or *Pax Indigena*?"

5. Militia Commissions, July 27, 1769, CMaA, Vol. 99:92, 436.

6. See Chapter 1.

7. *Perkins's Diary*, 1:3 June 1765; and Governor to the Board of Trade, 19 September 1765, NSARM, RG1, Vol. 37; and Joseph Edwards Plimsoll, "The Militia of Nova Scotia, 1749–1867," *Nova Scotia Historical Society Collections* 17 (1913): 71.

8. *Perkins's Diary*, 1:31 July 1769; 1:21 January 1774; 1:16 and 21 February 1774; 1:26 April 1774; 1:26 and 27 May 1774; and 1:19 June 1774.

9. *Perkins's Diary*, 1:21 January 1774; and 1:16 February 1774.

10. *Perkins's Diary*, 1:28 September 1774; 1:18 October 1774; Circular from Bulkeley, 30 August 1774, NSARM, RG 1, Vol. 136: 176; Commissions Book, NSARM, RG 1, Vol. 164: 104, 178, 179; Acknowledgement of Militia Return, 7 December 1774, NSARM, RG 1, Vol. 136: 183.

11. Governor Legge stated in a letter to Admiral Gage that he could not count on the Nova Scotia militia, NSARM, RG 1, Vol. 136: 222; Brebner, *The Neutral Yankees*, 243–290.

12. Circular Letter from Richard Bulkeley, NSARM, RG 1, Vol. 136: 217; Letter from R. Bulkeley, 11 September 1775, ibid., 224; *Perkins's Diary*, 1:5 October 1775 and 1:23 October 1775; 1:9 February 1776 and 1:29 March 1776; and Clarke, *The Siege of Fort Cumberland*, 1776, 13–17.

13. Circular letter from R. Bulkeley, 13 July 1775, NSARM, RG 1, Vol. 136: 201; Plimsoll, "The Militia of Nova Scotia," 68–69, 71.

14. Proclamation, 23 June 1775, NSARM, RG 1, Vol. 170: 166–167; Letter from R. Bulkeley to Elisha Freeman, Simeon Perkins, Seth Harding, Samuel Freeman, Nathan Tupper, William Johnstone, Edward Nickols, Esqs. in Liverpool, 3 July 1775, NSARM, RG 1, Vol. 136: 197–198; *Perkins's Diary*, 1:10, 14, and 19 July 1775; 1:19 December 1775; 1:2 January 1776.

15. *Perkins's Diary*, 1:26 July 1775; Harvey, ed. and intro., *The Diary of Simeon Perkins*, 2:xxx; Private letter from R. Bulkeley to Wm J[ohnsto]ne Esq., Liverpool, 20 September 1775, NSARM, RG 1, Vol. 136: 228; *Perkins's Diary*, 2: 23n.

16. Proclamations, NSARM, RG 1, Vol. 170: 167–168, 169, 188–190, 210–212.

17. Letter of John Allan, Machias, 17 August 1778, *DHMe*, 16: 73.

18. *Perkins's Diary*, 1:3 October 1776; Letter from Richard Bulkeley, 5 October 1776, NSARM, RG 1,170:218.

19. Letter from Massey, Halifax, 10 January 1778, NAC, British HQ Papers, MG 23, B1, doc. 861 on reel M-345.

20. *Perkins's Diary*, 1:16, 17, 18, 20, 21 October 1776; 1:5, 7, 8, February 1778.

21. *Perkins's Diary*, 1:8 March 1777.

22. *Perkins's Diary*, 1:23 March 1777.

23. *Perkins's Diary*, 1:16 and 25 March 1778; 1:7, 9, 19, and 20 April 1778.

24. *Perkins's Diary*, 1:31 May 1778.

25. *Perkins's Diary*, 1:31 May 1778.

26. *Perkins's Diary*, 1:31 May 1778; 1:1 June 1778.

27. *Perkins's Diary*, 1:3 June 1778.

28. *Perkins's Diary*, 2:1, 4, 11 June 1782.

29. *Perkins's Diary*, 1:3 July 1775.

30. *Perkins's Diary*, 1:30 July 1775; 1:19 October 1778.

31. *Perkins's Diary*, 1:25, 26 November 1778; 1:13, 14 December 1778; 1:12, 14, 15, 17, 20, 22, 24, 25, 31 May 1779; 1:1, 2, 4 June 1779; 1:3 November 1779; 2:24 May 1780; 2:13, 14, 15, 16, 27 February 1781; 2:2 April 1781; 2:27, 29 June 1781; 2:4 July 1781; 2:19 Aug 1783.

32. Clarke, *The Siege of Fort Cumberland*, passim.

33. *Perkins's Diary*, 1:4 June 1779; 2:4 June, 1780, 1781, 1782, 1783; see Richard L. Bushman, *King and People in Provincial Massachusetts* (Chapel Hill, NC: University of North Carolina Press, 1985), 11–25 for a discussion of celebrations in honor of the monarch in colonial Massachusetts.

34. *Perkins's Diary*, 2:30, 31 July 1780; Harvey, ed. and intro., *Perkins's Diary*, 2:xli–xlv, 2:31n.

35. Quoted in George E.E. Nichols, "Notes on Nova Scotian Privateers," *Collections of the Nova Scotia Historical Society* 13 (1908): 121; Dan Conlin, "A Private War in the Caribbean: Nova Scotia Privateering, 1793–1805," (M.A. thesis: Saint Mary's University, 1996); and Robert C. Ritchie, "Government Measures against Piracy and Privateering in the Atlantic Area, 1750–1850," in David J. Starkey, et al., eds., *Pirates and Privateers: New Perspectives on the War on Trade in the Eighteenth and Nineteenth Centuries* (Exeter: Exeter University Press, 1997), 10–28.

36. *Perkins's Diary*, 2:28, 29, 30 June 1780.

37. Edmund Duval Poole, *Annals of Yarmouth and Barrington, Nova Scotia In the Revolutionary War* (Yarmouth, NS: 1899), passim.

38. *Perkins's Diary*, 2:18 and 19 July 1780.

39. Invoice of Sundries Shipt by Caleb & Amasa Davis, 26 July 1773; Account of Joshua Davis, 3 and 30 September 1773; Shipping Orders to Capt. Joshua Davis, 29 December 1773; Dispersements at Gouldsboro, 7 February 1774; List of goods boarded at Gouldsboro, 26 February 1774, in the Caleb Davis Papers, Massachusetts Historical Society, Vol. 8.

40. Leamon, *Revolution Downeast*, 13–14.

41. Leamon, *Revolution Downeast*, 33–34.
42. Letter of Samuel Thompson, 29 April 1775, *DHMe*, 14:243–244; Motion of Capt. McCobb, Provincial Congress, 5 May 1775, *DHMe*, 14:246; Letter from Dummer Sewall to Provincial Congress, 6 May 1775, *DHMe*, 14:247; Letter from Edward Parry to Henry Mowat, 10 May 1775, *DHMe*, 14:247–248; Letter from Edward Parry to William Tyng, 10 May 1775, *DHMe*, 14:249; Letter from Edward Parry to Provincial Congress, 10 May 1775, *DHMe*, 249–250; Committee Resolution, Provincial Congress, 26 June 1775, *DHMe*, 14:287. See also, Leamon, *Revolution Downeast*, 63–64.
43. The literature on the *Margaretta* incident is voluminous. For a contemporary account see "Account of the Capture of the King's Cutter at Machias," 14 June 1775, Machias Committee of Safety, *DHMe*, 14: 280–283. I have used this account for most of the details of the event. For an 1822 account by Stephen Jones see "Historical Account of Machias," 44–56. For an assessment of the event's numerous renditions see Edwin A. Churchill, "The Historiography of the Margaretta Affair, Or, How Not To Let the Facts Interfere With a Good Story," *Maine Historical Society Quarterly* 15, 2 (1975): 60–74. The one addition I would make to Churchill's assessment is to note that the Machias incident was one of a number of incidents in Maine involving blocking the shipment of timber to the British. The Machias incident achieved its notoriety because of the taking of a British naval vessel. It was otherwise well within revolutionary action in other places in Maine.
44. Account of the Margaretta Affair, 14 June 1775, *DHMe*, 14:280–283; Letter from Machias to Provincial Congress, 17 June 1775, *DHMe*, 14:283–284; Resolve of the Provincial Congress, 26 June 1775, *DHMe*, 14:286–287; Petition of Benjamin Foster and others for Machias, 18 August 1775, in Frederic Kidder, ed., *Military Operations in Eastern Maine and Nova Scotia during the Revolution* (1867; rpt New York: Kraus Reprint, 1971), 47–48; Resolve to Man Two Vessels, n.d., ibid., 49–50.
45. Petition to the Provincial Congress, 1 July 1775, *Military Operations*, 6; Petition to the Governor and Company of Connecticut, 20 July 1775, *DHMe*, 24:164–165; Provincial Resolve on the Petition of Thomas Donnel, 8 July 1775, *DHMe*, 14:290.
46. Clarke, *The Siege of Fort Cumberland*, 5–6.
47. Letter from the Committee of Safety at Machias, 14 October 1775, *DHMe*, 14:311.
48. Leamon, *Revolution Downeast*, 69.
49. Demeritt, "Representing the "True" St. Croix," 515–548; and Francis M. Carroll, *A Good and Wise Measure: The Search for the Canadian-American Boundary, 1783–1842* (Toronto: University of Toronto Press, 2001), 3–31.
50. See Robert Greenlaugh Albion, *Forests and Sea Power: The Timber Problem of the Royal Navy, 1652–1862* (1926; rpt., Hamden, CT: Archon, 1965), 232, 289 for the impact of timber issues on imperial affairs.
51. Instructions to Lieut. Henry Mowat, 6 October 1775, NAC, British HQ Papers, MG 23, B1, doc. 63 on reel M-343; Declaration of William Gilly, 10 May 1777, *DHMe*, 15:90–91; Donald Yerxa, "The Burning of Falmouth, 1775: A Case Study in British Imperial Pacification," *Maine Historical Society Quarterly* 14, 3 (1975): 119–150; Leamon, *Revolution Downeast*, 70–73.
52. Letter from the Machias Committee of Safety, 9 July 1776, *DHMe*, 14:358–359. For similar expressions see Letter from Francis Shaw to the General Court, 28 August 1776, *DHMe*, 14:374–377; Letter from Lt. Col. Alexander Campbell, 13 July 1777, *DHMe*, 14:440–441; Letter from Francis Shaw, 15 July 1777, *DHMe*, 14:443.
53. Letter from James Lyon to the General Court, September 1776, *DHMe*, 14:383; Minutes of a Meeting at Maugerville, N.S., 14 May 1776, *Military Operations*, 62–65; Brebner, *The Neutral Yankees*, 321–322.
54. Letter from James Lyon, September 1776, *DHMe*, 14:379–385; Letter from Francis Shaw, 28 August 1776, *DHMe*, 14:374–377.
55. Clarke, *The Siege of Fort Cumberland*, 25, 32–33, 35, 37–38, 69–73.
56. Letter to the Massachusetts General Court from Jonathan Eddy, 5 January 1777, *DHMe*, 15:35–40; Clarke, *The Siege of Fort Cumberland*, 128–204.
57. Letter from William Tupper, 27 November 1776, *DHMe*, 14:399.
58. Kidder, ed. and intro., *Military Operations*, 12–13; Committee Report on Account of John Allan, 28 June 1777, *DHMe*, 422–424.

59. Letter from John Allan, 30 May 1777, *DHMe*, 14:414–417; and Report of the Committee of Both Houses, 5 June 1777, *DHMe*, 14:419–422; Letter to John Allan, 20 June 1777, *DHMe*, 14:437–438; Letter to the President of Congress from the Massachusetts Council, 13 August 1777, *DHMe*, 15:11–12; Letter to Stephen Smith, 19 August 1777, *DHMe*, 15:19–20.

60. Letter from Col. Benjamin Foster, 8 August 1777, *DHMe*, 15:8–10. See also Letter from Francis Shaw, 4 July 1777, *DHMe*, 14:439–440; and Letter from Col. Alexander Campbell, 13 July 1777, *DHMe*, 14:441–442.

61. Letter from Col. Jonathan Eddy, 17 August 1777, *DHMe*, 15:12–15; Letter from John Preble, 17 August 1777, *DHMe*, 15:15–16; Letter from Col. Benjamin Foster, 27 August 1777, *DHMe*, 15:25–26; Letter from the Committee at Machias, 29 August 1777, *DHMe*, 15:32–36; Letter from John Allan, 17 August 1777, *DHMe*, 15:169179. On the Natives' role in the war, see Clarke, *The Siege of Fort Cumberland*, 2–26, 59–62, 73–75.

62. Instructions to Maj. Small, 26 November 1777, NAC, British HQ Papers, doc. 765, reel M-345.

63. General Massey to General Howe, 2 January 1778, NAC, British HQ Paper, MG 23, B1, doc 830, reel M-345; Petition of a number of towns, 20 September 1777, *DHMe*, 15:219–220.

64. Letter from Col. Benjamin Foster, 27 August 1777, *DHMe*, 15:25–26. See also Letter from George Stillman, 27 August 1777, *DHMe*, 15:27–28; Letter from Stephen Smith, 28 August 1777, *DHMe*, 15:29–30; Letter from Benjamin Foster to Alexander Campbell, 28 August 1777, *DHMe*, 15:31–32; Letter from the Committee in Machias, 29 August 1777, *DHMe*, 15.

65. Stephen Jones's conduct justified, 16 July 1775, *DHMe*, 14:292; Letter from Stephen Jones, 22 July 1775, *DHMe*, 14:293.

66. Petition of Benajah Acley for land adjoining Machias on Holmes Bay [Cutler] May 13, 1784, and Petition from Chandler's River, May 7, 1784, CMaA, Eastern Lands Papers, Box 14.

67. Petition from Pleasant River Upper Township, 14 May 1784, CMaA, Eastern Lands Papers, Box 14. See also Petition from Pleasant River Township Six, 14 May 1784 and Petition from Township Four, 24 May 1784, CMaA, Eastern Lands Papers, Box 14.

68. For example, the copy of the petition for the abatement of taxes sent by the Town of Machias to the General Court, November 1787, Machias Town Minutes, Machias Town Hall.

69. *Perkins's Diary*, 2:5, 10, 22 November 1790; 1:15 March 1776; Letter of Wentworth to Castlereagh, 3 Feb 1806, NSARM, CB Ferguson Papers, Box 1897, F 1/5.

70. "Report of the Committee, 1791" and "Instructions to Mr. Phineas Bruce, 1791" in Drisko, *Narrative of the Town of Machias*, 147–157; and Ronald F. Banks, *Maine Becomes a State: The Movement to Separate Maine from Massachusetts, 1785–1820* (Middleton, CT: Wesleyan University Press, 1970), 57–67. For an exploration of war and American ideology see Reginald Stuart, *War and American Thought: From the Revolution to the Monroe Doctrine* (Kent, OH: Kent State University Press, 1982).

Chapter 6

1. Liverpool Proprietors' Records, 10 June 1761; 29 June 1761; 13 August 1761; 28 August 1761; 4 September 1761; and 19 September 1761; NSARM, MG4, Vol. 77.

2. The Proprietors' Book of Records of Machias, Letter to James Lyon, 6 June 1772, CMaA, 14:655; Letter from James Lyon, 8 June 1772, CMaA, 14:656; Letter from Machias to the General Court, 8 June 1772, CMaA, 14:653; Act to tax for support of the gospel, 4 July 1772, CMaA, 14:258–259.

3. See D.G. Bell, ed. and intro., *The Newlight Baptist Journals of James Manning and James Innis* (Hantsport, NS: Lancelot, 1984), xv–xvi for an explanation of "church," "society," and "congregation" in the Maritimes. In an eighteenth-century context see *Perkins's Diary*, 3:11, 12, 13, 14 January 1790. For an explanation of the Puritan background on church membership, see Edmund S. Morgan, *Visible Saints: The History of a Puritan Idea* (New York: New York University Press, 1963); and C.C. Goen, *Revivalism and Separatism in New England, 1740–1800* (1962; rpt., Hamden, CT: Archon, 1969), 3–6.

4. See Chapter 3 for a discussion of the meaning of proprietors in Liverpool and Machias.

5. Stephen A. Marini, *Radical Sects of Revolutionary New England* (Cambridge, MA: Harvard University Press, 1982).

6. Report of the Commissioners on Machias, 12 September 1771, *DHMe*, 14:139–140; Petition to Governor Hutchinson by the Inhabitants of the Fifth Township, n.d., *DHMe*, 14:92–93; Petition for Missionaries to the Eastward, *DHMe*, 182–185.

7. Machias Grant, 4 April 1770, CMaA, Vol. 118:446; Proprietors' Meetings, 20 November 1770 and 9 July 1771, Proprietors' Book of Records of Machias.
8. Oscar G.T. Sonneck, *Francis Hopkinson: The First American Poet-Composer (1737–1791) and James Lyon: Patriot, Preacher, Psalmodist (1735–1794)* (1905; rpt., New York: Da Capo, 1967), 124–133; John H. Ahlin, ed. and intro., *The Saint's Daily Assistant: James Lyon, His Life and Meditations* (1815; rpt., Machias, ME: Center Street Congregationalist Church, 1983), xiii–xxi; Drisko, *Narrative of the Town of Machias*, 195.
9. Sonneck, *Francis Hopkinson and James Lyon*, 132–133; Ahlin, *The Saint's Daily Assistant*, vii, xiv-xvi. Lyon was only one of several chairmen of the Machias Committee of Safety, although it is often implied that he was the only one. Cf. Ahlin, *The Saint's Daily Assistant*, xxvii; and *DHMe*, 14:283, 14:284, 14:314, 14:358, 19:228, 19:241.
10. Letter of Benjamin Foster et al., to Rev. James Lyon, 6 June 1772, *DHMe*, 14:172–173; Answer of James Lyon, 8 June 1772, *DHMe*, 14:174–175; Letter from B. Gerrish & Malachy Salter to Rev. Andrew Eliot, 18 January 1770, NSARM, MG 100, Vol. 121, No. 26; An Act to encourage the Preaching of the Gospel, 14 July 1772, *DHMe*, 14:185–186.
11. Letter from James Lyon to the General Court, 5 August 1777, *DHMe*, 15:7–9; Letter from James Lyon to James Avery, 13 May 1784, CMaA, Eastern Land Papers, Box 14; Proprietors' Meetings, 22 July 1773; 11 July 1781; 20 December 1781; and 12 May 1784, Proprietors' Records of Machias; Minutes, 16 March 1787 and Petition to the General Court March 1787, Machias Town Records. Many of the early minutes of the town are reprinted in Drisko, *Narrative of the Town of Machias*, 86–169.
12. Records of the Church of Christ at Machias, Porter Memorial Library, Machias, ME; Letter from Benjamin Foster and others to Rev. James Lyon, 6 June 1772, *DHMe*, 14:172–173.
13. Sonneck, *Francis Hopkinson and James Lyon*, 132–133; Benjamin Lincoln, "Copy of a Letter from the Hon. General Lincoln, on the Religious State of the Eastern Counties in the District of Maine," *Collections of the Massachusetts Historical Society*, 1st ser. 4 (1795): 153.
14. Stephen A. Marini, "Religious Revolution in the District of Maine, 1780–1820," in *Maine in the Early Republic: From Revolution to Statehood*, eds. Charles E. Clark, James S. Leamon, and Karen Bowden (Hanover, NH: University Press of New England, 1988), 121–128; Machias Church Records, 1.
15. Machias Church Records, 23, 200, 201.
16. See Nathan O. Hatch, *The Sacred Cause of Liberty: Republican Thought and the Millennium in Revolutionary New England* (New Haven, CT: Yale University Press, 1977) for a discussion of the clergy's response to the revolution.
17. Minutes, 5 November 1794, Machias Town Records; Machias Church Records, 2–14.
18. Machias Church Records, 17; Bell, ed., *The Newlight Baptist Journals of James Manning and James Innis*, 90–91; and Marini, *Radical Sects of Revolutionary New England*, passim.
19. Machias Church Records, 17, 50–53, 200.
20. The recording of baptisms attests to these distinctions. See Machias Church Records, 60, 84, 120, 140–141. On the Half-Way Covenant see Robert Pope, *The Half-Way Covenant: Church Membership in Puritan New England* (Princeton, NJ: Princeton University Press, 1969); for a summary see Francis J. Bremer, *The Puritan Experiment: New England Society from Bradford to Edwards*, rev. ed. (Hanover and London: University Press of New England, 1995), 161–165.
21. Minutes of the Church Meeting, 16 April 1797, Machias Church Records, 57–59.
22. Ibid.
23. Quoted in Bell, *The Newlight Baptist Journals of James Manning and James Innis*, 91–92.
24. Letter from Brown to the Church, 7 May 1797; Letter from Brown to the Church, 7 May 1797; Letter from Brown to the Church, 18 May 1797, in Machias Church Records, 80–82, 184–186, 192.
25. Machias Church Records, 80–81, 89, 184–186, 190, 192–193; Town Minutes, 1 August 1797, Machias Town Records.
26. Marini, "Religious Revolution," 118–145.
27. Machias Church Records, 210–212.
28. Proceedings of the Ecclesiastical Council, 2 September 1800, Machias Church Records, 213.
29. Machias Confession of Faith, 2 September 1800, Machias Church Records, 214–217.
30. Minutes, 1799–1812, Machias Town Records, 1:72–216.
31. Minutes, June 1800, Machias Town Records, 1:86–89; Letter from Steele to the Church and Congregation at Machias, 16 September 1799, Machias Church Records, 7–8, 209–211.
32. Minutes of a Church Meeting, 7 October 1800, Machias Church Records, 219–221.

33. Notice for Annual Meeting and Minutes of Annual Meeting, 2 April 1804, Machias Town Records, 1:126–30.
34. Petition of Abraham Fletcher for a Baptist Society in Machias, June 1810, CMaA, Senate Unenacted Business, 1810, No. 4037.
35. Annual Meeting, 6 April 1812, Machias Town Records, 1:214–216.
36. Town Minutes, 1812–1817, Machias Town Records, 1:214–304.
37. Petition for "An Act to Incorporate the Machias Congregational Society," Chapter 79, Massachusetts Acts and Resolves, 1817; Petition for "An Act to Incorporate the First Baptist Society in Machias," Chapter 10, Massachusetts Acts and Resolves, 1819; CMaA, Legislative Papers.
38. Report of the Selectmen respecting the Ministerial Funds, 7 May 1817, Machias Town Records, 1:299–304; and Machias Town Records, 1816–1824.
39. Machias Town Records, 1802–1805; Petition for "An Act to Incorporate the Proprietors of the Machias Meeting House," Massachusetts Acts and Resolves, 1810; CMaA, Legislative Papers.
40. Robert Drew Simpson, ed., *American Methodist Pioneer: The Life and Journals of The Rev. Freeborn Garrettson, 1752–1827* (Rutland, VT: Academy, 1984), 127.
41. For overviews of the religious history of the Maritimes in this period see George A. Rawlyk, *The Canada Fire: Radical Evangelicalism in British North America, 1775–1812* (Kingston and Montreal: McGill–Queen's University Press, 1994); idem, *Ravished by the Spirit: Religious Revivals, Baptists, and Henry Alline* (Kingston and Montreal: McGill–Queen's Univeristy Press, 1984); idem, "A Total Revolution in Religious and Civil Government: The Maritimes, New England, and the Evolving Evangelical Ethos, 1776–1812" in Mark A. Noll, David W. Bebbington, and George A. Rawlyk, eds., *Evangelicalism: Comparative Studies of Popular Protestantism in North America, the British Isles, and Beyond, 1700–1900* (New York and Oxford: Oxford University Press, 1994) 137–155; and Bell, ed., *The Newlight Baptist Journals of James Manning and James Innis*, xi–xvii, 2–53.
42. Liverpool Proprietors' Records, 4 September 1761, NSARM, MG 4, Vol. 77; *Perkins's Diary*, 1:4 and 11 October 1767.
43. "The Memorial of the Congregational Church of Cornwallis in the County of Kings County in the Province of Nova Scotia [8 November 1769]," and "Benjamin Gerrish and Malachy Salter to the Reverend Mr. Andrew Eliot, Halifax, January 18, 1770," in Gordon T. Stewart, ed., *Documents Relating to the Great Awakening in Nova Scotia, 1760–1791* (Toronto: Champlain Society, 1982), 4–7; Stewart and Rawlyk, *'A People Highly Favoured of God,'* 31–33.
44. *Perkins's Diary*, 1:26 and 28 April 1772; 1:1, 3, 7, 21 May 1776; 1:1 and 25 August 1776.
45. *Perkins's Diary*, 1:30 and 31 August 1776; 1:18, 19 and 29 September 1776.
46. Liverpool Proprietors' Records, 29 June and 13 July 1761, NSARM, MG 4, Vol. 77; and Perkins's Diary, 1:22 June 1761; 1:3 July 1766. See Christine Leigh Heyrman, *Commerce and Culture: The Maritime Communities of Colonial Massachusetts, 1690–1750* (New York: Norton, 1984), 143–181 for a discussion of a dispute over pews in Gloucester, Massachusetts.
47. Liverpool Proprietors' Records, 26 September 1774 and 25 November 1774, NSARM, MG 4, Vol. 77; *Perkins's Diary*, 1:28 September 1774; 1:5, 13, 23, 25, and 26 November 1774.
48. *Perkins's Diary*, 1:30 and 31 August 1776, 1:1, 18, 29, and 29 September 1776, 1:4, 5, and 6 October 1776.
49. *Perkins's Diary*, 1:4, 5, 6, 23, 24, 28 October 1776; 1:3 November 1776.
50. *Perkins's Diary*, 1:10 & 17 November 1776; 1:11, 26, and 30 April 1777; 1:14 May 1777.
51. J.M. Bumsted, *Henry Alline 1748–1784* (Toronto: University of Toronto Press, 1971).
52. Perkins recorded in his diary that Alline arrived in Liverpool on 5 December and dined with him that evening. Alline recorded in his journal that he arrived in Liverpool on 11 December, but his entries were often synoptic and tended to telescope time, whereas Perkins's entries were almost daily and are therefore a more reliable record of when Alline actually arrived in Liverpool. As David G. Bell notes in "All Things New: The Transformation of Maritime Baptist Historiography," *Nova Scotia Historical Review* 4, 2 (1984): 69–81, Alline's journal is "pious redaction … intended for the use of saints rather than historians."
53. *Perkins's Diary*, 2:5, 9, and 15 December 1781.
54. *Perkins's Diary*, 2:14 and 30 December 1781, 2:3, 4, 5, 6, and 7 January 1782.
55. *Perkins's Diary*, 2:17, 20, 27 and 31 January 1782, 2:3 February 1782.
56. *Perkins's Diary*, 2:5, 6, 12, 24, and 26 February 1782.

57. *Perkins's Diary*, 2:3, 7, 10, 14, 17, 24, 28, and 31 March 1782; 2:7, 21, 25, 28 April 1782; 2:2, 9, 12, 19, 23, 26, and 30 May 1782; 2:9, 13, 16, 23, and 30 June 1782; Letter from Liverpool to Jonathan Scott, Yarmouth, NS, 7 August 1782, in Stewart, ed., *Documents Relating to the Great Awakening*, 146.

58. *Perkins's Diary*, 2:13, 14, 15, 17, 19, 21, 23, and 24 November 1782; 2:1, 25, and 29 December 1782; 2:26 and 30 January 1783; 2:8, 9, 12, 13, 14, and 16 February 1783. Cf. *Perkins's Diary*, 2:25 December 1782 and Alline's journal entry for 20 November 1782 entry, Stewart, ed., *Documents of the Great Awakening*, 277–278.

59. *Perkins's Diary*, 2:16 and 17 February 1783.

60. *Perkins's Diary*, 2:30 January 1783; 2:13 March 1783; and Brian C. Cuthbertson, ed., *The Journal of the Reverend John Payzant (1749–1834)* (Hantsport, NS: Lancelot, 1981), 59. Frank C. Burnett in "Henry Alline's Articles and Covenant of a Gospel Church," *Nova Scotia Historical Review* 4, 2 (1984): 13–24; argues that the last churches which Alline gathered were in Argyle and Barrington in 1782, although the evidence in Perkins's diary indicates otherwise.

61. Cuthbertson, ed., *The Journal of the Reverend John Payzant*, 59; "The Faith, Church Order, Discipline, and Covenant, of the Congregational Church, Liverpool, N.S." n.d. NSARM, MG 4, Vol. 125, No. N, No.14. An "open communion" plan meant that all professed Christians could commune in the church and not just those of the same denomination; see Bell, ed., *New Light Baptist Journals*, xvi.

62. *Perkins's Diary*, 2:28 and 29 May 1783; 2:1, 3, 22, and 25 June 1783; 2:7 December 1783. For disputes over other ministers see *Perkins's Diary*, 2:1 April 1784; 2:27 June 1784.

63. *Perkins's Diary*, 2:17 and 23 March 1784. For earlier complaints about Firmage, see *Perkins's Diary*, 2:14, 21, 23, 28 September 1783; 2:7 December 1783; 2:11 January 1784.

64. *Perkins's Diary*, 2:26 March 1784; 2:4, 24, 28 April 1784; 2:19, 26 December 1784; 2:10, 11, 12, 14,15 September 1784; 2:23 October 1787; 2:9 August 1788; 2:1, 26 October 1788; 2:10, 11, 17 August 1789; 2:1 September 1789; 2:25, 26, 27, 29, 30 November 1789; 2:6, 13, 27, December 1789; 3:3, 10, 11, 12, 13 January 1790; 3:6, 20 June 1790.

65. *Perkins's Diary*, 2:7 January 1785; 2:29 May 1785; 2:1, 3, 6, 7, 8, 15, 22 July 1787.

66. *Perkins's Diary*, 3:23, 26, 27, 28, 29 August 1790; 3:3 October 1790.

67. *Perkins's Diary*, 3:21, 25, 26 December 1790; 3:2, 9, 16, 21, 23, 26, 30 January 1791; 3:2, 6, 9, 13, 14, 16, 17, 20, 21, 24, 27, 18 February 1791.

68. *Perkins's Diary*, 3:28 February 1791; 3:1 March 1791; 3:17, 25, 29 Februray 1792; 3:7 March 1792; 3:27 February 1793, 3:1, 5, 7, 8, 12, 13 March 1791; 3:3, 28 May 1793; 3:3, 4, 7, 8, 9, 10, 11, 12, 13 June 1793.

69. Marini, *Radical Sects of Revolutionary New England*, 36–39.

70. Stewart and Rawlyk, *'A People Highly Favoured of God'*, 79–97, 154–192. Some of these issues can be found in James Beverly and Barry Moody, eds., *The Life and Journal of the Rev. Mr. Henry Alline* (Hantsport, NS: Lancelot, 1982), 13.

71. A copy of the subscription list for the support of the Rev. John Payzant, Zion Congregational Church, Liverpool, Nova Scotia, NSARM, MG 4, Vol. 77; A List of the early subscribers of the Methodist Church, Liverpool, Nova Scotia, NSARM, MG 4, Vol. 79. The genealogical data are taken from *Perkins's Diary*, Vol. 1–3, passim. For an examination of the possible socioeconomic underpinnings of the Allinite revival see Gordon Stewart, "Socio-Economic Factors in the Great Awakening: The Case of Yarmouth, Nova Scotia," *Acadiensis* 3, 1 (1973): 19–34.

72. Stephen Foster, "New England and the Challenge of Heresy, 1630 to 1660: The Puritan Crisis in Transatlantic Perspective," *William and Mary Quarterly*, 3d ser., 38 (1981): 624–660; idem, *The Long Argument: English Puritanism and the Shaping of New England Culture, 1570–1700* (Chapel Hill: University of North Carolina Press, 1991), 155–230; Philip F. Gura, *A Glimpse of Sion's Glory: Puritan Radicalism in New England, 1620–1660* (Middletown, CT: Wesleyan University Press, 1984), 1–14.

73. Harvey, ed. and intro., *Perkins's Diary*, 2:lvi. Allen B. Robertson, "Methodism Among Nova Scotia's Yankee Planters," in Conrad, ed., *They Planted Well*, 179.

74. Rhys Isaac, *The Transformation of Virginia* (Chapel Hill: University of North Carolina Press, 1982), 260–264; Goldwin French, *Parsons and Politics: The Role of the Wesleyan Methodists in Upper Canada and the Maritimes from 1780 to 1855* (Toronto: Ryerson, 1962), 21, 39, 278–287; Robertson, "Methodism Among Nova Scotia's Yankee Planters," 182–189; and David Hempton, "Methodist Growth in Transatlantic Perspective, ca. 1770–1850," in Nathan O. Hatch and John H. Wigger, eds., *Methodism and the Shaping of American Culture* (Nashville, TN: Kingswood, 2001), 41–85.

75. S.D. Clark, *Church and Sect in Canada* (Toronto: University of Toronto Press, 1948), 30–45; Daniel Goodwin, "From Disunity to Integration: Evangelical Religion and Society in Yarmouth, Nova Scotia, 1761–1830," in *They Planted Well*, 190–200.

76. Marini, "Religious Revolution," 120, 137.

77. Foster, *The Long Argument*, 155–230; and Gura, *A Glimpse of Sion's Glory*, passim. Gura argues that during the synods of 1648 and 1662 the Puritan radicals in Massachusetts and Connecticut were suppressed by Puritan orthodoxy. Richard Archer, *Fissures in the Rock: New England in the Seventeenth Century* (Hanover, NH, and London: University Press of New England, 2001), 27–58, argues that New England had considerable religious diversity, but questions whether the various early groups can be legitimately included under the Puritan umbrella as Gura groups them. The example from Liverpool, and probably from other towns settled in Northern New England and Nova Scotia, suggests that the divergence of doctrinal sensibilities within New England Puritanism/Congregationalism may have been greater than people realized and had one of its strongest manifestations when people moved some distance to a new town.

78. See Paul R. Lucas, *Valley of Discord: Church and Society along the Connecticut River, 1636–1725* (Hanover, NH: University Press of New England, 1976) for an argument about the shift from clerical to lay control in congregations, including over "doctrine and discipline" (p. 20–21).

79. Quoted in Maurice W. Armstrong, *The Great Awakening in Nova Scotia, 1776–1809* (Hartford, CT: American Society of Church History, 1948) 18–21.

80. Margaret Ells, *A Study of Early Provincial Taxation: Being a Tabular Statement of Fiscal Legislation in Nova Scotia Between 1751 and 1815, with an Introduction and an Appendix* (Halifax: Provincial Archives, 1937), 1–5.

81. Judith Fingard, *The Anglican Design in Loyalist Nova Scotia, 1783– 1816* (London: Church Historical Society, 1972), 87–98.

82. Rawlyk, *Ravished by the Spirit*, 116–118.

83. John Payzant, pastor of Zion Congregationalist Church in Liverpool, Henry Alline's brother-in-law, and the only ordained New Light minister in Nova Scotia, developed an acrimonious relationship with Baptists when they tried to get him to become a Baptist and wanted converts from his parishioners to become Baptists; see George A. Rawlyk, *Wrapped Up In God: A Study of Several Canadian Revivals and Revivalists* (Burlington, ON: Welch, 1988), 78–89.

84. For example, see Marini, *Radical Sects of Revolutionary New England*, 5, 25–39; and Taylor, *Liberty Men and Great Proprietors*, 131–142.

85. I use this term "frontier" cautiously, and only within the context of the historiographical discussion. In general, "frontier" is not a useful descriptor, much less analytic category, for studying eighteenth-century Maine and Nova Scotia.

86. "Machias Settlers," *Collections of the Maine Historical Society*, 1st ser. 3 (1853), 179–180; E. P. White, "Nova Scotia Settlers from Chatham, Massachusetts 1759–1760," *National Genealogical Society Quarterly* 62 (1974): 96–117.

87. On the maintenance of internal religious cohesion in New England towns see Michael Zuckerman, *Peaceable Kingdoms: New England Towns in the Eighteenth Century* (New York: Knopf, 1970), 51–65. Clark in *Church and Sect in Canada*, 14–15, suggests that Nova Scotia inherited the schisms within New England Congregationalism.

88. Marini, "Religious Revolution," 137; and Taylor, *Liberty Men and Great Proprietors*, 124–127.

89. William Henry Kilby, ed., *Eastport and Passamaquoddy: A Collection of Historical and Biographical Sketches* (1888; reprint ed., Eastport, ME: Border History Fathom Series, 1982), 70–72, 490–491.

90. David Jaffee, *People of the Wachusett: Greater New England in History and Memory, 1630–1860* (Ithaca and London: Cornell University Press, 1999), 3 and passim, argues that New England's process of expansion was basically conservative with "serial town settlement."

91. Taylor, *Liberty Men and Great Proprietors*; and Bellesiles, *Revolutionary Outlaws*.

Chapter 7

1. T.H. Breen, "Persistent Localism: English Social Change and the Shaping of New England Institutions," *William and Mary Quarterly*, 3d ser., 32 (1975): 3–28. David Thomas Konig challenges Breen's contention that town organization was an early priority of Puritan leaders in "English Legal Change and the Origins of Local Government in Northern Massachusetts," in Bruce C. Daniels, ed., *Town and County: Essays on the Structure of Local Government in the American Colonies* (Middletown, CT: Wesleyan University Press, 1978), 12–43. On royal challenges to municipal charters in England, see Paul D. Halliday, *Dismembering the Body Politic: Partisan Politics in England's Towns, 1650–1730* (Cambridge: Cambridge University Press, 1998).
2. Brebner, *New England's Outpost*, 72–73, 134, 239, quote on 73. British policy in Nova Scotia was not a sudden shift, but part of a long process of trying to gain greater control over the colonial ventures that were chartered in the seventeenth century; see Mancke, "Chartered Enterprises and the Evolution of the British Atlantic World." British officials, however, faced extreme difficulty in crafting a government for Nova Scotia between 1713 and 1749; see Mancke, "Imperial Transitions."
3. J. Murray Beck, *The Evolution of Municipal Government in Nova Scotia, 1749–1973* (Halifax, Nova Scotia: Royal Commission on Education, Public Services, and Provincial-Municipal Relations, 1973). Except for Nova Scotia, scholars of municipal governments in Canada have not paid heed to the imperial context in shaping their development. See Kenneth Grant Crawford, *Canadian Municipal Government* (Toronto: University of Toronto Press, 1954), 1–47; and C.R. Tindal and S. Nobes Tindal, *Local Government in Canada*, 2d ed. (Toronto: McGraw-Hill Ryerson, 1984), 11–25. For an important caveat, see C.F.J. Whebell, "The Upper Canada District Councils Act of 1841 and British Colonial Policy," *Journal of Imperial and Commonwealth History* 17 (1989): 185–209.
4. Brown, *Revolutionary Politics in Massachusetts*, passim.
5. Mancke, "Early Modern Imperial Governance and the Origins of Canadian Political Culture," 7–20.
6. Daniels, "Introduction," in *Town and County*, 7; Daniels, "The Political Structure of Local Government in Colonial Connecticut," in *Town and County*, 44–71; and Brown, *Revolutionary Politics in Massachusetts*, 3–6.
7. On the commonalities among local governments in colonial British America see the essays in Daniels, ed., *Town and County*.
8. Daniels, *The Connecticut Town*, 67.
9. David Ammerman, *In the Common Cause: American Response to the Coercive Acts of 1774* (Charlottesville: University Press of Virginia, 1974), 7–8; Brown, *Revolutionary Politics in Massachusetts*, 190, 192; and Jack N. Rakove, *The Beginnings of National Politics: An Interpretive History of the Continental Congress* (New York: Knopf, 1979), 44–47.
10. Machias Town Records, 1784 and 1794, Machias Town Office; East Machias Town Records, 1826 and 1834, East Machias Town Office; Records of the Clerk of the Court of Sessions, Liverpool, Nova Scotia, 1826, NAC; "Officers Appointed and Regulations Made by The General Sessions of the Peace Held at Liverpool, April Term, for the Town of Liverpool and County of Queens for the Year 1834," NSARM, RG 34-319, O.1.
11. On the changing nature of town officers, see Daniels, "The Political Structure of Local Government in Colonial Connecticut," in *Town and County*, 53–68.
12. There is no good study of the timber trade in eastern Maine or Nova Scotia for the late eighteenth century and the first two decades of the nineteenth century. The best regional account for this period is Graeme Wynn, *Timber Colony: A Historical Geography of Early Nineteenth Century New Brunswick* (Toronto: University of Toronto Press, 1981).
13. Brown, *Revolutionary Politics in Massachusetts*, 4–6.
14. Edward M. Cook, Jr., *Fathers of the Towns: Leadership and Community Structure in Eighteenth Century New England* (Baltimore: Johns Hopkins University Press, 1976); and Bruce C. Daniels, "Diversity and Democracy: Officeholding Patterns among Selectmen in Eighteenth-Century Connecticut," in Daniels, ed., *Power and Status: Officeholding in Colonial America*, (Middletown, CT: Wesleyan University Press, 1986), 36–52.

15. Proprietors' Records of Liverpool, 1 July 1760; *Perkins's Diary*, 3:4n.

16. Harvey, ed., and intro., *Perkins's Diary*, 2:xxiv–xxv, 11n., 38n, 238n; Proprietors' Records of Liverpool, 1 July 1760; Book of Commissions, NSARM, RG 1, Vol. 164: 104, 106, 178, 233–235, 238, 246–252.

17. Machias Town Records, 6 April 1795; 16 August 1784; Property Valuations in Washington County, 1798, Papers of John Cooper, Maine Historical Society; Proprietors' Records of Machias, 12 May 1784; County Commissioners Records, Vol. 1, Washington County Court House; Letter from George Stillman, *DHMe*, 14:436–437.

18. *Perkins's Diary*, 2:207n; 2:18 July to 7 November 1789, passim; 3:18 January to 18 May 1790, passim; 3:24 October 1792.

19. Daniels, *The Connecticut Town*, 34–44.

20. For sites of the annual town meeting, see Machias Town Records, passim. For evidence of alternating church services see Minutes for 13 May 1799, ibid.

21. "An Act to divide the town of Machias and incorporate the towns of West Machias, East, Machias, and Machiasport," 26 January 1826, Chapter CCCLXVII, *Private or Special Laws of the State of Maine, from 1820 to 1828 inclusive, Vol. 1* (Portland, 1828). The petition is in the Legislative Papers, 1/1, 1826, Chapter 8, Box 39, Maine State Archives (hereafter MeSA).

22. Petition that the name of the town of West Machias be changed to Machias, 6 January 1827, MeSA, 1/3, 1827, Env. 26; Remonstrance from East Machias, n.d., Legislative Graveyard, MeSA, 1/1, 1830, Chapter 39, Box 65; An Act to Change the Name of West Machias, 10 March 1830, *Private or Special Laws*, and Petition, 25 February 1830.

23. Minutes, 1 November 1839, 12 February 1840, and 6 April 1841, East Machias Town Records.

24. *Maine State Yearbook and Legislative Manual for the Year 1875–6* (Portland, 1875); *Maine Register, State Yearbook and Legislative Manual*, No. 66 (Portland: Fred G. Towers Companies, 1935).

25. Council Minutes, NSARM, RG 1, Vol. 188: 94–96, 317, 413; Yarmouth Petition, NSARM, RG 1, Vol. 222, No. 59; Beck, *The Government of Nova Scotia*, 302–303; and Charles Morse, "Provincial and Local Government," in Adam Shortt and Arthur G. Doughty, eds., *Canada and Its Provinces: A History of the Canadian People and Their Institutions, Vol. 14., Atlantic Provinces* (Edinburgh: University of Edinburgh Press, 1914), 14:479–480.

26. Haliburton, *An Historical and Statistical Account of Nova Scotia*, 2:277; and *Fifth Census: Or, Enumeration of the Inhabitants of the United States, as Corrected at the Department of State, 1830* (Washington, DC, 1832).

27. Martin, Robert Montgomery, *History of the Colonies of the British Empire in the West Indies, South America, North America, Asia, Austral-Asia, Africa, and Europe* (London, 1843), 154–155, 185–195, 216, 238; and *Fifth Census: Or, Enumeration of the Inhabitants of the United States, as Corrected at the Department of State*, 1830, passim.

28. On the structure of colonial local government that those states inherited see the essays in Daniels, ed., *Town and County*.

29. Commissioners Minute Books, Vol. 1, Washington County Court House. The papers on the licenses are stored loose in the Court House with the supplemental papers on county roads.

30. Records of the Clerk of the Court of Sessions, Liverpool, Nova Scotia, 1816–1828, NAC.

31. Minutes, 27 February 1785 and 27 April 1786, Machias Town Records; Letter from James Avery, et al., to Caleb Davis, 22 May 1786, Vol. 13a, Caleb Davis Papers, MHS; Letter from Avery to Davis, 8 June 1786, Vol. 13a, ibid.; Letter from Avery to Davis, 9 June 1786, Vol. 13a, ibid.; and Letter from Avery and Stephen Jones to Davis, 24 November 1787, Vol. 14b, ibid.

32. Minutes, 5 May 1819 and 31 December 1821, Machias Town Records.

33. *Maine State Yearbook and Legislative Manual for the Year 1875–6*.

34. Kenneth Lockridge, *A New England Town: The First Hundred Years, Dedham, Massachusetts, 1636–1736* (New York: Norton, 1970), 16–17; Douglas Lamar Jones, "The Strolling Poor: Transiency in Eighteenth-Century Massachusetts," *Journal of Social History* 8 (1975): 28–54; Martin, *Profits in the Wilderness*, 218–227, 236–237, 245–253, 257–293.

35. Sydney V. James, *The Colonial Metamorphoses in Rhode Island: A Study of Institutions in Change* (Hanover, NH, and London: University Press of New England, 2000), 197–199, 207–225.

36. Handlin and Handlin, *Commonwealth*, 91–92, 87–105; and Akagi, *The Town Proprietors of New England Colonies*, 50–84.

37. Chapter CXXXI, "An act to incorporate the proprietors of the East Meeting House in Machias, February 7, 1822," in *Private or Special Laws*, Vol. 1; and Chapter CCXXIX, "An act to incorporate the owners and proprietors of the East Meeting House in Machias, January 26, 1824," ibid., 179–180. See also the Legislative Record, MeSA, Box 19, 1822, Chapter 63, and Box 27, 1824, Chapter 4.

38. Chapter 79, "An Act to Incorporate the Machias Congregational Society," *Massachusetts Acts and Resolves*, 1820; and Legislative Papers, MeSA, 1/3, 1820, Env. 22.

39. John D. Cushing, "Notes on Disestablishment in Massachusetts, 1780–1833," *William and Mary Quarterly* 3d ser., 26 (1969): 169–190.

40. Armand Budington DuBois, *The English Business Company after the Bubble Act, 1720–1800* (1931; rpt., New York: Octagon, 1971).

41. Records of the Clerk of the Court of Sessions, Liverpool, Nova Scotia, 1818, NAC; Liverpool School Records, NSARM, RG 14, Vol. 56; Charles Bruce Fergusson, "The Inauguration of the Free School System in Nova Scotia," *Bulletin of the Public Archives of Nova Scotia*, No. 21 (Halifax, 1964); A.H. MacKay, "History of Education in Nova Scotia and Prince Edward Island," in *Canada and Its Provinces*, Vol. 14, *Atlantic Provinces*, 515, 520–524; and G.U. Hay, "History of Education in New Brunswick," in ibid., 547–548, 552–554.

42. Records of the Clerk of the Court of Sessions, 1816–28, Liverpool, Nova Scotia, NAC. For road building in Nova Scotia, see W.R. Bird, "History of the Highways of Nova Scotia," (Halifax: Department of Highways and Public Works, n.d., unpublished typescript), 1–52.

43. Summary of Rate Bills, NSARM, RG 34-319, A.4.

44. Ells, *A Study of Early Provincial Taxation*, passim.

45. East Machias Town Records, East Machias, Maine.

46. J. Murray Beck, "Ups and Downs of Halifax Influence in Nova Scotia Government, 1749–1981," *Transactions of the Royal Society of Canada*, 4th ser., 19 (1981): 72; and idem, *The Government of Nova Scotia*, 302–303. In 1879, the assembly finally decided to force municipal government on the province, and passed the County Incorporation Act. That legislation transferred bridge and road service to municipal councils and reduced the provincial road expenditures from $140,000 to $85,000 per year.

47. Quoted in Dale A. Oesterle, "Formative Contribution to American Corporate Law by the Massachusetts Supreme Judicial Court from 1806 to 1810," in *The History of the Law in Massachusetts: The Supreme Judicial Court 1692–1992*, Russell K. Osgood, ed. (Boston: Supreme Judicial Court Historical Society, 1992), 136n47.

48. Handlin and Handlin, *Commonwealth*, 153–155.

49. For essays on state formation in nineteenth-century British North America and the Dominion of Canada, see Allan Greer and Ian Radforth, eds., *Colonial Leviathan: State Formation in Mid-Nineteenth-Century Canada* (Toronto: University of Toronto Press, 1992).

Conclusion

1. Harvey, "The Struggle for the New England Form of Township Government in Nova Scotia," 184–194.

2. Ammerman, *In the Common Cause*, 7–8.

3. Greene, "Political Mimesis;" and Greene, "Metropolis and Colonies," 50–52, 54–55, 57–58. Harvey, ed., "Governor Lawrence's Case Against an Assembly in Nova Scotia," passim;

4. Greene, *Peripheries and Center*, 55–76.

5. Jack P. Greene, "The Jamaica Privilege Controversy, 1764–66: An Episode in the Process of Constitutional Definition in the Early Modern British Empire," *Journal of Imperial and Commonwealth History* 22 (1994): 16–53.

6. Bailyn, *The Ideological Origins of the American Revolution*, 162–175.

7. See Chapters 4 and 5.

8. Mancke, "Imperial Transitions," passim.

9. John Bartlet Brebner, "Nova Scotia's Remedy for the American Revolution," *Canadian Historical Review* 15 (1934): 171–181.

10. Archibald Kennedy, *An essay on the government of the colonies: fitted to the latitude of forty-one, but may, without sensible error, serve all the northern colonies* (New York, 1752); Thomas Pownall, *The administration of the colonies*, 3d ed. (London, 1766); and William Smith, *Thoughts upon the present contest, between administration, and the British colonies in America: addressed to the merchants of the city of London, and all the seaport, trading, and manufacturing towns, in Great Britain and Ireland* (London, 1775).

11. Timothy J. Shannon, *Indians and Colonists at the Crossroads of Empire: The Albany Congress of 1754* (Ithaca, NY, and London: Cornell University Press, 2000), 174–233.

12. Janice Potter, *The Liberty We Seek: Loyalist Ideology in Colonial New York and Massachusetts* (Cambridge, MA: Harvard University Press, 1983), 153–180.

13. Mancke, "Early Modern Imperial Governance and the Origins of Canadian Political Culture," 3–20.

Bibliography

Manuscript Sources

I. Nova Scotia Archives and Records Management (NSARM)

A. Record Group (RG) Series—Government Documents

RG 1, Vol. 22: Council Minutes
RG 1, Vol. 37: Dispatches from the Governors to the Board of Trade and Plantations
RG 1, Vol. 136: Inland Letter Book, 1760–1784
RG 1, Vol. 163: Commission Book, 1749–1759
RG 1, Vol. 164: Commission Book, 1749–1766
RG 1, Vol. 165: Commission Book, 1759–1766
RG 1, Vol. 170: Orderly Book, 1768–1792
RG 1, Vol. 171: Commission Book, 1793–1796
RG 1, Vol. 188: Council Minutes, 1757–1766
RG 1, Vol. 204: Council Minutes, Land, 1761–1763
RG 1, Vol. 211: Council Minutes, 1757–1766
RG 1, Vol. 212: Council Minutes, 1766–1783
RG 1, Vol. 222: Papers of the township grants, memorials, militia, and repeal of laws against Catholics, 1757–1781
RG 1, Vol. 443: Census and Assessment Roles, 1767–1794
RG 14, Vol. 56: School Papers
RG 20, Series C: Land Papers
RG 34–319: Queens County Government Papers

B. Manuscript Group (MG) Series—Town Records and Non-Government Documents

MG 4, Vol. 77: Liverpool Records, Queens County
MG 4, Vol. 79: Liverpool Methodist Church
MG 4, Vol. 125: Pictou County Miscellaneous
MG 100, Vol. 121: Miscellaneous Private Papers
MG 100, Vol. 176: Miscellaneous Private Papers

C. C.B. Ferguson Collection

II. Muncipality of Queens, Registry of Deeds
Proprietors' Allotment Book
Proprietors' Record Book

III. Acadia University Archives
 Edward Manning Papers

IV. National Archives of Canada (NAC)
 British Headquarter Papers
 Queens County Court of Sessions Records

V. Massachusetts Historical Society (MHS)
 Caleb Davis Papers

VI. Commonwealth of Massachusetts Archives (CMaA)
 Vol. 14
 Vol. 26
 Vol. 27
 Vol. 118
 Eastern Land Papers, Box 14
 Unenacted Legislative Papers
 Enacted Legislative Papers

VII. Maine Historical Society (MeHS)
 John Cooper Papers
 Boston and Eastern Mill and Land Company Papers

VIII. Maine State Archives (MeSA)
 Legislative Papers

IX. Washington County Court House
 The Proprietors' Book of Records of Machias
 Commissioners' Minute Books
 Land Deeds

X. Machias Town Hall
 Records of the Town of Machias

XI. East Machias Town Hall
 Records of the Town of East Machias

XII. Porter Memorial Library
 Records of the Church of Christ at Machias

Published Primary Sources

Ahlin, John Howard, ed. *The Saint's Daily Assistant: James Lyon, His Life and Meditations*. Machias, ME: Center Street Congregationalist Church, 1983.

Baxter, James P., ed. *Documentary History of the State of Maine*, 24 vols. Portland: Maine Historical Society, 1889–1916 (*DHMe*).

Belknap, Jeremy. *The History of New Hampshire*, 2 vols. Boston: 1784–1792.

Bell, D. G., ed. *The Newlight Baptist Journals of James Manning and James Innis*. Hantsport, NS: Lancelot, 1984.

Beverly, James and Barry Moody, eds. *The Life and Journal of the Rev. Mr. Henry Alline*. Hantsport, NS: Lancelot, 1982.

Cooper, John. "A Topographical Description of Machias, in the County of Washington." *Collections of the Massachusetts Historical Society,* 1st ser., 3 (1794): 144–148.

Crèvecoeur, J. Hector St. John de. *Letters from an American Farmer*. New York: Dutton [1912].

Cuthbertson, Brian C., ed. *The Journal of the Reverend John Payzant (1749–1834)*. Hantsport, NS: Lancelot, 1981.

Greenleaf, Moses. *A Survey of the State of Maine in Reference to Its Geographical Features, Statistics and Political Economy*. 1829. Reprint. Augusta: Maine State Museum, 1970.

Haliburton, Thomas C. *An Historical and Statistical Account of Nova Scotia*. 2 vols. Halifax: Joseph Howe, 1829.

The Importance of Settling and Fortifying Nova Scotia; With a Particular Account of the Climate, Soil, and Native Inhabitants of the Country. By a Gentleman lately arrived from the colony. London, 1751.

Jones, Stephen. "Historical Account of Machias." *Maine Historical Society Quarterly*, 15, 2 (1975): 44–56.

Kennedy, Archibald. *An essay on the government of the colonies: Fitted to the latitude forty-one, but may, without sensible error, serve all the northern colonies*. New York, 1752.

Kidder, Frederic, ed. *Military Operations in Eastern Maine and Nova Scotia During the Revolution*. 1867. Reprint. New York: Kraus Reprint, 1971.

Labaree, Leonard Woods, ed. *Royal Instructions to British Governors, 1670–1776*. 2 vols. 1935. Reprint. New York: Octagon, 1967.

Lincoln, Benjamin. "Observations on the Climate, Soil and Value of the Eastern Counties, in the District of Maine; written in the Year 1789." *Collections of the Massachusetts Historical Society*, 1st ser. 4 (1795): 142–153.

Lincoln, Benjamin. "Copy of a Letter from the Hon. General Lincoln, on the Religious State of the Eastern Counties in the District of Maine." *Collections of the Massachusetts Historical Society*, 1st ser. 4 (1795): 153–156.

Lockwood, Anthony. *A brief description of Nova Scotia, with plates of the principal Harbors including a particular account of the island of Grand Manan*. London, 1818.

Maine State Yearbook and Legislative Manual for the Year 1875–6. Portland, 1875.

Maine Register, State Yearbook and Legislative Manual. No. 66. Portland, 1935.

Martin, Robert Montgomery. *History of the Colonies of the British Empire in the West Indies, South America, North America, Asia, Austral-Asia, Africa, and Europe*. London, 1843.

"Miscellaneous Remarks and Observations on Nova Scotia, New Brunswick, and Cape Breton. Supposed to Be Written by the Surveyor General of Nova Scotia." *Collections of the Massachusetts Historical Society*, 3 (1794): 98.

Morris, Charles. "Description and State of the New Settlements in Nova Scotia in 1761." Canadian Archives *Report* (1904): 289–300.

Nova Scotia. "Statistics of Each County of the Province of Nova Scotia." *Journals and Proceedings of the House of Assembly*. Halifax, 1851.

Perkins, Simeon. *The Diary of Simeon Perkins, 1766–1780*. Vol. 1. Ed. Harold A. Innis. Toronto: Champlain Society, 1948.

Perkins, Simeon. *The Diary of Simeon Perkins, 1780–1789*. Vol. 2. Ed. D. C. Harvey. Toronto: Champlain Society, 1958.

Perkins, Simeon. *The Diary of Simeon Perkins, 1790–1796*. Vol. 3. Ed. Charles Bruce Ferguson. Toronto: Champlain Society, 1961.

Perkins, Simeon. *The Diary of Simeon Perkins, 1797–1803*. Vol. 4. Ed. Charles Bruce Ferguson. Toronto: Champlain Society, 1967.

Perkins, Simeon. *The Diary of Simeon Perkins, 1804–1812*. Vol. 5. Ed. Charles Bruce Ferguson. Toronto: Champlain Society, 1978.

Poole, Edmond Duval. *Annals of Yarmouth and Barrington, Nova Scotia, in the Revolutionary War*. Yarmouth, NS, 1899.

Pownall, Thomas. *The administration of the colonies*. 3rd ed. London, 1766.

Private or Special Laws of the State of Maine, from 1820 to 1828 inclusive. Vol. 1. Portland, 1828.

"Return of the Men, Women and Children in the County of Queens made by Order of His Excellancy, the Lieutenant-Governor, April 30, 1787." Public Archives of Nova Scotia *Report* (1937): 56–61.

Simpson, Robert Drew, ed. *American Methodist Pioneer: The Life and Journals of the Rev. Freeborn Garrettson, 1752–1827*. Rutland, VT: Academy, 1984.

Smith, William. *Thoughts upon the present contest, between administration, and the British colonies in America: addressed to the merchants of the city of London, and all the seaport, trading, and manufacturing towns, in Great Britain and Ireland*. London, 1775.

"State and Condition of the Province of Nova Scotia Together With Some Observations … October 29, 1763." Public Archives of Nova Scotia *Report* (1933): 21–26.

"Statistics of Each County of the Province of Nova Scotia." *Journals and Proceedings of the House of Assembly*. Halifax, 1851. Appendix 16.

Stewart, Gordon, ed. *Documents Relating to the Great Awakening in Nova Scotia, 1760–1791*. Toronto: Champlain Society, 1982.

United States. *Heads of Families at the First Census of the United States, taken in the year 1790, Maine.* 1908. Reprint. Baltimore: Genealogical Publishing, 1966.

United States. *Second Census of the United States, Return of the Whole Number of Persons within the Several Districts of the United States.* Facsimile. Washington, 1801.

United States. *Aggregate Amount of Persons Within the United States in the Year 1810.* Facsimile. Washington, 1811.

United States. *Census for 1820, Fourth Census, Book I.* Facsimile. Washington, 1821.

United States. *Fifth Census: Or, Enumeration of the Inhabitants of the United States, as Corrected at the Department of State, 1830.* Facsimile. Washington, 1832.

Secondary Sources

Ahlin, John H. *Maine Rubicon: Downeast Settlers During the American Revolution.* Calais, ME: Calais Advertiser Press, 1966.

Ajzenstat, Janet and Peter J. Smith, eds. *Canada's Origins: Liberal, Tory, or Republican?* Ottawa: Carlton University Press, 1985.

Akagi, Roy Hidemichi. *The Town Proprietors of the New England Colonies: A Study of Their Development, Organization, Activities and Controversies, 1620–1770.* 1924. Reprint. Gloucester, MA: Peter Smith, 1963.

Albion, Robert Greenlaugh. *Forests and Sea Power: The Timber Problem of the Royal Navy, 1652–1862.* 1926. Reprint. Hamden, CT: Archon, 1965.

Allis, Frederick S., Jr. *William Bingham's Maine Lands, 1790–1820,* 2 vols. Boston: Colonial Society of Massachusetts, 1954.

Ammerman, David. *In the Common Cause: American Response to the Coercive Acts of 1774.* Charlottesville: University Press of Virginia, 1974.

Anderson, Fred. *A People's Army: Massachusetts Soldiers and Society in the Seven Years' War.* Chapel Hill: University of North Carolina Press, 1984.

Anderson, Fred. *Crucible of War; The Seven Years' War and the Fate of Empire in British North America, 1754–1766.* New York: Knopf, 2000.

Andrews, Charles M. *The Colonial Period of American History.* 4 vols. New Haven, CT: Yale University Press, 1934–1938.

Archer, Richard. *Fissures in the Rock: New England in the Seventeenth Century.* Hanover, NH and London: University Press of New England, 2001.

Armstrong, Maurice W. *The Great Awakening in Nova Scotia, 1776–1809.* Hartford, CT: American Society of Church History, 1948.

Bailyn, Bernard. *The Ideological Origins of the American Revolution.* Cambridge, MA: Belknap, 1967.

Bailyn, Bernard. *Voyagers to the West: A Passage in the Peopling of America on the Eve of the Revolution.* New York: Vintage, 1988.

Baker, Emerson W. and John G. Reid. "Amerindian Power in the Early Modern Northeast: A Reappraisal." *William and Mary Quarterly,* 3d ser., 61 (2004): 77–106.

Banks, Ronald F. *Maine Becomes a State: The Movement to Separate Maine from Massachusetts, 1785–1820.* Middletown, CT: Wesleyan University Press, 1970.

Beck, J. Murray. *The Government of Nova Scotia.* Toronto: University of Toronto Press, 1957.

Beck, J. Murray. *The Evolution of Municipal Government in Nova Scotia, 1749–1973.* Halifax: Nova Scotia Royal Commission on Education, Public Services, and Provincial-Municipal Relations, 1973.

Beck, J. Murray. "Ups and Downs of Halifax Influence in Nova Scotia Government, 1749–1981." *Transactions of the Royal Society of Canada,* 4th ser., 19 (1981).

Bell, D. G. *Early Loyalist Saint John: The Origin of New Brunswick Politics, 1783–1786.* Fredericton, NB: New Ireland, 1983.

Bell, D. G. "All Things New: The Transformation of Maritime Baptist Historiography." *Nova Scotia Historical Review,* 4, 2 (1984): 69–81.

Bell, Winthrop P. *The Foreign Protestants and the Settlement of Nova Scotia: The History of a Piece of Arrested British Colonial Policy in the Eighteenth Century.* Toronto: University of Toronto Press, 1961.

Bellesiles, Michael A. *Revolutionary Outlaws: Ethan Allen and the Struggle for Independence on the Early American Frontier.* Charlottesville and London: University Press of Virginia, 1993.

Bird, W. R. "History of the Highways of Nova Scotia." Halifax: Department of Highways and Public Works, n.d. unpublished typescript.

Blakeley, Phyllis. "Silvanus Cobb." In *Dictionary of Canadian Biography, Vol. 3, 1741–1770*. Toronto: University of Toronto Press, 1974, 128–130.

Borque, Bruce J. *Twelve Thousand Years: American Indians in Maine*. Lincoln and London: University of Nebraska Press, 2001.

Braddick, Michael J. "The English Government, War, Trade, and Settlement, 1625–1688." In *The Oxford History of the British Empire, Vol. 1, The Origins of Empire: British Overseas Enterprise to the Close of the Seventeenth Century*. Ed. Nicholas Canny. Oxford: Oxford University Press, 1998, 286–308.

Brebner, John Bartlet. *New England's Outpost: Acadia before the Conquest of Canada*. 1927. Reprint. New York: Burt Franklin, 1973.

Brebner, John Bartlet. "Nova Scotia's Remedy for the American Revolution." *Canadian Historical Review*, 15 (1934), 171–181.

Brebner, John Bartlet. *The Neutral Yankees of Nova Scotia: A Marginal Colony during the Revolutionary Years*. 1937. Reprint. New York: Russell & Russell, 1970.

Breen, T. H. "Persistent Localism: English Social Change and the Shaping of New England Institutions." *William and Mary Quarterly*, 3d ser., 32 (1975): 3–28.

Breen, T. H. "The Baubles of Britain: The American and Consumer Revolutions of the Eighteenth Century." In *Of Consuming Interests: The Style of Life in the Eighteenth Century*. Eds. Carey Carson, Ronald Hoffman, and Peter J. Albert. Charlottesville: University Press of Virgina, 1994, 444–482.

Bremer, Francis J. *The Puritan Experiment: New England Society from Bradford to Edwards*. Rev. Ed. Hanover, NH and London: University Press of New England, 1995.

Brewer, John. *The Sinews of Power: War, Money, and the English State, 1688–1783*. London and Boston: Unwin, 1989.

Brown, Richard D. *Revolutionary Politics in Massachusetts: The Boston Committee of Correspondence and the Towns, 1772–1774*. Cambridge, MA: Harvard University Press, 1970.

Brown, Richard Maxwell. *The South Carolina Regulators*. Cambridge, MA: Harvard University Press, 1963.

Buckner, Phillip A. and John G. Reid, eds. *The Atlantic Region to Confederation: A History*. Toronto: University of Toronto Press, 1994.

Bumsted, J. M. *Henry Alline, 1748–1784*. Toronto: University of Toronto Press, 1971.

Bumsted, J. M. *Understanding the Loyalists*. Sackville, NB: Centre for Canadian Studies, Mount Allison University, 1986.

Bumsted, J. M. "1763–1783 Resettlement and Rebellion." In *The Atlantic Region to Confederation: A History*. Eds. Phillip A. Buckner and John G. Reid. Toronto: University of Toronto Press, 1994, 156–183.

Burnett, Frank C. "Henry Alline's Articles and Covenant of a Gospel Church." *Nova Scotia Historical Review*, 4, 2 (1984): 13–24.

Bushman, Richard. *King and People in Provincial Massachusetts*. Chapel Hill: University of North Carolina Press, 1985.

Carroll, Francis M. *A Good and Wise Measure: The Search for the Canadian–American Boundary, 1783–1842*. Toronto: University of Toronto Press, 2001.

Cell, Gillian T. *English Enterprise in Newfoundland, 1577–1660*. Toronto: University of Toronto Press, 1969.

Churchill, Edwin A. "The Historiography of the Margaretta Affair, or, How Not to Let the Facts Interfere With a Good Story."*Maine Historical Society Quarterly*, 15, 2 (1975): 60–74.

Clark, Andrew Hill. *Acadia: The Geography of Early Nova Scotia to 1760*. Madison: University of Wisconsin Press, 1968.

Clark, Charles E. *The Eastern Frontier: The Settlement of Northern New England, 1610–1763*. New York: Knopf, 1970.

Clark, S. D. *Church and Sect in Canada*. Toronto: University of Toronto Press, 1948.

Clarke, Ernest A. *The Siege of Fort Cumberland, 1776: An Episode in the American Revolution*. Montreal and Kingston: McGill–Queen's University Press, 1995.

Clarke, Ernest A. and Jim Phillips. "Rebellion and Repression in Nova Scotia in the Era of the American Revolution." In *Canadian State Trials: Law, Politics, and Security Measures, 1608–1837*. Eds. F. Murray Greenwood and Barry Wright. Toronto: University of Toronto Press, 1996, 172–220.

Cole, John W. and Eric R. Wolf. *The Hidden Frontier: Ecology and Ethnicity in an Alpine Valley.* New York: Academic, 1974.

Condon, Ann Gorman. "1783–1800: Loyalist Arrival, Acadian Return, Imperial Reform." In *The Atlantic Region to Confederation: A History.* Phillip A. Buckner and John G. Reid, Eds. Toronto: University of Toronto Press, 1994, 184–209.

Conlin, Dan. "A Private War in the Caribbean: Nova Scotia Privateering, 1793–1805." M.A. thesis: Saint Mary's University, 1996.

Cook, Edward M., Jr. *The Fathers of the Towns: Leadership and Community Structure in Eighteenth Century New England.* Baltimore: Johns Hopkins University Press, 1976.

Crawford, Kenneth Grant. *Canadian Municipal Government.* Toronto: University of Toronto Press, 1954.

Cushing, John D. "Notes on Disestablishment in Massachusetts, 1780–1833." *William and Mary Quarterly,* 3d ser., 26 (1969): 169–190.

Cuthbertson, Brian. *Johnny Bluenose at the Polls: Epic Nova Scotian Elections Battles, 1758–1848.* Halifax: Formac, 1994.

Daigle, Jean. "Acadia, 1604–1763: An Historical Synthesis." In *The Acadians of the Maritimes: Thematic Studies.* Ed. Jean Daigle. Moncton, NB: Centre d'études acadiennes, 1982, 17–46.

Daigle, Jean and Robert LeBlanc. "Acadian Deportation and Return." In *The Historical Atlas of Canada. Vol. 1. From the Beginning to 1800.* Ed. R. Cole Harris. Toronto: University of Toronto, 1987. Plate 30.

Daniels, Bruce C., ed. *Town and County: Essays on the Structure of Local Government in the American Colonies.* Middletown, CT: Wesleyan University Press, 1978.

Daniels, Bruce C. *The Connecticut Town: Growth and Development, 1635–1790.* Middletown, CT: Wesleyan University Press, 1979.

Daniels, Bruce C. "Diversity and Democracy: Officeholding Patterns among Selectmen in Eighteenth-Century Connecticut." In *Power and Status: Officeholding in Colonial America.* Ed. Bruce C. Daniels. Middletown, CT: Wesleyan University Press, 1986, 36–52.

Daniels, Christine and Michael V. Kennedy, eds. *Negotiated Empires: Centers and Peripheries in the New World, 1500–1820.* New York: Routledge, 2002.

Davis, Harold A. *An International Community on the St. Croix, 1604–1930.* Orono: University of Maine Press, 1950.

Day, Clarence A. *A History of Maine Agriculture, 1604–1860.* Orono: University of Maine Press, 1954.

Demeritt, David. "Representing the 'True' St. Croix: Knowledge and Power in the Partition of the Northeast." *William and Mary Quarterly,* 3d ser., 54 (1997): 515–548.

Desserud, Donald. "Nova Scotia and the American Revolution: A Study of Neutrality and Moderation in the Eighteenth Century." In *Making Adjustments: Change and Continuity in Planter Nova Scotia, 1759–1800.* Ed. Margaret Conrad. Fredericton, NB: Acadiensis, 1991, 89–112.

Drisko, George W. *Narrative of the Town of Machias.* 1904. Reprint. Somersworth, NH: New Hampshire Publishing, 1979.

DuBois, Armand Budington. *The English Business Company after the Bubble Act, 1720–1800.* 1931. Reprint. New York: Octagon, 1971.

Ells, Margaret. "Clearing the Decks for the Loyalists." Canadian Historical Association *Report* (1933): 43–58.

Ells, Margaret. *A study of early provincial taxation: Being a tabular statement of fiscal legislation in Nova Scotia between 1751 and 1815, with an introduction and an appendix.* Halifax: Provincial Archives, 1937.

Ells, Margaret. "Governor Wentworth's Patronage." *Collections of the Nova Scotia Historical Society,* 25 (1942): 49–73.

Ertman, Thomas. *Birth of the Leviathan: Building States and Regimes in Medieval and Early Modern Europe.* Cambridge: Cambridge University Press, 1997.

Eves, Jamie H. "The Acquisition of Wealth, or of a Comfortable Subsistence: The Census of 1800 and the Yankee Migration to Maine, 1760–1825." *Maine History* 35 (1995): 6–25.

Fergusson, Charles Bruce. *The Origin of Representative Government in Canada.* Halifax: The Committee on the Bicentenary of Representative Government, 1958.

Fergusson, Charles Bruce. "Early Liverpool and Its Diarist." *Bulletin of the Public Archives of Nova Scotia.* No. 16. Halifax: 1961.

Fergusson, Charles Bruce. "Local Government in Nova Scotia." *Bulletin of the Public Archives of Nova Scotia.* No. 17. Halifax: 1961.

Fergusson, Charles Bruce. "The Inauguration of the Free School System in Nova Scotia." *Bulletin of the Public Archives of Nova Scotia.* No. 21. Halifax: 1964.

Fergusson, Charles Bruce. "Pre-Revolutionary Settlements in Nova Scotia." *Collections of the Nova Scotia Historical Society* 37 (1970): 5–22.

Fingard, Judith. *The Anglican Design in Loyalist Nova Scotia, 1783–1816.* London: Church Historical Society, 1972.

Fisher, Lewis R. "Revolution without Independence: The Canadian Colonies, 1749–1775." In *The Economy of Early America: The Revolutionary Period, 1763–1790.* Eds. Ronald Hoffman et al., Charlottesville: University Press of Virginia, 1988.

Foster, Stephen. "New England and the Challenge of Heresy, 1630 to 1660: The Puritan Crisis in Transatlantic Perspective." *William and Mary Quarterly,* 3d ser., 38 (1981): 624–660.

Foster, Stephen. *The Long Argument: English Puritanism and the Shaping of New England Culture, 1570–1700.* Chapel Hill: University of North Carolina Press, 1991.

Fox, Catherine. "The Great Fire in the Woods: A Case Study in Ecological History." M.A. thesis, University of Maine, 1984.

French, Goldwin. *Parsons and Politics: The Role of the Wesleyan Methodists in Upper Canada and the Maritimes from 1780 to 1855.* Toronto: Ryerson, 1962.

Gates, Lillian F. *Land Policies of Upper Canada.* Toronto: University of Toronto Press, 1968.

Goen, C. C. *Revivalism and Separatism in New England, 1740–1800.* 1962. Reprint. Hamden, CT: Archon, 1969.

Goodwin, Daniel. "From Disunity to Integration: Evangelical Religion and Society in Yarmouth, Nova Scotia, 1761–1830." In *They Planted Well: New England Planters in Maritime Canada.* Ed. Margaret Conrad. Fredericton, NB: Acadiensis, 1988, 190–200.

Gould, Eliga H. "Revolution and Counter-Revolution." In *The British Atlantic World, 1500–1800.* Eds. David Armitage and Michael J. Braddick. Basingstoke, UK and New York: Palgrave, 2002, 196–213.

Graham, Dominick. "Charles Lawrence." In *Dictionary of Canadian Biography. Vol. 3, 1741–1770.* Toronto: University of Toronto Press, 1974, 361–366.

Greene, Jack P. "The Role of the Lower Houses of Assembly in Eighteenth-Century Politics." *Journal of Southern History* 27 (1961): 451–474.

Greene, Jack P. "Political Mimesis: A Consideration of the Historical and Cultural Roots of Legislative Behavior in the British Colonies in the Eighteenth Century." *American Historical Review* 75 (1969): 337–367.

Greene, Jack P. *The Quest for Power: The Lower Houses of Assembly in the Southern Royal Colonies, 1689–1776.* 1963. Reprint. New York: Norton, 1972.

Greene, Jack P. ""A Posture of Hostility": A Reconsideration of Some Aspects of the Origins of the American Revolution." *Proceedings of the American Antiquarian Society* 87 (1977), 27–68.

Greene, Jack P. *Peripheries and Center: Constitutional Development in the Extended Polities of the British Empire and the United States, 1607–1788.* Athens: University of Georgia Press, 1986.

Greene, Jack P. *Pursuits of Happiness: The Social Development of Early Modern British Colonies and the Formation of American Culture.* Chapel Hill: University of North Carolina Press, 1988.

Greene, Jack P. "Metropolis and Colonies: Changing Patterns of Constitutional Conflict in the Early Modern British Empire, 1607–1763." In *Negotiated Authorities: Essays in Colonial Political and Constitutional History.* Charlottesville and London: University Press of Virginia, 1994, 43–77.

Greene, Jack P. "The Jamaica Privilege Controversy, 1764–66: An Episode in the Process of Constitutional Definition in the Early Modern British Empire." *Journal of Imperial and Commonwealth History* 22 (1994), 16–53.

Greer, Allan and Ian Radforth, eds. *Colonial Leviathan: State Formation in Mid-Nineteenth-Century Canada.* Toronto: University of Toronto Press, 1992.

Greven, Philip J., Jr. "The average size of families and households in the Province of Massachusetts in 1764 and in the United States in 1790: An overview." In *Household and Family in Past Time.* Eds. Peter Laslett and Richard Wall. Cambridge: Cambridge University Press, 1972, 545–560.

Griffiths, Naomi E. S. *The Acadian Deportation: Deliberate Perfidy or Cruel Necessity?* Toronto: Copp Clark, 1969.

Griffiths, Naomi E. S. "The Acadians of the British Seaports." *Acadiensis* 4, 1 (1976), 67–84.

Griffiths, Naomi E. S. *The Contexts of Acadian History, 1686–1784.* Montreal and Kingston: McGill–Queen's University Press, 1992.

Gura, Philip F. *A Glimpse of Sion's Glory: Puritan Radicalism in New England, 1620–1660.* Middletown, CT: Wesleyan University Press, 1984.

Gwyn, Julian. *Excessive Expectations: Maritime Commerce and the Economic Development of Nova Scotia, 1740–1870.* Montreal and Kingston: McGill–Queen's University Press, 1998.

Halliday, Paul D. *Dismembering the Body Politic: Partisan Politics in England's Towns, 1650–1730.* Cambridge: Cambridge University Press, 1998.

Handlin, Oscar and Mary Flug Handlin. *Commonwealth, A Study of the Role of Government in the American Economy: Massachusetts, 1774–1861.* Rev. Ed. Cambridge, MA: Belknap, 1969.

Harris, R. Cole, ed. and Geoffrey J. Matthews, cartographer. *Historical Atlas of Canada, Vol. I, From the Beginning to 1800.* Toronto: University of Toronto Press, 1987.

Hartz, Louis. *The Liberal Tradition in America: An Interpretation of American Political Thought Since the Revolution.* New York: Harcourt, Brace and World, 1955.

Hartz, Louis. *The Founding of New Societies: Studies in the History of the United States, Latin America, South Africa, and Canada.* New York: Harcourt, Brace and World, 1964.

Harvey, D. C., ed. "Governor Lawrence's Case Against an Assembly in Nova Scotia." *Canadian Historical Review* 13, 2 (1932): 184–194.

Harvey, D. C., ed. "The Struggle for the New England Form of Township Government in Nova Scotia." Canadian Historical Association *Report* (1933), 15–23.

Hatch, Nathan O. *The Sacred Cause of Liberty: Republican Thought and the Millennium in Revolutionary New England.* New Haven: Yale University Press, 1977.

Hay, G. U. "History of Education in New Brunswick," In *Canada and Its Provinces: A History of the Canadian People and Their Institutions*, Vol. 14 *The Atlantic Provinces.* Eds. Adam Shortt and Arthur G. Doughty. Edinburgh: Edinburgh University Press, 1914, 545–558.

Head, C. Grant. *Eighteenth Century Newfoundland.* Toronto: McClelland and Stewart, 1976.

Hempton, David. "Methodist Growth in Transatlantic Perspective, ca. 1770–1850." In *Methodism and the Shaping of American Culture.* Eds. Nathan O. Hatch and John H. Wigger. Nashville, TN: Kingswood, 2001, 41–85.

Heyrman, Christine Leigh. *Commerce and Culture: The Maritime Communities of Colonial Massachusetts, 1690–1750.* New York: Norton, 1984.

Horowitz, Gad. "Conservatism, Liberalism, and Socialism in Canada: An Interpretation." *Canadian Journal of Economics and Political Science* 32 (1966): 143–171.

Innis, Harold A. *The Cod Fisheries: The History of An International Economy.* Rev. Ed. Toronto: University of Toronto Press, 1954.

Isaac, Rhys. *The Transformation of Virginia, 1740–1790.* Chapel Hill: University of North Carolina Press, 1982.

Jaffee, David. *People of the Wachusett: Greater New England in History and Memory, 1630–1860.* Ithaca and London: Cornell University Press, 1999.

James, Sidney V. *The Colonial Metamorphoses in Rhode Island: A Study of Institutions in Change.* Hanover, NH, and London: University Press of New England, 2000.

Jones, Douglas Lamar. "The Strolling Poor: Transiency in Eighteenth-Century Massachusetts." *Journal of Social History* 8 (1975): 28–45.

Judd, Richard W., Edwin A. Churchill, and Joel W. Eastman, eds. *Maine: The Pine Tree State from Prehistory to the Present.* Orono: University of Maine Press, 1995.

Kerr, Wilfred Brenton. *The Maritime Provinces of British North America and the American Revolution.* 1941. Reprint. New York: Russell & Russell, 1970.

Kershaw, Gordon E. *The Kennebeck Proprietors, 1749–1775.* Portland: Maine Historical Society, 1975.

Kilby, William Henry. *Eastport and Passamaquoddy: A Collection of Historical and Biographical Sketches.* 1888. Reprint. Eastport, ME: Border History Fathom Series, no. 2, 1982.

Konig, David Thomas. "English Legal Change and the Origins of Local Government in Northern Massachusetts." In *Town and County: Essays on the Structure of Local Government in the American Colonies.* Ed. Bruce C. Daniels. Middletown, CT: Wesleyan University Press, 1978, 12–43.

Kulik, Gary. "Dams, Fish, and Farmers: The Defense of Public Rights in Eighteenth-Century Rhode Island." In *The New England Working Class and the New Labor History.* Eds. Herbert G. Gutman and Donald H. Bell. Urbana: University of Illinois Press, 1987, 187–213.

Leamon, James S. "The Search for Security: Maine After Penobscot." *Maine Historical Society Quarterly* 21, 3 (1982): 119–153.

Leamon, James S. "Revolution and Separation: Maine's First Efforts at Statehood." In *Maine in the Early Republic: From Revolution to Statehood.* Eds. Charles E. Clark, James S. Leamon, and Karen Bowden. Hanover, NH: University Press of New England, 1988.

Leamon, James S. *Revolution Downeast: The War for American Independence in Maine.* Amherst: University of Massachusetts Press, 1993.

Lipset, Seymour Martin. *Continental Divide: The Values and Institutions of the United States and Canada.* Washington, DC: Canadian American Committee, 1989.

Lipset, Seymour Martin. *American Exceptionalism: A Double-Edged Sword.* New York: Norton, 1996.

Lockridge, Kenneth. "Land, Population and the Evolution of New England Society 1630–1790." *Past and Present* 39 (1968): 62–80.

Lockridge, Kenneth. *A New England Town: The First Hundred Years, Dedham, Massachusetts, 1636–1736.* New York: Norton, 1970.

Long, Robert J. *The Annals of Liverpool and Queens County, 1760–1867.* West Medford, MA: Private, 1926.

Lucas, Paul R. *Valley of Discord: Church and Society Along the Connecticut River, 1636–1725.* Hanover, NH: University Press of New England, 1976.

McDonnell, Michael A. "Popular Mobilization and Political Culture in Revolutionary Virginia: The Failure of the Minutemen and the Revolution from Below." *Journal of American History* 85 (1998): 946–981.

McGuigan G., "Administration of Land Policy and the Growth of Corporate Economic Organization in Lower Canada, 1791–1809." Canadian Historical Association *Report* (1963): 65–73.

"Machias Settlers." *Collections of the Maine Historical Society,* 1st ser., 3 (1853): 179–180.

MacKay, A. H. "History of Education in Nova Scotia and Prince Edward Island." In *Canada and Its Provinces: A History of the Canadian People and Their Institutions,* Vol. 14, *The Atlantic Provinces.* Eds. Adam Shortt and Arthur G. Doughty. Edinburgh: Edinburgh University Press, 1914, 511–542.

MacKinnon, Ian F. *Settlements and Churches in Nova Scotia, 1749–1776.* Montreal: Walker Press, 1930.

MacKinnon, Neil. *This Unfriendly Soil: The Loyalist Experience in Nova Scotia, 1783–1791.* Kingston and Montreal: McGill–Queen's University Press, 1986.

McLennan, J. S. *Louisbourg: From Its Foundation to Its Fall, 1713–1758.* 4th ed. Halifax: Book Room, 1979.

McNabb, Debra Anne. "Land and Families in Horton Township, N.S., 1760–1830." M.A. thesis, University of British Columbia, 1986.

McNabb, Debra Anne. "The Role of the Land in Settling Horton Township, Nova Scotia, 1766–1830." In *They Planted Well: New England Planters in Maritime Canada.* Ed. Margaret Conrad. Fredericton, NB: Acadiensis, 1988, 151–160.

MacNutt, W. S. *The Atlantic Provinces: The Emergence of Colonial Society, 1712–1857.* Toronto: McClelland and Stewart, 1965.

McRae, Kenneth D. "The Structure of Canadian History." In *The Founding of New Societies: Studies in the History of the United States, Latin America, South Africa, Canada, and Australia.* Ed. Louis Hartz. New York: Harcourt, Brace & World, 1964, 219–274.

Maier, Pauline. *From Resistance to Revolution: Colonial Radicals and the Development of American Opposition to Britain, 1765–1776.* New York: Knopf, 1973.

Maier, Pauline. "The Revolutionary Origins of the American Corporation." *William and Mary Quarterly,* 3d ser, 50 (1993): 51–84.

Malone, Joseph J. *Pine Trees and Politics: The Naval Stores and Forest Policy in Colonial New England, 1691–1775.* Seattle: University of Washington Press, 1964.

Mancke, Elizabeth. "Another British America: A Canadian Model for the Early Modern British Empire." *Journal of Imperial and Commonwealth History* 25 (1997): 1–36.

Mancke, Elizabeth. "Early Modern Imperial Governance and the Origins of Canadian Political Culture." *Canadian Journal of Political Science/Revue canadienne de science politique* 32, 1 (1999): 3–20.

Mancke, Elizabeth. "The American Revolution in Canada." In *A Companion to the American Revolution.* Eds. Jack P. Greene and J. R. Pole. Malden, MA and Oxford: Blackwell, 2000, 503–510.

Mancke, Elizabeth. "Negotiating an Empire: Britain and Its Overseas Peripheries, c.1550–1780." In *Negotiated Empires: Centers and Peripheries in the New World, 1500–1820*. Eds. Christine Daniels and Michael V. Kennedy. New York: Routledge, 2002, 235–265.

Mancke, Elizabeth. "Imperial Transitions." In *The 'Conquest' of Acadia, 1710: Imperial, Colonial, and Aboriginal Contructions*. John G. Reid et al. Toronto: University of Toronto Press, 2003, 178–202.

Mancke, Elizabeth. "Chartered Enterprises and the Evolution of the British Atlantic World." In *The Creation of the British Atlantic World*. Eds. Elizabeth Mancke and Carole Shammas. Baltimore: Johns Hopkins University Press, 2005.

Mancke, Elizabeth and John G. Reid. "Elites, States, and the Imperial Contest for Acadia." In *The 'Conquest' of Acadia: 1710: Imperial, Colonial, and Aboriginal Constructions*. John G. Reid et al. Toronto: University of Toronto Press, 2003.

Mannion, John and Selma Barkham. "The 16th Century Fishery." In *Historical Atlas of Canada, Vol. I, From the Beginning to 1800*. Ed. R. Cole Harris and Geoffrey J. Matthews, cartographer. Toronto: University of Toronto Press, 1987. Plate 22.

Mannion, John and Gordon Handcock. "The 17th Century Fishery." In *Historical Atlas of Canada, Vol. I, From the Beginning to 1800*. Ed. R. Cole Harris and Geoffrey J. Matthews, cartographer. Toronto: University of Toronto Press, 1987. Plate 23.

Marini, Stephen A. *Radical Sects of Revolutionary New England*. Cambridge, MA: Harvard University Press, 1982.

Marini, Stephen A. "Religious Revolution in the District of Maine, 1780–1820." In *Maine in the Early Republic: From Revolution to Statehood*. Eds. Charles E. Clark, James S. Leamon, and Karen Bowden. Hanover, NH: University Press of New England, 1988.

Martell, J. S. "Pre-Loyalist Settlements around the Minas Basin." M.A. thesis, Dalhousie University, 1933.

Martin, John Frederick. *Profits in the Wilderness: Entrepreneurship and the Founding of New England Towns in the Seventeenth Century*. Chapel Hill, NC: University of North Carolina Press, 1991.

"Mills at the Eastward Prior to 1800." *Bangor Historical Magazine* 6, 1–3 (1890): 18–21.

Moody, Robert Earle and Richard Clive Simmons, eds. *The Glorious Revolution in Massachusetts: Selected Documents, 1689–1692*. Boston: Colonial Society of Massachusetts, 1988.

Morgan, Edmund S. *Visible Saints: The History of a Puritan Idea*. New York: New York University Press, 1963.

Morse, Charles. "Provincial and Local Government." In *Canada and Its Provinces: A History of the Canadian People and Their Institutions. Vol. 14. The Atlantic Provinces*. Eds. Adam Shortt and Arthur G. Doughty. Edinburgh: Edinburgh University Press, 1914, 435–508.

Mullins, Janet E. *Some Liverpool Chronicles*. 1941. Reprint. Hantsport, NS: Lancelot, 1980.

Nichols, George E.E. "Notes on Nova Scotian Privateers." *Collections of the Nova Scotia Historical Society* 13 (1908).

Oesterle, Dale A. "Formative Contribution to American Corporate Law by the Massachusetts Supreme Judicial Court from 1806 to 1810." In *The History of the Law in Massachusetts: The Supreme Judicial Court 1692–1992*. Ed. Russell K. Osgood. Boston: Supreme Judicial Court Historical Society, 1992, 127–152.

Onuf, Peter S. "Settlers, Settlements, and New States." In *The American Revolution: Its Character and Limits*. Ed. Jack P. Greene. New York: New York University Press, 1987, 171–196.

Onuf, Peter S. *Statehood and Union: A History of the Northwest Ordinance*. Bloomington: University of Indiana Press, 1987.

Patterson, Stephen E. "1744–1763: Colonial Wars and Aboriginal Peoples." In *The Atlantic Region to Confederation: A History*. Eds. Phillip A. Buckner and John G. Reid. Toronto: University of Toronto Press, 1994, 125–155.

Paul, Daniel N. *We Were Not the Savages: A Micmac Perspective on the Collision of European and Aboriginal Civilizations*. Halifax: Nimbus, 1993.

Paulsen, Kenneth S. "Settlement and Ethnicity in Lunenburg, Nova Scotia, 1753–1800: A History of the Foreign-Protestant Community." Ph.D. dissertation, University of Maine, 1996.

Plank, Geoffrey. *An Unsettled Conquest: The British Campaign Against the Peoples of Acadia*. Philadelphia: University of Pennsylvania Press, 2001.

Plimsoll, Joseph Edwards. "The Militia of Nova Scotia, 1749–1867." *Nova Scotia Historical Society Collections* 17 (1913): 63–106.

Pope, Robert. *The Half-Way Covenant: Church Membership in Puritan New England*. Princeton, NJ: Princeton University Press, 1969.

Potter, J. "The Growth of Population in America, 1700–1860." In *Population in History: Essays in Historical Demography*. Eds. D. V. Glass and D. E. C. Eversley. Chicago: Aldine, 1965.

Potter, Janice. *The Liberty We Seek: Loyalist Ideology in Colonial New York and Massachusetts*. Cambridge, MA: Harvard University Press, 1983.

Raddal, Thomas H. *A Brief History of Zion Church, Liverpool, N.S., 1760–1967*. Liverpool, NS: Zion United Church of Canada, 1967.

Rakove, Jack N. *The Beginnings of National Politics: An Interpretive History of the Continental Congress*. New York: Knopf, 1979.

Rawlyk, George A. *Revolution Rejected 1775–1776*. Scarborough, ON: Prentice-Hall, 1968.

Rawlyk, George A. *Nova Scotia's Massachusetts: A Study of Massachusetts–Nova Scotia Relations, 1630 to 1784*. Montreal: McGill–Queen's University Press, 1973.

Rawlyk, George A. *Ravished by the Spirit: Religious Revivals, Baptists, and Henry Alline*. Kingston and Montreal: McGill–Queen's University Press, 1984.

Rawlyk, George A. *Wrapped Up in God: A Study of Several Canadian Revivals and Revivalists*. Burlington, ON: Welch, 1988.

Rawlyk, George A. "1720–1744: Cod, Louisbourg, and the Acadians." In *Atlantic Region to Confederation: A History*. Eds. Phillip A. Buckner and John G. Reid. Toronto: University of Toronto Press, 1994, 107–124.

Rawlyk, George A. *The Canada Fire: Radical, Evangelicalism in British North America, 1775–1812*. Kingston and Montreal: McGill–Queen's University Press, 1994.

Rawlyk, George A. "A Total Revolution in Religious and Civil Government: The Maritimes, New England, and the Evolving Evangelical Ethos, 1776–1812." In *Evangelicalism: Comparative Studies of Popular Protestantism in North America, the British Isles, and Beyond, 1700–1900*. Eds. Mark A. Noll, David W. Bebbington, and George A. Rawlyk. New York and Oxford: Oxford University Press, 1994, 137–155.

Reid, John G. *Acadia, Maine, and New Scotland: Marginal Colonies in the Seventeenth Century*. Toronto: University of Toronto Press, 1981.

Reid, John G. "1686–1720: Imperial Intrusions." In *The Atlantic Region to Confederation: A History*. Eds. Phillip A. Buckner and John G. Reid. Toronto: University of Toronto Press, 1994, 78–103.

Reid, John G. "*Pax Britannica* or *Pax Indigena*? Planter Nova Scotia and Competing Strategies of Pacification." *Canadian Historical Review*, 85 (2004).

Reid, John G. et al. *The 'Conquest' of Acadia, 1710: Imperial, Colonial, and Aboriginal Constructions*. Toronto: University of Toronto Press, 2003.

Ritchie, Robert C. "Government Measures against Piracy and Privateering in the Atlantic Area, 1750–1850." In *Pirates and Privateers: New Perspectives on the War on Trade in the Eighteenth and Nineteenth Centuries*. Eds. David J. Starkey, E. S. van Eyck van Heslinga, and J. A. de Moor. Exeter: University of Exeter Press, 1997, 10–28.

Rivard, Paul E. *Maine Sawmills*. Augusta, ME: Maine State Museum, 1990.

Robertson, Allen Barry. "Charles Inglis and John Wesley: Church of England and Methodist Relations in Nova Scotia in the Late Eighteenth Century." *Nova Scotia Historical Review* 7, 1 (1987): 48–63.

Robertson, Allen Barry. "Methodism Among Nova Scotia's Yankee Planters." In *They Planted Well: New England Planters in Maritime Canada*. Ed. Margaret Conrad. Fredericton, NB: Acadiensis, 1988, 178–189.

Robertson, Barbara R. "Trees, Treaties and the Timing of Settlement: A Comparison of the Lumber Industry in Nova Scotia and New Brunswick, 1784–1867." *Nova Scotia Historical Review* 4, 1 (1984): 37–55.

Robinson, Mark Power. "Maritime Frontiers: The Evolution of Empire in Nova Scotia, 1713–1758." Ph.D. dissertation, University of Colorado, 2000.

Rutman, Darrett B. "People in Process: The New Hampshire Towns of the Eighteenth Century." *Journal of Urban History* 1, 3 (1975): 268–292.

Sahlins, Peter. *Boundaries: The Making of France and Spain in the Pyrenees*. Berkeley: University of California Press, 1989.

Salisbury, Neal. *Manitou and Providence: Indians, Europeans, and the Making of New England, 1500–1643*. New York and Oxford: Oxford University Press, 1982.

Shannon, Timothy J. *Indians and Colonists at the Crossroads of Empire: The Albany Congress of 1754*. Ithaca and New York: Cornell University Press, 2000.

Shortt, Adam. "Municipal History, 1791–1867." In *Canada and Its Provinces: A History of the Canadian People and Their Institutions, Vol. 18, Province of Ontario.* Eds., Adam Shortt and Arthur G. Doughty. Edinburgh: University of Edinburgh Press, 1914, 405–452.

Shy, John. *A People Numerous and Armed: Reflections on the Military Struggle for Independence.* Rev. Ed. Ann Arbor: University of Michigan Press, 1990.

Skocpol, Theda. *States and Social Revolution: A Comparative Analysis of France, Russia, and China.* Cambridge: Cambridge University Press, 1974.

Smith, A. Tanner. "Transportation and Communication in Nova Scotia, 1749–1815." M.A. thesis, Dalhousie University, 1936.

Snowdon, James D. "Footprints in the Marsh Mud: Politics and Land Settlement in the Township of Sackville, 1760–1800." M.A. thesis, University of New Brunswick, 1974.

Sonneck, Oscar G. T. *Francis Hopkinson: The First American Poet-Composer (1737–1791) and James Lyon: Patriot, Preacher, Psalmodist (1735–1794).* 1905. Reprint. New York: Da Capo, 1967.

Stewart, Gordon. "Socio-Economic Factors in the Great Awakening: The Case of Yarmouth, Nova Scotia." *Acadiensis* 3, 1 (1973): 19–34.

Stewart, Gordon. *The Origins of Canadian Politics: A Comparative Approach.* Vancouver: University of British Columbia Press, 1986.

Stewart, Gordon. *United States Expansionism and British North America, 1775–1871.* Chapel Hill and London: University of North Carolina Press, 1988.

Stewart, Gordon. *The American Response to Canada Since 1776.* East Lansing, MI: Michigan State University Press, 1992.

Stewart, Gordon, and George A. Rawlyk. *'A People Highly Favoured of God': The Nova Scotia Yankees and the American Revolution.* Toronto: Macmillan of Canada, 1972.

Stuart, Reginald. *War and American Thought: From the Revolution to the Monroe Doctrine.* Kent, OH: Kent State University Press, 1982.

Taylor, Alan S. *Liberty Men and Great Proprietors: The Revolutionary Settlement on the Maine Frontier, 1760–1820.* Chapel Hill: University of North Carolina Press, 1990.

Thompson, John Herd and Stephen J. Randall. *Canada and the United States: Ambivalent Allies.* 3d ed. Athens, GA and London: University of Georgia Press, 2002.

Throughton, Michael J. "From Nodes to Nodes: The Rise and Fall of Agricultural Activity in the Maritime Provinces." In *Geographical Perspectives on the Maritime Provinces.* Ed. Douglas Day. Halifax, NS: St. Mary's University, 1988, 25–46.

Tindal, C. R. and S. Nobes Tindal, *Local Government in Canada.* 2d ed. Toronto: McGraw-Hill Ryerson, 1984.

Upton, L. F. S. *Micmacs and Colonists: Indian-White Relations in the Maritimes, 1713–1867.* Vancouver: University of British Columbia Press, 1979.

Vickers, Daniel. "Work and Life on the Fishing Periphery of Essex County, Massachusetts, 1630–1675." In *Seventeenth Century New England.* Eds. David G. Allen and David Hall. Boston: Colonial Society of Massachusetts, 1985, 83–117.

Vickers, Daniel. "Competency and Competition: Economic Culture in Early America." *William and Mary Quarterly,* 3d ser., 47 (1990): 3–29.

Vickers, Daniel. *Farmers and Fishermen: Two Centuries of Work in Essex County, Massachusetts, 1630–1850.* Chapel Hill: University of North Carolina Press, 1994.

Wells, Robert V. *The Population of the British Colonies in America before 1776: A Survey of Census Data.* Princeton, NJ: Princeton University Press, 1975.

Whebell, C. F. J. "The Upper Canada District Councils Act of 1841 and British Colonial Policy." *Journal of Imperial and Commonwealth History* 17 (1989): 185–209.

White, E. P. "Nova Scotia Settlers from Chatham, Massachusetts 1759–1760." *National Genealogical Society Quarterly* 62 (1974): 96–117.

Wicken, William C. *Mi'kmaq Treaties on Trial: History, Land, and Donald Marshall Junior.* Toronto: University of Toronto Press, 2002.

Williamson, William D. *The History of the State of Maine; From Its First Discovery, A.D. 1602, to The Separation, A.D. 1820, Inclusive,* 2 vols. 1832. Reprint. Freeport, ME: Cumberland, n.d.

Wright, Esther Clark. "Without Intervention of Prophet, Priest or King." In *Repent and Believe: The Baptist Experience in Maritime Canada.* Ed. Barry Moody. Hantsport, NS: Lancelot, 1980.

Wynn, Graeme. "'Deplorably Dark and Demoralized Lumberers'?: Rhetoric and Reality in Early Nineteenth Century New Brunswick." *Journal of Forest History* 24, 4 (1980): 168–187.

Wynn, Graeme. *Timber Colony: A Historical Geography of Early Nineteenth Century New Brunswick.* Toronto: University of Toronto Press, 1981.

Wynn, Graeme.. "A Province Too Much Dependent on New England." *The Canadian Geographer/ Le Geographe Canadien* 31, 2 (1987): 98–113.

Wynn, Graeme. "A Region of Scattered Settlements and Bounded Possibilities: Northeastern America, 1775–1800." *The Canadian Geographer/Le Geographe Canadien,* 31, 4 (1987): 319–338.

Wynn, Graeme and Debra McNabb. "Pre-Loyalist Nova Scotia." In *Historical Atlas of Canada, Vol. I, From the Beginning to 1800.* Ed. R. Cole Harris and Geoffrey J. Matthews, cartographer. Toronto: University of Toronto Press, 1987. Plate 31.

Yerxa, Donald. "The Burning of Falmouth, 1775: A Case Study in British Imperial Pacification." *Maine Historical Society Quarterly* 14, 3 (1975): 119–150.

Zuckerman, Michael. *Peaceable Kingdoms: New England Towns in the Eighteenth Century.* New York: Knopf, 1970.

Zuckerman, Michael. "The Fabrication of Identity in Early America." *William and Mary Quarterly,* 3d ser., 34 (1977): 183–214.

Index